Reaching for
Power

Yitzhak Nakash

Reaching for Power

The Shiʻa in the Modern Arab World

PRINCETON UNIVERSITY PRESS
PRINCETON AND OXFORD

Library of Congress Cataloging-in-Publication Data

Nakash, Yitzhak.
Reaching for power : the shi'a in the modern Arab world / Yitzhak Nakash.
p.   cm.
Includes bibliographical references and index.
ISBN-13: 978-0-691-12529-9 (hardcover : alk. paper)
ISBN-10: 0-691-12529-5 (hardcover : alk. paper)
1. Shiites—Middle East. 2. Islam and politics—Middle East. I. Title.
DS59.S55N35   2006
320.956′088′29782—dc22   2005021393

British Library Cataloging-in-Publication Data is available

This book has been composed in Sabon with Friz Quadrata display

Printed on acid-free paper. ∞

pup.princeton.edu

Printed in the United States of America

1 3 5 7 9 10 8 6 4 2

To Beth

And to Neta and Talya

Contents

Preface

A month before the January 2005 elections in Iraq, and a few days after gunmen brazenly shot to death election officials in broad daylight at the heart of Baghdad, the Ansar al-Sunna militant group issued a statement denouncing democracy as un-Islamic because it idolized human beings. "Democracy," the statement read, "is a Greek word indicating the rule of the people, which means that the people do as they see fit. This concept of government is apostasy because it defies the Muslim doctrinal belief that sovereignty rests with God." The statement was endorsed by two other Sunni insurgent groups. It warned that anyone who participates in the elections will not be safe, and was clearly aimed at countering the rulings of Shi'i clerics that voting in the elections was the duty of every Iraqi.

Both this statement, and the mounting violence in Iraq in the period before and after the elections, underscore the fierce struggle that is raging today among Muslims for the soul of Islam—a struggle that is taking shape at a time when America is attempting to play an assertive role in the Middle East, and as the geopolitics of the region are shifting. The outcome of this war of ideas within Islam will have a profound impact not only on the people of the

Middle East, but also on the relations between Muslim and Western societies.

This book illuminates some of the historical dimensions of this struggle. It focuses on the Shi'is, who constitute the minority sect within Islam, and who stand today at the center of a U.S. government attempt to remake the Middle East. The history discussed here shows how Shi'is in the Arab world have responded to the upheaval resulting from the collapse of the Ottoman Empire and the rise of the nation-state in the twentieth century. It introduces us to Shi'i political communities whose members had to take on a new identity and redefine their relations with newly emerging states, and to non-Shi'i ruling elites backed by Western powers who were unwilling to accommodate the Shi'is within the modern state. The repercussions of this upheaval, and of the shortcomings of the nation-state, are in full play today in the Middle East.

The analysis presented here demonstrates the sociopolitical transformation experienced by Arab Shi'is in the period preceding the rise of the nation-state in the Middle East and continuing through it to the January 2005 elections in Iraq. The book captures the surge of Shi'ism as a political force since the Iranian Islamic Revolution of 1978–79. It draws attention to the pivotal change in Shi'i attitudes toward the West, most notably the shift of focus among Shi'is since the 1990s from confrontation to accommodation—a development that stands in stark contrast to the growing militancy among Sunni groups, and which carries implications for the U.S. endeavor in the Middle East. At the same time, the book seeks to alert readers and policymakers to the strong nationalist sentiments of Shi'is in the Arab world, underscoring the tough challenge that the United States faces in attempting to impose a new order in the region.

The book takes up the cases of Shi'is in Saudi Arabia, Bahrain, Iraq, and Lebanon. It highlights the reciprocal influences shaping the political development of Shi'is in these states, and assesses the impact that the revival of Shi'ism has had on the larger Arab world. The narrative begins with a prologue on the 2003 U.S. invasion of Iraq and the vision of government offered by Shi'is under the leadership of Grand Ayatollah 'Ali Sistani for the post-Ba'th period. The prologue incorporates background information on Shi'i Islam and on the states discussed in the book, and is intended to introduce the nonspecialist reader to the topic. The purpose of chapter 1 is to illustrate the vicissitudes that Shi'is experienced before the twentieth century and which affected their position in the modern state. Chapters 2, 3, and 4 illuminate the distinct political experience of Shi'is in Saudi Arabia, Bahrain, Lebanon, and Iraq before the U.S. invasion and the tensions underlying Shi'i-government relations in each country. The attempts of Shi'is to carve out a political space for themselves in the wake of the Gulf War of 1991 and the recent war in Iraq are the focus of chapter 5. A concluding chapter highlights the risks and possibilities arising from the assertion of Shi'i power in Iraq and from the declared intention of the United States to bring democracy to the Middle East.

In the ten years of researching and drafting this book, I met scores of Shi'i writers and activists of different countries and political persuasions; many of them were forced to live and publish their works in exile. The writing of the exiles has often built on and extended the work of Shi'is inside the Arab world, resulting in a rich literature that has shaped the contemporary aspirations of Saudi, Bahraini, Iraqi, and Lebanese Shi'is. This literature stands as testimony to the aspiration of people in the Middle East to adapt Islam to modern times and be the masters of their future and their political destiny.

A Note on Transliteration

In transcribing Arabic and Persian into English, I have kept the general reader in mind. The system used here is a simplified form of the one adopted by the *International Journal of Middle East Studies*. I have kept the diacritic (') for the Arabic consonant *'ayn* in words such as 'Ali and Shi'is, as well as (') for *hamza*, the character designating the glottal stop, as in *ta'rikh*. The plural of Arabic words has been marked by an addition of an "s" to the singular, except in such cases as "ulama," where the plural form has become standard. The article "al-" has been omitted from last names indicating a person's non-Arab place of origin, such as Sistani, Khoei, Khomeini, or Shirazi, and from Arabic names that have been widely cited in the Western media without the "al-," such as Iyad 'Allawi. Readers should also note the difference between the article "al-" and the word "Al," which means "the house of," and is used in this book in reference to Arab tribes and, in the cases of the Al Sa'ud and the Al Khalifa, the ruling families of Saudi Arabia and Bahrain respectively.

Map 1. Iraq

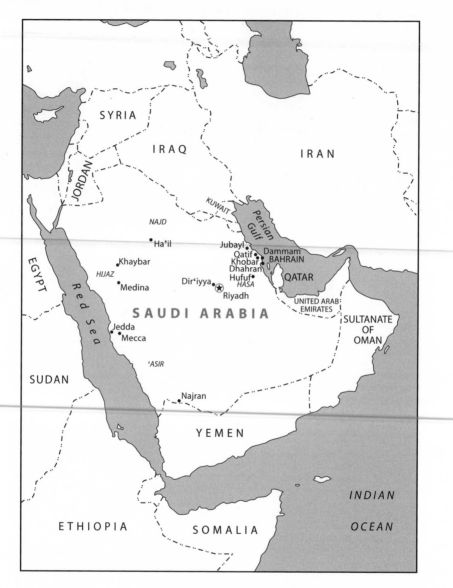

Map 2. Saudi Arabia

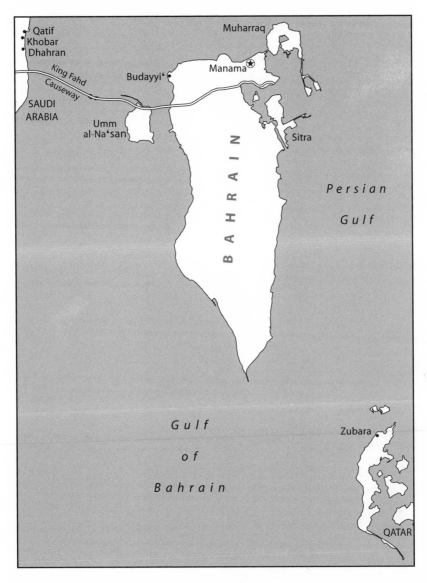

Map 3. Bahrain

Map 4. Lebanon

Reaching for
Power

A Shiʻi-Led Reformation

When U.S. marines stormed into Baghdad in April 2003, there was strong anticipation of political change among Shiʻis in the Arab world. America had pledged to bring reform to the Middle East and put the region on course to democracy. In the initial euphoria that followed the collapse of the Baʻth, Iraqi Shiʻis vowed to replace the tyranny of the former regime with just governance based on freedom and equality. Saudi and Bahraini Shiʻis contended that a Shiʻi-led government in Iraq would force their own governments to introduce serious reforms that would improve their position in the state. In Lebanon, the leading Shiʻi cleric Muhammad Hussein Fadlallah was reportedly considering moving from Beirut to Najaf in Iraq. Fadlallah openly expressed the wish of many Arab Shiʻis that a revival of Najaf as the center of Shiʻi learning should end more than a quarter of a century of Iranian domination of Shiʻism and offer a more resilient interpretation of the faith.

Yet if Shiʻis expected the war in Iraq to quickly change the political realities of the Middle East, they were proven wrong. Within a year, it turned out that the Bush administration was poorly prepared for the mission that it had taken upon itself, and unwilling to commit the necessary resources to implement its prewar vision of Iraq as a beacon of democracy in the Arab world. Instead, Iraq had become the central front in the U.S.-led war on terrorism, and Iraqi politics were subordinated to the administration's agenda and timetable in the run-up to the American elections of November 2004. Meanwhile, the initial goodwill shown by Iraqi Shi'is toward the United States gave way to an insurrection against the occupation. The Saudi and Bahraini governments rebuffed advocates of reforms, depicting them as dissenters who undermined national unity. And Fadlallah suspended his plan to move to Najaf, citing lack of security in Iraq and conceding that it would be years before Najaf could rival Qum as the center of Shi'i thought.

Despite these setbacks, reform in the Middle East is still within reach. But the seeds of reform will be planted by the people of the region, not by an outside power, even one as mighty as America. The U.S. experience in Iraq in the period leading up to the January 2005 elections underscored the fact that Iraq's Shi'i majority is destined to lead the reform process, which is bound to be long and painful. Yet that experience also demonstrated that America is still haunted by memories of its encounter with Shi'i radicalism in Iran and Lebanon in the late 1970s and 1980s. The Bush administration did not acknowledge the crucial changes that took place among Shi'is from the 1990s, and failed to seize the momentum created by the invasion to build early bridges to those Shi'i Islamists who sought to contain the radicals in their midst and fuse Islamic and Western concepts of government. That failure was evident in the clash between the administration's policies in Iraq and the expectations of Shi'is in the post-Ba'th period. Whereas the administration sought to rebuild Iraq as a state with a secular pro-U.S. government, dominated by former exiles and led by a strong prime minister, Shi'is sought an independent Iraq with a government system that reflected their own culture and traditions, and which did not serve as a base for U.S. troops in the Persian Gulf. The administration's insistence on its vision, and its policies of marginalizing Shi'i Islamists and controlling the political process so as to block majority rule, had the effect of radicalizing Iraqi Shi'is and leading them to believe that the Americans sought to block their bid for power. The sense of Shi'is that America had broken faith with them was behind the two rebellions of the cleric Muqtada al-Sadr between April and August 2004, turning him into the symbol of Iraqi Shi'i resistance to the occupation. Nevertheless, in what turned out to be a test of will for the Shi'is of Iraq, pragmatism prevailed. Sadr succumbed to the call of Grand Ayatollah 'Ali Sistani to end the rebellion, and agreed to a truce with the coalition forces. Sadr's followers have since entered politics—in stark contrast to the Sunni rebels, who renounced the political process, and were willing to push Iraq into civil war and fight the Americans to the bitter end.

The development of the Sadr movement thus far is reminiscent of the transformation of the Lebanese Shi'i organization Hizballah from a populist movement entertaining revolutionary ideas into a mainstream political party that accepted both the power-sharing arrangement governing Lebanon and the new political reality created by the departure of Syrian troops from the country in April 2005. As part of that change, which began to take shape in the decade between 1982 and 1992, Hizballah has also mended fences with the West—a fact noted by Shi'i and Western writers as well as by Sunni radicals hostile to the Shi'i organization. The decrease in acts of violence by Hizballah against Western targets since the mid-1990s has stood in contrast to the growth of Sunni-sponsored terrorism by al-Qaeda and other militant groups, including the 9/11 attacks in the United States, the bombings in Bali, Madrid, Riyadh, and London, as well as the gruesome beheadings of hostages in Iraq, Pakistan, and Saudi Arabia—a strategy that all Shi'i groups, including the Sadr movement, have condemned. There are indeed salient differences between Hizballah and those radical Sunni groups influenced by the Wahhabi-Hanbali school dominant in Saudi Arabia and the writings of the Egyptian Sayyid Qutb. Unlike Sunni radicals who view Muslims who do not conform to their Islamic vision as infidels, and who consider secular Muslims as apostates who deserve death, Hizballah has neither declared its adversaries unbelievers nor equated secularism with sin. Whereas al-Qaeda adheres to the mission of changing the world to make it safer for Islam, Hizballah has recast itself as a national liberation movement confined to Lebanon and seeking to make it safe for Shi'is in their local environment. Moreover, in contrast to radical Sunni movements, like the Taliban in Afghanistan, that have rejected modernity and proved that they would rather perish than seek accommodation with the West, Hizballah has selectively accepted Western values, and its members have attended Western institutions of learning including the American University of Beirut.

Hizballah's transformation is part of a shift of focus among Shi'is in the Middle East since the early 1990s from violence to accommodation, coupled with a desire to carve out a political space for themselves. That shift is evident not only in the Arab world, but also in Iran, which has long lost its revolutionary fervor, and acted as America's silent partner during the Gulf War of 1991 and in the recent wars in Afghanistan and Iraq. A regional power to reckon with, Iran today is very different from the embattled Islamic Republic of the early 1980s, with the vast majority of Iranians now clamoring for reform and socioeconomic justice, and a widespread women's movement overshadowing its Sunni counterpart in the Arab world. What is more, the hard-line clerical establishment in Tehran shares the U.S. goal of bringing stability to Iraq—a fact that should not be obscured by the debates over Iran's nuclear intentions, its aid to Shi'i groups in Iraq, and the election of the populist Mahmud Ahmadinejad as Iran's president in June 2005.

The trend within Shi'ism away from confrontation and toward a dialogue with the West is indeed unmistakable, raising a critically important question for American foreign policy: Can Shi'is, who historically have been a minority within Islam, take the lead in inspiring reform in the Arab world? The distinct history and organizational features of Shi'ism suggest that they certainly have the potential and motivation to do so.

Shi'ism grew out of a quarrel among Arab Muslims over the question of succession to the Prophet Muhammad. When Muhammad died in A.D. 632, one group asserted that legitimate succession belonged to 'Ali ibn Abi Talib, the Prophet's cousin and son-in-law, and after him to the Prophet's descendants. But 'Ali was passed over for succession three times in a row before he became caliph. In 661 'Ali was assassinated in a mosque in Kufa in southern Iraq, and the caliphate subsequently shifted from Iraq to Syria whence the Umayyad dynasty ruled for the best part of a century. Some twenty years after 'Ali's death, his partisans in Kufa, known as the *Shi'at 'Ali*, or simply the Shi'a, encouraged his son Hussein to challenge the Syrian claim to the caliphate. Hussein raised the banner of revolt in 680, but the people of Kufa broke their promise to rally to his side, leaving him to meet his death at the battle of Karbala at the hand of forces loyal to the Umayyads. Shi'ism was born of Hussein's defeat in Karbala. It developed as the minority sect while Sunnism grew to be the majority sect in Islam. At the core of Shi'i history, then, lies a tale of betrayal and political dispossession, and of people seeking justice. The drama of Hussein's martyrdom has become the focus of religious devotion for the faithful, comparable to the Passion of Jesus in Christianity, reenacted yearly in rituals of lament and remembrance among the world's 170 million Shi'is.

The impulse to redress historic wrong is important in distinguishing Shi'ism from Sunnism. But more crucial in explaining why Shi'is could lead a reform today is the special relationship between clerics and followers in Shi'i Islam. The main (Twelver) branch of Shi'ism came to believe in a line of twelve imams stretching from 'Ali to Muhammad the Mahdi, who is hidden from view and expected to return one day as a messianic figure. The imam is the religious and political leader of the community, and he is believed to be infallible. Unlike Sunnis, who in theory are expected to obey their rulers and even tolerate a tyrant in order to avoid civil strife and preserve the cohesion of the Muslim community, observant Shi'is recognize no authority on earth except that of the imam. In his absence there can be no human sovereign who is fully legitimate. Yet in reality, the Shi'i clerics, or ulama, have long acted as representatives of the imam and fulfilled some of his functions. Those clerics who are well advanced in their religious studies can become mujtahids, meaning doctors of Islamic law and jurisprudence. Yet only a few mujtahids have succeeded at any given time in gaining the acceptance of a large number of followers. Such a mujtahid is known as a *marja' al-taqlid*, a "model" who can give his followers authoritative opinions on disputed questions and bears the title of Ayatollah. Although in theory only the attributes of knowledge, probity, and piety should be factors in advancing one mujtahid over another, in practice charisma and the ability to lead have played a part in the competition and affected the number of followers that a mujtahid could gather around himself. This special relationship between clerics and followers in Shi'ism has helped Shi'i mujtahids to maintain independence from the government. Whereas Sunni clerics are usually appointed and paid by the government, which thereby confers legitimacy on them, in Shi'ism the followers select the mujtahid of their choice, pay their religious dues to him, and abide by his rulings. While this process has empowered Shi'i followers to bring clerics into line with their interests, it has also enabled the religious leaders to build up their intellectual and financial strength in relation to the state. In this duality lies the essence of democracy: the freedom of ordinary people to play a prominent role in deciding who is to have religious authority—an authority that, in turn, can be used to check the executive and hold rulers accountable.

For well over a century, Shi'i clerics have led many of the movements advocating constitutionalism, parliamentary rule, and just governance in the Middle East. In post-Ba'th Iraq, clerics have again taken the lead, in large part because there scarcely exists a secular civil society in the country that can act as the nucleus of an Iraqi democratic system. In its thirty-five years of rule, the Ba'th wiped out all forms of civil organization not directly controlled by the party. To make matters worse, the twelve years of sanctions that preceded the U.S. invasion of 2003, reinforced by insecurity and an unemployment rate of some 50 percent in its wake, have reduced the Iraqi middle class to bare subsistence. It will be years before a viable secular middle class can reemerge and check the power of the religious groups, who are now the most vocal, organized, and politically mobilized force in Iraq. The participation of clerics in Iranian politics in 1978–79 resulted in a theocracy. But clerical participation in Iraqi politics today may give birth to a strong parliamentary system and to an elected government accountable to the electorate—a development that could transform relations between people and government both in Iraq and in the larger Arab world.

Amid the turmoil that followed the U.S. invasion of Iraq, and in the absence of a national leader with the stature to unite Iraqis, Grand Ayatollah ʿAli Sistani has asserted himself as the most revered leader of Iraqi Shiʿis. This reclusive seventy-five-year-old cleric, who enjoys the largest following in the Shiʿi world today, has assumed something of the role of a Shiʿi "pope," providing counsel to his followers and responding to the political aspirations of his constituency. For many Americans, who still remember the rise to power of the virulently anti-American Ayatollah Ruhollah Khomeini of Iran, Sistani's growing power may seem worrisome. Yet unlike Khomeini, who articulated the idea that clerics should rule (*wilayat al-faqih*), and implemented it in the Islamic Republic of Iran, Sistani represents the quietist school of thought within Shiʿism, and he has been reluctant to get directly involved in worldly affairs. The other three senior Shiʿi clerics in Najaf—Muhammad Saʿid al-Hakim, Muhammad Ishaq Fayyad, and Bashir Najafi—have all advocated a similar line. Sistani has shown pragmatism in dealing with the U.S. presence in Iraq, urging Shiʿis not to take up arms against the occupiers and—in sharp contrast to Khomeini—refusing to insult America. His rise as the authoritative and moral voice of Iraq was evident in the truce that Sistani brokered in August 2004, upon his dramatic return to Iraq following medical treatment in London. That truce ended three weeks of fighting around the imam 'Ali shrine in Najaf between U.S. marines and rebels loyal to Muqtada al-Sadr, averted an imminent attack on the shrine, and saved the Bush administration from political embarrassment on the eve of the Republican convention.

Still, despite his basic belief that clerics should stay out of politics, Sistani was drawn into the power vacuum in Iraq. And he has made clear his opinion on government and constitution making. On several occasions during 2003–4, Sistani bumped up against the plans of L. Paul Bremer III, the top American administrator in Iraq. In June 2003 Sistani issued a ruling forbidding the appointment of drafters to write the constitution, sanctioning their election by Iraqis instead. This move dealt a blow to the American plan to quickly introduce a new constitution. When in November Bremer unveiled a plan to elect a transitional national assembly through caucuses, Sistani insisted on direct elections and forced the Americans to scrap their proposal. Sistani also objected to the interim constitution (Transitional Administrative Law) signed by the Iraqi Governing Council in March 2004, stating that the elected assembly would not be bound by a document written by an institution appointed under occupation. His objection in effect annulled the interim constitution. In his actions, Sistani has engaged reluctant U.S. policymakers in a debate over the meaning of democracy. And as it turned out, his clout has fundamentally altered Washington's plans for Iraq, resulting in the transfer of sovereignty to an Iraqi interim government in June 2004 (to which Sistani gave his conditional approval), the elections to a transitional national assembly in January 2005, and the rise of Shi'is as the politically dominant community in post-Ba'th Iraq.[1]

Although Sistani has a vision of what an Islamic government should be, he is not inspired by Khomeini. Like his mentor, Abu al-Qasim Khoei, who died in 1992, Sistani has accepted the political reality of a modern nation-state led by lay politicians. He sees Iran's theocracy as a departure from centuries of Shi'i thought and does not advocate that clerics should be the final arbiters of state affairs. Unlike Khomeini's, Sistani's ideas are in tune with those of Muhammad Hussein Naʼini, author of *Tanbih al-umma wa-tanzih al-milla* (The Awakening of the Islamic Nation and the Purification of the Islamic Creed), published in Najaf around 1909.[2] Like Naʼini, Sistani's emphasis is on ensuring government accountability and protecting Islam. Hence his repeated calls for direct elections to a national assembly—an institution that would check the government and the process of legislation in Iraq. Nevertheless, in a break with both Naʼini's theory and the current political system in Iran, Sistani has not called for a council of guardians to scrutinize the bills that would be introduced in the assembly. If he continues to stick to this pragmatic stance, Sistani will in effect be recognizing the complex social reality of Iraq with its substantial Sunni and Kurdish minorities, and tacitly acknowledging that there should be limits on clerical participation in state affairs. Indeed, an Iraq that ends up with a strong national assembly capable of checking the executive, and guarding minority and women's rights, will be a radical departure from the political realities in both Iran and the Arab world, where rulers have been free to impose their will on legislatures and disregard human rights.

It is difficult to divine exactly where Sistani wants Shiʻism to go, but he seems determined to avoid the pitfalls of the Iranian revolution, which enabled an individual cleric like Khomeini to monopolize religious and political power, gain access to government funds, and boost his position within the universal Shiʻi religious leadership (the *marjaʻiyya*) vis-à-vis the more senior clerics. Following Khomeini's death in 1989, Iran's leaders have attempted to further blur the lines between religious and political leadership, as was evident in the hasty elevation of ʻAli Khamenei from the rank of a midlevel mujtahid to that of Ayatollah, and his subsequent appointment as the supreme religious leader of the Islamic Republic. Yet the Iranian government's attempt to encourage Shiʻis to follow Khamenei reinforced divisions within the clergy and alienated the lay population throughout the Shiʻi Muslim world.

Like the majority of Iranians, who have refused to fall in line behind Khamenei, their coreligionists elsewhere have not recognized him as the preeminent religious leader. This has worked to the advantage of Sistani and the clerics around him in Najaf today.

Najaf is a special place for Shi'is. For one thing, it contains the shrine of 'Ali, the first Shi'i imam. Moreover, the city has maintained a tradition of Shi'i scholarship for more than a millennium. Before the rise of the modern state in the twentieth century, Najaf was the preferred seat of the most learned Shi'i clerics. It enjoyed a semiautonomous status and viewed itself as the great nerve center of the Shi'i world. The establishment of modern Iraq under Sunni minority rule in 1921, and the subsequent demarcation of the border with Iran, dealt a blow to Najaf's semiautonomous status and to its economic welfare and academic standing. Najaf spiraled into a socioeconomic and intellectual decline, and in the middle of the twentieth century was superseded by Qum in Iran as the major Shi'i academic center. While the number of students in Qum increased, Najaf's student population dropped from some eight thousand early in the twentieth century to fewer than two thousand in 1957—the equivalent of a decline from a major research university to a small college. Under the Ba'th, and especially after the Iranian revolution, the number of students in Najaf dwindled further to a few hundred. Qum became the center for disseminating Shi'i ideas. Najaf, by contrast, turned inward.

In the wake of the U.S. invasion of Iraq, Shi'is around the globe have been eagerly anticipating the revival of Najaf as the leading academic center. Their hope is that a renaissance in Najaf will embolden the reform movement in Iran and encourage Sistani and the clerics around him to adapt Shi'ism to modern times. Shi'is have argued that change must begin in the religious leadership itself, advocating that the *marja'iyya* in Najaf should evolve into an institution similar to the papacy in the Vatican.[3] The idea of a Shi'i religious institution independent of the government was first proposed by the Iraqi cleric Muhammad Baqir al-Sadr shortly before his execution by the Ba'th in 1980. It was elaborated in the 1990s by Muhammad Hussein Fadlallah of Lebanon. Both Sadr and Fadlallah observed that the specialized curriculum in the Shi'i seminaries did not prepare religious leaders to deal with modern life. Today's religious leaders, Fadlallah argued, must have a commanding grip of world affairs, and the knowledge to answer a wide range of questions from followers all over the world. Yet the religious leaders have lagged behind the development of their followers and have failed to respond to their sociopolitical aspirations. To deal with that problem, Fadlallah proposed a universal Shi'i leadership established as a single institution with a permanent headquarters that would support the religious leader. The leader himself would be assisted by experts in all fields of life, and he would have representatives in various countries acting as ambassadors. Like John Paul II, who was an active pope, the Shi'i religious leader would travel throughout the Muslim world, reaching out to the faithful and addressing their concerns. Upon the death of the leader, the institution would provide continuity and enable the new leader to begin where his predecessor had left off.[4]

Sistani may prefer to keep the informal and loose organization that has characterized the Shi'i religious leadership for centuries, but the reforms that he and his successors choose to introduce will have a profound impact on Shi'is in the Arab world—the focus of this book. In contrast to Iran, where Shi'is are more than 80 percent of the population and Shi'ism is the state religion, in the Arab world Shi'is have been dominated by Sunni governments, or even by Christians, as was the case in Lebanon until the mid-1970s. Unlike Iranians, who are for the most part Persian-speakers, the Arab Shi'is share ethnic attributes with their Sunni counterparts. Yet they have not had the political opportunities enjoyed by Sunnis in the state and have therefore often contested the legitimacy of the government.

The Arab Shi'is are spread in large pockets from Lebanon to Iraq to the oil monarchies of the Persian Gulf. While they include small heterodox groups like the 'Alawis in Syria, the Isma'ilis in south-western Arabia, and the Zaydis in Yemen, this book focuses on the Twelvers, who adhere to the main branch of Shi'ism and form the vast majority of Shi'is. My purpose is to highlight the dialectics of change, and the reciprocal influences, that have shaped the development of Shi'ism in Saudi Arabia, Bahrain, Iraq, and Lebanon from the mid–eighteenth century to the 2005 elections in Iraq. I have chosen these four cases because of the different numerical and sociopolitical weight that Saudi, Bahraini, Iraqi, and Lebanese Shi'is have had within their respective countries, and because of the contrasts in nature among these states. Small Twelver Shi'i communities can be found in other Arab countries, but for the most part they are not as politically mobilized as their coreligionists in the four countries discussed here. I will compare political aspirations among Saudi, Bahraini, Iraqi, and Lebanese Shi'i communities, and assess the repercussions that the new Iraq is likely to have on Shi'is in the larger Arab world and on their view of America.

In Saudi Arabia, the challenge that the modern state posed to the Shi'i minority (estimated at around 8 percent of the population) has occasionally manifested itself in open religious hostility directed by the rulers and the state clergy against Saudi Shi'is, who live mainly in the eastern province of Hasa where the country's oil is found. The Saudi rulers' adoption of Wahhabi-Hanbali Islam as the religious ideology of Saudi Arabia in the eighteenth century has had direct bearing on the inferior status of Shi'is within the kingdom. From the Wahhabi point of view, Shi'is are considered either extremists or infidels. The severe restrictions imposed on Shi'i sociopolitical mobility in the state, as well as on basic Shi'i religious practices, have led Shi'is to consider themselves as second- and even third-class citizens. In a religiously oriented and politically conservative monarchy, where the strategies of the ruling family of the Al Sa'ud seem intended to isolate rather than include the Shi'is, the dilemma of the Shi'i minority has been how to survive as a viable group while maintaining a clear distinction between their dislike of the dominant Sunni Wahhabi religious ideology and their loyalty to the state. The major survival strategy pursued by Saudi Shi'is has appeared in their attempts to attach themselves to ideological movements that promised sweeping sociopolitical change. Whereas in the 1950s and 1960s Saudi Shi'is were influenced by communism, and by Nasserite and Ba'thist ideas of Pan-Arabism, in the late 1970s and 1980s they espoused Islamist ideology. Against the background of talk of a new world order after the Gulf War of 1991, Saudi Shi'is flaunted the regional component of their identity. The upheaval created by the 2003 U.S. invasion of Iraq has reenergized Saudi Shi'is, who have joined other Saudis in calling for reforms. Although the government has cracked down on the reformers, in the long run it will not be able to ignore the political change in Iraq, and it is likely to introduce reforms that would go beyond the limited municipal elections of 2005, and which would improve the sociopolitical rights of all Saudis, including the status of the Shi'i minority.

The case of Bahrain, where Shi'is form as much as 70 percent of the native population, illustrates the challenge of attempting to introduce constitutional reforms and a strong parliamentary system in the Arab world. It also underscores the sociopolitical tensions widespread in several of the Persian Gulf monarchies as a result of the employment of large numbers of foreigners, who in 2002 constituted some 65 percent of the Bahraini workforce. Bahrain is a small archipelago of 255 square miles off the eastern shore of Saudi Arabia, and the home port of the U.S. Fifth Fleet in the Persian Gulf. The Shi'i majority in the islands has been dominated by the Sunni Al Khalifa ruling family since their conquest of Bahrain in 1783. The tension between the Shi'is and the rulers came to a head after the emir suspended the constitution and dissolved parliament in 1975, and during the uprising of 1994–99, which led the government to introduce reforms. Yet the reform process has stalled, largely because of the government's refusal to reinstate the 1973 constitution and allow a strong parliamentary system in the country. Like their Saudi counterparts, Bahraini Shi'is have been eagerly anticipating the political outcome in Iraq. But more than in Saudi Arabia, the depth of reforms in Bahrain will be influenced both by the fate of the Iraqi constitution that was drafted during 2005 and by the evolving relations between the national assembly and the government in Iraq. Moreover, the negotiations that are bound to take place between an elected Iraqi government and the United States over the future of American bases in Iraq will inevitably have a strong impact on the U.S. military presence in Bahrain and on the Bahraini Shi'i view of America.

In Lebanon, Shi'is constitute the largest sect, or around 40 percent of the population. They predominate in Beirut, as well as in the Jabal 'Amil in the south and in the Bekaa Valley and Baalbek in the northeast. This case reveals the profound change that has taken place over the past thirty years in the politics of Lebanese Shi'is, who have shed their political quietism and emerged as leading players in the national arena. It also underscores the victory of pragmatism over Shi'i radicalism—an outcome that has important implications for the reconstruction of Iraq. Shi'i expressions of identity, and the progress Shi'is have made in the state, reflect the unique Lebanese reality in which political power has been apportioned according to ethnic and sectarian affiliation. Lebanese Shi'i expression took on a sectarian character from the mid-1970s—a development consonant with the increasing militancy of Lebanon's other major communities at a time when the country was disintegrating. The civil war of 1975–90 radicalized Lebanese Shi'is, as is evident in the emergence of Hizballah in the early 1980s. Yet in the course of two decades, Hizballah evolved from a militant movement seeking to establish an Islamic government in Lebanon into a political party. And in doing so, it accepted the Lebanese reality based on a pact among the country's seventeen sects, vying not only for the votes of Shi'is but also for those of Sunnis and Christians in mixed areas.

The Shi'i experience in Lebanon has direct bearing on postwar Iraq, where the newly empowered Shi'i majority will need to conclude a political deal with Sunnis and Kurds as a precondition for turning the country into a more tolerant and inclusive place than Ba'thist Iraq. Shi'is constitute some 60 percent of the population, spread over southern and central Iraq. Yet between 1921 and 2003, the Iraqi Shi'is (like the Kurds in the north) were dominated by a Sunni minority elite of barely 20 percent, with its base in central Iraq. In those years, Arab Shi'is and Sunnis fought over the right to rule and to define the meaning of nationalism in the country. That struggle, and the feeling of Shi'is that they have been robbed of power in modern Iraq, explain their drive to dominate the politics of the new Iraq. Nevertheless, the events leading up to the January 2005 elections demonstrated the rise of 'Ali Sistani as the Shi'i leader who understood the importance of compromise among Iraq's social groups as the only way to realize Shi'i political aspirations. Although Sistani is a Muslim cleric, and not an advocate of Jeffersonian democracy, his vision of a representative government and a strong parliament, put in power by free elections, could inspire revolutionary change in Iraq and the larger Arab world.

In the wake of the U.S. invasion of Iraq, the stakes are high. Iraq could descend into a civil war that would quash the aspirations of people in the Middle East for reform, or it could end up with just governance based on a compromise among Iraqis. America's pledge to bring democracy to Iraq and the Middle East turned out to be hollow in the face of events on the ground. It was left for Sistani and his followers to take the lead in charting the political future of Iraq and the larger Middle East. They can hardly afford to fail.

Chapter 1

The Burden of the Past

◈

This chapter illuminates the history underlying the uneasy relations between Shi'is and governments in modern Bahrain, Saudi Arabia, Iraq, and Lebanon. It shows that Shi'is and ruling elites have used the past to deny or legitimize the existing social order and hierarchy of power. Both the debates between Shi'is and the governing elite, and the history discussed here, illustrate that Shi'is in the Arab world entered nationhood feeling excluded from power and seeking to redress political wrong. I will start with Bahrain and Saudi Arabia, where debates about the past between Shi'is and ruling families have lasted more than two hundred years.

Whose Homeland?

The Shi'is of Bahrain and Saudi Arabia were bound together for many centuries. In early Islamic history, the name Bahrain applied loosely to the area embracing the oases of Hasa and Qatif on the eastern coast of Arabia as well as to the archipelago lying just a few miles offshore. Later the name came to be restricted to the islands. Yet the Shi'i population, which forms a majority both on the islands and in Hasa and Qatif, retained many similarities long after Bahrain and Saudi Arabia came under the rule of the Al Khalifa and the Al Sa'ud, respectively. These two dynastic families originated in Najd in central Arabia, claiming descent from the 'Anaza tribal confederation. They made their appearance roughly in the mid–eighteenth century, when the modern history of Bahrain and Saudi Arabia begins.

The Al Khalifa's conquest of Bahrain in 1783 came more than a century after a famine had forced the family to leave central Arabia and migrate eastward. The family constitute a branch of the 'Utub, a subtribe of the 'Anaza. The name 'Utub means roamers or wanderers, indicating the vast distances that the tribe had covered after leaving Najd. Before their arrival in Bahrain, the Al Khalifa were based in Kuwait, departing in 1766 to settle in Zubara in northwestern Qatar. Their settlement in Zubara was an important stage in a process by which the Al Khalifa gave up their nomadic lifestyle and acquired prominence as sailors and traders in the Persian Gulf.[1]

Bahrain was an Iranian possession for most of the seventeenth and eighteenth centuries, beginning in 1602 when the Safavids expelled the Portuguese from the islands. Actual rule was in the hands of Arab tribes who submitted to provincial governors in southern Iran. On the eve of the Al Khalifa's conquest, the Arab Madhkur family of Bushire governed the islands in the shah's name. The Al Khalifa's success in gaining a monopoly over the pearl trade off the coasts of Qatar and Bahrain, and their crossing from Zubara to Bahrain to trade, provoked the animosity of Sheikh Nasr Madhkur. In 1782 an incident in the Sitra island of Bahrain led to the death of an Al Khalifa member. Madhkur subsequently put Zubara under siege for a month, but he failed to occupy the town. In 1783 Sheikh Ahmad ibn Muhammad Al Khalifa counterattacked, defeating Madhkur's army and conquering Bahrain. Nevertheless, the Al Khalifa did not move immediately into Bahrain; for several years they ruled the islands from Zubara, paying a small annual tribute to the governor of Shiraz and not openly denying Iran's claim to Bahrain. Although in 1796 Salman ibn Ahmad Al Khalifa moved from Zubara to Bahrain, the Al Khalifa's rule was still not secured. The sultan of Oman occupied the islands in 1800, and between 1802 and 1811 the Al Khalifa submitted to the Al Saʿud. The Al Khalifa managed to consolidate their rule only after the British government guaranteed the security of their territories in treaties signed in 1861, 1880, and 1892, amounting to a British protectorate that lasted until 1971, when Bahrain gained independence.[2]

By the time of the Al Khalifa's conquest of Bahrain, the Al Saʿud had already established themselves as a power in Arabia. In the early eighteenth century, a religious reformer, Muhammad ibn ʿAbd al-Wahhab (1703–92), began calling Muslims to return to an Islam based on what he regarded as strict Sunni teachings. The reformer made an alliance with Muhammad ibn Saʿud, the ruler of Dirʿiyya, a small market oasis in Najd, and this led to the formation of the first Saudi state (1745–1818). Twice during the nineteenth century the power of the Al Saʿud was reduced, but each time the family managed to regain its dominance. A second Saudi state existed for most of the period between 1823 and 1887, and in 1902 ʿAbd al-ʿAziz ibn Saʿud formed the third state, which became the basis for modern Saudi Arabia. The Al Saʿud first conquered Hasa and Qatif in 1795, defeating the sheikhs of the Banu Khalid tribe who had governed the Hasa province in the name of the Ottoman sultan. Between 1795 and 1913 Hasa and Qatif changed hands several times, and were also included in the second Saudi state. Ibn Saʿud's occupation of the Hasa province in 1913 put an end to Ottoman rule there. The Shiʿa of Hasa and Qatif subsequently became part of Saudi Arabia, followed by the small Shiʿi community around Medina in the Hijaz, which Ibn Saʿud annexed in 1925.[3]

The rise of the Al Khalifa and the Al Saʿud was a blow to the Shiʿis in Bahrain and Saudi Arabia. Whereas in Bahrain a Sunni minority came to dominate the Shiʿi majority, in Saudi Arabia a Shiʿi minority was subjected to a Wahhabi reform that considered the Shi'is as infidels who should be forced to conform to the Wahhabi version of Islam. In both countries, Shi'is and ruling elites offered different interpretations regarding the emergence of modern Bahrain and Saudi Arabia, each trying to lay claim to the homeland.

The Al Khalifa's account of the 1783 conquest of Bahrain is presented in a series of articles written during the Iran-Iraq War of 1980–88 (which exacerbated tensions between Sunnis and Shi'is and between Arabs and Persians), and also in a book on the history of Bahrain that grew out of a conference held in Manama in 1983 to mark the two hundredth anniversary of the family's arrival in the islands. In their writings, the Al Khalifa members and other writers in their camp lengthened the historical past of the ruling family in Bahrain. They emphasized that sections of the 'Utub tribe were already living in Bahrain in 1700—eighty-three years before Ahmad ibn Muhammad Al Khalifa had conquered the islands. The failed siege that Sheikh Nasr Madhkur laid to Zubara in December 1782 is given special consideration, and the Al Khalifa are presented as a noble people whose courageous defense of the city reflected the attributes of ideal manhood of the Arabs. We are told that Madhkur assembled a force of between two thousand and four thousand fighters in preparation for the battle of Zubara. All attempts to end the siege peacefully failed because Madhkur insisted on the total and unconditional submission of the Al Khalifa, including the surrender of their women and children—a humiliating demand that the elders of the family rejected. The Al Khalifa braced themselves for the worst, and the men prepared to put their women and children to death in the event of defeat. For the Al Khalifa the choice was clear: either victory and life with honor or a brave and dignified death. Fortunately, the Al Khalifa repelled Madhkur's army and then proceeded to "liberate" Bahrain. The conquest of the islands is presented in the context of the old rivalry between Arabs and Persians, and as a landmark in Arab history. Sheikh Ahmad ibn Muhammad Al Khalifa is named the victorious conqueror (*fatih*) who rescued Bahrain from Iranian hands and brought it back "once and for all to the Arab fold." We are told that Bahrain's history prior to 1783, when the Al Khalifa established a new administrative power in the islands, was "full of troubles." By contrast, the conquest brought swift commercial progress to Bahrain thanks to the aptitude of the 'Utub tribe for trade and political stability, and the connection of Bahrain to Zubara where the Al Khalifa had created conditions for "free trade and the duty-free movement of merchandise."[4]

If the Al Khalifa were the liberators of Arab lands, the Al Sa'ud were the unifiers of Islam. The Al Sa'ud claim to this role is apparent in Saudi government accounts that narrate 'Abd al-'Aziz Ibn Sa'ud's conquest of Hasa and Qatif in May 1913. The first account was provided in that very year by Ibn Sa'ud himself. In an interview for the Carmelite journal *Lughat al-'Arab*, he explained that he had reclaimed a territory that belonged to his family, one which the Ottomans had seized in 1871 from his uncle 'Abdallah ibn Sa'ud. The timing of his attack was influenced by requests that he had received from clerics and notables in Hasa and Qatif, urging him to rescue them from corrupt Ottoman officials and the menacing power of the tribes.[5] Modern Saudi historiography has elaborated this story, presenting it as part of a process of Saudi state formation that began with the establishment of the first Saudi state in 1745. Ibn Sa'ud is portrayed as a legendary figure and as the founding father of modern Saudi Arabia. A man of special virtues, he is compared both to the Prophet Muhammad, who converted the pagan Arab tribes to Islam, and to Saladin, the twelfth-century Muslim leader who defeated the Crusaders and established the Ayyubid dynasty in Egypt, Syria, and parts of western Arabia. Ibn Sa'ud is depicted as the greatest Islamic reformer and Arab leader of modern times—a hero who was injured many times in the wars that he waged in the name of Islam and Arabism. We are told that he rebelled against Ottoman and British imperialism, fought heretics, subdued the tribes, and unified Arabia, making it a secure and stable state governed by principles of social justice. His creation of Saudi Arabia stood as the major achievement of the Arabs in modern history. At the same time, the conquest of Hasa and Qatif is said to have opened a new page in the history of the Wahhabi movement, enabling Ibn Saʿud to control the trade routes leading from the Persian Gulf coast to inner Arabia, and thereby securing the future of the country. His move on Hasa and Qatif is presented as holy war against Shiʿi heretics, who cooperated with foreign imperialists to weaken Islam, and as a response to the sad plight of the people.[6]

The accounts of the Al Khalifa and the Al Saʿud are intended to legitimize the rule of the two families and discredit the Arab origin and Muslim credentials of Bahraini and Saudi Shiʿis. While the Al Khalifa's case rests on the assertion that the family has turned Bahrain into a prospering state and a bastion of Arabism, the Al Saʿud's is built around the commitment of the family to spreading and preserving the "true spirit" of Islam. Whereas the Al Khalifa's account suggests that the Shiʿis of Bahrain have an indelible "Persian connection" going back to 1602, when the islands became an Iranian possession, the accounts narrating Ibn Saʿud's "liberation" of Hasa and Qatif depict the Shiʿis as heretics who are beyond the pale of Islam. This type of presentation of the past has cast doubts on the national credentials of Shiʿis in Bahrain and Saudi Arabia, and undermined their sociopolitical position in the state.

In coping with this challenge, Shiʿis claimed to be the indigenous populations of Bahrain, Hasa, and Qatif, pointing to the long history of sedentarization in the area as proof that their civilization was more enlightened than the brusque tribal culture of the Al Khalifa and the Al Saʿud. Bahraini and Saudi Shiʿis asserted that their Arab origin was evident from the similarities between their dialect and the early dialects of central and southern Arabia. They emphasized their shared historical past, the family relations tying Shiʿis on the islands to those on the mainland, and the fact that until the mid–eighteenth century they were commonly known as Baharna, Bahrainis.[7] To give further credence to their Arab origin and right to the homeland, Shiʿis highlighted the fact that their Shiʿism is very old. Tradition has it that after the death of the

Prophet Muhammad in 632, members of the 'Abd al-Qays tribe, who were spread in Bahrain, Hasa, and Qatif, were strong support- ers of 'Ali ibn Abi Talib's right to the caliphate. Some of the families in the area, Shi'is relate, are descendants of the 'Abd al-Qays.[8]

While it is generally accepted that Shi'ism first appeared in Iraq around the mid–seventh century, and sometime later in Bahrain, Hasa, and Qatif, it is not clear when Shi'is became a majority in this region. The rise of the Carmathians in the late ninth century probably gave a boost to Shi'ism in the area. The Carmathians were a branch of Isma'ili Shi'ism. They defeated the 'Abd al-Qays who ruled Bahrain, Hasa, and Qatif, establishing their own powerful state in the region. This state was destroyed in 1077 by 'Abdallah ibn 'Ali al-'Uyuni, who recognized the suzerainty of the Fatimids of Egypt—adherents of a different branch of Isma'ilism. It is possible that parts of the population of the former Carmathian state accepted Twelver Shi'ism during the 'Uyunid period, which lasted until around 1237.[9] In any case, the development of Shi'ism on both the islands and the mainland was influenced by the emer- gence of Bahrain as a center of Shi'i learning in the thirteenth and fourteenth centuries, and by its status as an Iranian possession in the seventeenth and eighteenth centuries. The increase in the num- ber of Shi'is may also be attributed to the settlement of Sunni no- madic tribes whose members subsequently converted to Shi'ism. This pattern is more evident, however, on the Saudi mainland, where a third of the Shi'i population are said to be descendants of settled tribes. A good example is the Banu Khalid. After the Al Sa'ud broke the power of this powerful tribe in the nineteenth cen- tury, some of its sections settled down around Hasa and Qatif and espoused Shi'ism.[10] The makeup of modern Shi'i society in the area reflected migration waves between Bahrain, Hasa, and Qatif, as well as emigrations from Iraq and Iran to both the islands and the mainland. The long history of Shi'ism in Bahrain, Hasa, and Qatif is evident in the rich Shi'i endowment (*waqf*) property in the area. In Bahrain, the sizable Shi'i *waqf* stands in marked contrast to the scarcity of Sunni endowments. That property has sustained the activity of Shi'i religious institutions (*ma'tams*), several of which are reported to be quite ancient.[11]

At the time they encountered the Al Khalifa and the Al Sa'ud in the mid–eighteenth century, the Shi'is of Bahrain did not form one community with those of Hasa and Qatif. The differences between Shi'is on the islands and those on the mainland were already evident when the Portuguese arrived in the area. The Portuguese ruled the islands for eighty-one years beginning in 1521, but they did not establish themselves in Hasa and Qatif. While the islands were an Iranian possession between 1602 and 1783, Hasa and Qatif were under Ottoman rule, starting in 1534 when the chief of Qatif traveled to Baghdad to swear allegiance to Sultan Suleiman the Magnificent.[12] In the eighteenth century there was apparently no single religious figure accepted by the Shi'is of the islands and those of the mainland. This may be attributed in part to the role of Bahrain and the city of Qatif as the strongholds of the Akhbari Shi'i ulama. Unlike the Usuli ulama, their Akhbari rivals prohibited the following of living mujtahids, thus rendering the emergence of a charismatic religious leader difficult.[13] The rise of the Al Khalifa and the Al Sa'ud further pulled Bahraini and Saudi Shi'is apart, and since the mid–eighteenth century they have used different self-designations. While Shi'is on the mainland increasingly came to be known as the Hasawiyya, the term Baharna has been used almost exclusively for Shi'is on the islands. The Baharna have further used this term to distinguish themselves from Sunnis of Bahrain, and to make the point that they were the native islanders and hence the legal owners of the land confiscated by the Al Khalifa.[14]

The writings of Bahraini Shi'is tell the story of a settled people who succumbed to the humiliating supremacy of Sunni nomads. The anthropologist Fuad Khuri recorded a tradition which relates that Bahrain had three hundred villages and thirty cities before 1783, each ruled by a jurist who was well versed in Shi'i law. These 330 jurists were organized into a hierarchy headed by a council of three, elected by an assembly of thirty-three who, in turn, held power thanks to acclamation by the jurists of the entire country.

Land was held individually under the Islamic law of usufruct, according to which whoever cultivates or continues to cultivate a plot of land earns the right to its use and can pass it on to his children.[15] Shi'is claim that the raids of the 'Utub tribe in 1700, followed by the Al Khalifa's occupation in 1783, destroyed this just government-system, and ruined Bahrain and its civilization. This point was developed during the 1990s when Shi'i opposition groups depicted the Al Khalifa as "foreign invaders" and "medieval rulers" who established their Sunni minority rule thanks to British and Saudi help. The conquest, which the Al Khalifa presented as the liberation of Arab lands from Persian control, was thus labeled the destruction of Bahrain and a calamity worse than the invasion of the islands by the Christian Portuguese. Shi'is alleged that the Al Khalifa failed to gain legitimacy in Bahrain and established a system of "political apartheid based on racial, sectarian, and tribal discrimination."[16]

The Shi'i development of a myth of a golden age in Bahrain just before the Al Khalifa's arrival may very well be a reaction to the social agonies that they experienced after 1783. This myth was probably inspired by Bahrain's Carmathian past. It is known that the prosperity of the Carmathian state invoked the envy of its enemies. The state had vast fruit and grain estates both on the islands and in Hasa and Qatif. Nasir-i Khusru, who visited Hasa in 1051, recounted that these estates were cultivated by some thirty thousand Ethiopian slaves. He mentions that the people of Hasa were exempt from taxes. Those impoverished or in debt could obtain a loan until they put their affairs in order. No interest was taken on loans, and token lead money was used for all local transactions. The Carmathian state had a powerful and long-lasting legacy. This is evidenced by a coin known as *Tawila*, minted around 920 by one of the Carmathian rulers, and which was still in circulation in Hasa early in the twentieth century.[17]

The myth of a glorious Shi'i past stood in sharp contrast to the modern reality of Bahrain where a Sunni tribal elite has dominated the settled Shi'i population. As will be shown in the next chapter, the Al Khalifa encouraged the migration of Sunni nomadic tribes into the islands, thus altering the ratio of Sunnis to Shi'is in the country. Bahraini society remained divided along sectarian, geographical, and class lines well into the twentieth century, with the Sunni population tending to concentrate in cities and Shi'is living mainly in rural areas. Intermarriage between the two groups was almost unheard-of until the late 1960s. Segregation was a way of life that preserved not only the Al Khalifa's minority rule but also the distinct identity of the Shi'i majority.

In contrast to Bahrain, where the Al Khalifa have not entertained any grand religious vision, in Saudi Arabia Wahhabism posed a threat to the survival of the Shi'i minority as a viable religious group. Saudi rulers attempted not only to isolate the Shi'is but to dissolve their identity as well. During the first and second Saudi states the Shi'i religious seminaries in Qatif were closed down and their libraries burned. Tombs of Shi'i saints, as well as mosques and other religious institutions, were destroyed. Shi'is were forbidden to perform their rituals in public, as special judges and prayer-leaders were appointed in Hasa and Qatif to enforce Sunni Islam. The Saudis installed new governors, sent from Najd, in the two cities. They broke the power of prominent Shi'i families and exiled their members to Dir'iyya. By the time of the third Saudi state, the power of the Shi'i elite in Hasa and Qatif had been greatly reduced, and many religious scholars left for Iran and Iraq.[18]

Saudi Shi'is offer their own version of the events leading to Ibn Sa'ud's conquest of Hasa and Qatif in 1913. In contrast to official Saudi accounts which maintain that the leaders of Hasa urged Ibn Sa'ud to occupy the city, Shi'is claim that in April of the same year Ibn Sa'ud and the senior mujtahid of Hasa, Musa Bu Khamsin, signed a contract stipulating the peaceful submission of Shi'is in return for a guarantee of their lives and religious freedom. Life around Hasa and Qatif in the years just before 1913 had been insecure because of the growing power of the tribes. The Ottoman garrison was too weak to subdue the tribes, let alone defend the two cities against Ibn Sa'ud's army. The Shi'is were thus in dire straits, divided between Usulis and Akhbaris and between those who favored surrender and those who advocated resistance. While the majority of clerics and notables in both cities were willing to pledge allegiance to Ibn Sa'ud, there was a minority that refused to submit; it was led by Hasan 'Ali Al Badr, the senior mujtahid of Qatif, and by 'Abd al-Hussein al-Jum'a. The view of the majority prevailed, however. Hasa surrendered in April, and Qatif followed a month later. Those few ulama who did not submit to Ibn Sa'ud fled to Bahrain. In the writings of contemporary Shi'i Islamic opposition groups, those ulama who refused to surrender became the heroes whose conduct inspired modern Shi'i opposition to the Al Sa'ud. By contrast, those who pledged allegiance to Ibn Sa'ud in 1913 have been depicted as people whose families did not originate in the area of Hasa and Qatif, and whose Shi'ism was weak.[19]

As will be shown in chapter 2, the Al Sa'ud did indeed break their contract with the Shi'is. Saudi Shi'is became a persecuted religious minority and did not reap the fruits of the economic boom that followed the 1938 discovery of oil in their province.

Two notable differences distinguish Iraq from Bahrain and Saudi Arabia. First, in contrast to the drawn-out processes of state formation in the latter two countries, which amounted to conquest and territorial expansion by the Al Khalifa and the Al Sa'ud, Iraq was created as a British mandate in 1921 following the collapse of the Ottoman Empire. In the five preceding centuries Iraq had been a cultural-religious contact zone between the Sunni Ottoman Empire and Shi'i Iran. Because Ottoman rule was often nominal, Safavid, and later Qajar, Iran was able to claim that the shah should be the protector of Shi'i interests in Iraq, at the core of which stood the shrine cities of Najaf and Karbala. Second, unlike Bahraini and Saudi Shi'is, who have a long history as a settled people, the majority of Iraqi Shi'is are of recent tribal origin. This development is a result of the emergence of Najaf and Karbala during the eighteenth and nineteenth centuries as the bases of Shi'i propagation among the Arab nomadic tribes of central and southern Iraq. By the twentieth century, Shi'is had become a majority in the country as the bulk of Iraq's tribes settled down and espoused Shi'ism.[20] This means that the debate between Shi'is and the ruling elite over the formative years in Iraq covered a shorter period than that in Bahrain and Saudi Arabia; it focused on the events surrounding the fall of the Ottoman Empire, covered later in this chapter, and on the 1920 revolt against the British, discussed in chapter 3. Moreover, whereas Bahraini Shi'is despised "the tribal mentality" of the Al Khalifa, Iraqi Shi'is took pride in their tribal attributes and protested the government's attempt to play down the role of tribes in the struggle for independence against the British.

The Iraqi monarchy that the British put together was built around King Feisal, a son of Sharif Hussein of Mecca, and a Sunni elite whose members for the most part lacked a strong social base in the country. Before coming to Iraq Feisal had been installed as king in Syria at the end of World War I, but the French evicted him in 1920. The Sharifian officers around Feisal were too few to govern Iraq on their own, and they had to share power with some five hundred ex-Ottoman officers and officials. These either deserted to Feisal during the war or joined him in Damascus after the destruction of the Ottoman Empire. The lieutenants and clerks of 1914 were transformed in the course of a few years into generals, governors, and high-ranking officials and ministers. Among the officials, there were a good number of non-Iraqis who were unfamiliar with the ways of the country and its people. Most notable among these was Sati' al-Husri, who was entrusted with shaping Iraq's educational system. The Sunni politicians were drawn mainly from among the ex-Ottoman officers, and they rose to prominence with British support. While the majority were Iraqis who had been absent from the country for a long time before 1921 (as was the case with 'Abd al-Muhsin al-Sa'dun, Yasin al-Hashimi, and Nuri Sa'id), some were of Turkish or mixed origin—most notably Hikmat Sulayman and Ja'far al-'Askari.[21] These Sharifians and ex-Ottoman officers ruled Iraq until 1958. A decade of instability followed the collapse of the monarchy, leading to the Ba'th rise to power and the subsequent emergence of the Sunni Takriti clan whose members, led by Saddam Hussein, ruled Iraq until 2003.

As will be seen in chapter 3, the formation of modern Iraq generated a heated debate between Shi'is and the ruling Sunni elite over the question "Who is an Iraqi?" The repercussions of this debate are still evident today in the difficulty Iraqis have in accepting the proportionally high number of returning exiles in the administration and government, and in agreeing on the national identity of post-Ba'th Iraq.

Like Iraq, Lebanon was created as a mandate following World War I, administered by France. But Lebanon was different in a fundamental way from Iraq as well as from the other countries discussed in this book, which were ruled by Muslim elites. In Lebanon the Christian Maronites emerged as the dominant political sect, retaining that position until the civil war of 1975–90. This means that unlike Bahrain, Saudi Arabia, or Iraq, where the debate over history and national identity took place among Muslims, in Lebanon Christians played a leading role in reconstructing the past. Christian and Muslim Lebanese have disagreed over what constitutes the Lebanese heritage. Whereas the majority of Christians viewed Lebanon as an entity in its own right, Muslims insisted that what history Lebanon could claim for itself was Arab and Islamic. The difficulty of the Lebanese in agreeing on a common history has manifested itself even among members of the same sect, as the case of the Shi'i community demonstrates.

During most of the Ottoman period, the name Lebanon was restricted to the mountain region, the country constituting part of the Damascus province. Among the seventeen sects that make up modern Lebanese society, the Maronites, the Druzes, the Sunnis, and the Shi'is represent the largest groups. Their struggle for land and political hegemony is an old one, dating back to the eleventh century. The Maronites, as a Christian community in historical Syria, are roughly as old as Islam, but Mount Lebanon became their principal territory only around the eleventh century. That period also marked the appearance in Lebanon, around 1017, of the Druzes, who broke off from the Shi'i Isma'ilis. The expansion of Sunnism, in Syria and along the coast of Lebanon, was spurred by the rise of the Sunni Mamluks, and later the Ottoman Empire, starting in the late thirteenth century.[22] In subsequent centuries leading up to the mid–twentieth, these three communities grew in importance and managed to overshadow the Shi'is, who experienced religious and cultural decline.

Shi'is claim that the seeds of Shi'ism in Syria and Lebanon were planted as early as the mid–seventh century by Abu Dharr al-Ghifari, whom the caliph 'Uthman had exiled to Syria. Abu Dharr's success in propagating Shi'ism in Syria led its governor, Mu'awiya ibn Abi Sufyan, to expel him to Lebanon. Yet Abu Dharr did not stop preaching in Lebanon and was especially successful among the population of the Jabal 'Amil. This tradition has become part of the collective memory of Shi'is in Lebanon, who still call themselves "Shi'at Abi Dharr."[23] But this story does not explain the historical growth of Shi'ism in Syria and Lebanon—a development that took place between the tenth and the thirteenth centuries. The expansion of Shi'ism was spurred by the rise of three Shi'i dynasties: the Hamdanids in the north of Syria and Iraq from 906 to 1004, the Fatimids who ruled Egypt and parts of Syria and Lebanon between 969 and 1171, and the Buyids who ruled most of Iraq between 945 and 1055. It is the establishment of Shi'ism as the religion of the rulers in large parts of the Fertile Crescent that accounts for the spread of Shi'ism in Syria and Lebanon. In Lebanon, Shi'is became concentrated in four areas: the Jabal 'Amil in the south, the Bekaa Valley and Baalbek in the northeast, Kisrawan in the northwest, and the Maronite districts in the north.[24]

Yet the growth of Shi'ism in Lebanon stopped around the late thirteenth century, and subsequently Shi'i communities decreased in size. This development may be traced to 1291 when the Sunni Mamluks sent the first of three expeditions to subdue the Shi'is of Kisrawan, a mountain region overlooking the coastal area north of Beirut. These Mamluk expeditions, sanctioned by the respectful jurist Ibn Taymiya, forced Shi'is in Kisrawan to conceal their identity and follow the Sunni teaching of the Shafi'i law school during the fourteenth century. Kisrawan began to lose its Shi'i character under the Assaf Sunni Turkomans whom the Mamluks appointed as overlords of the area in 1306. The process intensified around 1545 when the Maronites started migrating from northern to southern Lebanon, encouraged by the Assafs, who sought to use them as a counterweight to the Shi'i Himada sheikhs who ruled Kisrawan.[25] When in 1605 the Druze emir Fakhr al-Din Ma'n II took over Kisrawan, he entrusted its management to the Khazin Maronite family. The Khazins gradually colonized Kisrawan, purchasing Shi'i lands and founding churches and monasteries. They emerged as the predominant authority in the region at the expense of the Shi'i Himada clan, starting a process that led to the eviction of Shi'is from Kisrawan. By the end of the eighteenth century, the Khazins owned Kisrawan and only a few Shi'i villages survived. As Shi'is left Kisrawan, the position of their coreligionists in the Maronite districts further north weakened, and Shi'is were forced to leave that area too. Kisrawan and northern Lebanon thus became predominantly Maronite. The Shi'is withdrew further south and eventually had to abandon even Jezzin, which until the mid–eighteenth century had functioned as a center of Shi'i learning in Lebanon.[26]

It was probably in reaction to the setback to their position in Lebanon that Shi'is began calling themselves Mutawalis—a name which means followers of imam 'Ali. The name was apparently not in use before the early seventeenth century, and it did not include the Shi'i communities of Syria. The appearance of the name was said to be connected to the fighting over land and political hegemony, when the Shi'i Nassar, Harfush, and Himada clans in the

Jabal ʿAmil, Baalbek, and Kisrawan united in opposition to the rule of the Druze Maʿn and the Sunni Shihab dynasties. Shiʿi fighters used the name to motivate themselves in battle, considering it a blessing to die as devotees of imam ʿAli.[27]

Although the Jabal ʿAmil enjoyed a degree of autonomy in the eighteenth century, this ended with the Ottoman appointment of Ahmad al-Jazzar as governor of Sidon province (1775–1804). Jazzar crushed the military power of the Shiʿi clan leaders and burned the libraries of the religious scholars. He established a centralized administration in the Shiʿi areas and brought their revenues and cash crops under his domain. By the late eighteenth century, the Shiʿis of the Jabal ʿAmil lost their independent spirit and adopted an attitude of political defeat. Like the Shiʿis of Bahrain, who spoke of a glorious past before the Al Khalifa conquered the islands, the Shiʿis of the Jabal ʿAmil evoked their own memory of a golden age that preceded Jazzar's time. In both cases the myth carried the nostalgic glow that settled communities confer on an imagined era of justice and prosperity.[28]

At the turn of the nineteenth century, Shiʿis in Lebanon were confined to the Jabal ʿAmil in the south and to the Bekaa Valley and Baalbek in the northeast. The two communities were separated by geography and distinguished by their different economic orientation and socioreligious organization. The Jabal ʿAmil was part of Sidon province and looked to Palestine and the Mediterranean; the Bekaa and Baalbek were part of Damascus province and their economy was tied to the Syrian interior. Shiʿi society in the Jabal ʿAmil was composed mainly of peasants and had clearer structures of authority than its counterpart in the Bekaa and Baalbek, which was more clannish in nature. In the late nineteenth and early twentieth centuries members of the two communities observed religious rituals differently. While Shiʿis in the Jabal ʿAmil began publicly observing the rituals of ʿAshuraʾ in commemoration of Hussein, including the *taʿziya* play, those in the Bekaa and Baalbek exhibited more restraint in their rituals and mainly read literature of lament. Unlike the Maronites and the Druzes, whose political organization was reinforced by strong religious institutions, until the second half of the twentieth century Lebanese Shi'is lacked socioreligious and political unity. The Jabal 'Amil had a long tradition of religious scholarship, but during the Ottoman period Shi'i religious life declined and the ulama were eclipsed by the notable leaders. The Shi'i ulama of the Jabal 'Amil became famous not because of their activities in Ottoman Lebanon, but because of the role they played in spreading Shi'ism in Iran following the establishment of the Safavid state in 1501. In the Bekaa Valley, no tradition of organized religious learning is known to have existed among the Shi'i clans, even under the Harfush emirs who ruled Baalbek between 1516 and 1866, first as Ottoman-appointed governors and later as virtual vassals of the Ma'n and Shihab dynasties.[29] The Jabal 'Amil and the Bekaa remained the major concentrations of Shi'is in Lebanon before migrants from these areas established the Shi'is as the largest community of Beirut in the second half of the twentieth century. As will be seen in chapter 4, this migration set the stage for the development of Shi'i mass politics in the country.

The discussion thus far shows how processes of society and state formation have influenced the position of Shi'is in the four countries under consideration. It also underscores the difficulty experienced by the Shi'is and governing elites of Bahrain, Saudi Arabia, Iraq, and Lebanon in agreeing on a common historical past. That difficulty becomes further evident in the controversies surrounding the fall of the Ottoman Empire and the role of Shi'is and ruling elites in resisting or assisting the Christian powers who brought it about.

The Destruction of the Ottoman Empire

In 1922 the Turkish nationalist regime abolished the Ottoman Sultanate, an act that officially ended four centuries of Ottoman rule of the Arab lands. This development had little bearing on Bahrain, which remained a British protectorate. But it generated debates between Shi'is and ruling elites in Saudi Arabia, Iraq, and Lebanon, because the emergence of these states was tied both to the fate of the Ottoman Empire and to the subsequent remaking of the Middle East by Britain and France. The themes varied according to the specific historical experience of each of these states, but the discussion essentially focused on one question: Who defended the Ottoman Empire in its difficult hour, and who acted to bring about the demise of this last great Muslim state?

In Saudi Arabia, the debate between Shi'is and the rulers focused on Ibn Sa'ud's foreign contacts between 1902 and 1918, and on the circumstances surrounding the rise of Saudi Arabia. Following his capture of Riyadh in 1902, Ibn Sa'ud adopted a strategy intended to safeguard his independence from the Ottomans through the support and protection of Britain. On several occasions in the period prior to 1913 Ibn Sa'ud tried to assess the British reaction to a possible Saudi conquest of the Hasa province. If he were to obtain independence from the Ottomans, he had to occupy a seaport in Hasa and establish treaty relations with Britain. In May 1913, just days before his move on Hasa, Ibn Sa'ud met with Captain Shakespear, the British political agent in Kuwait. Ibn Sa'ud told Shakespear that the misfortunes and weakness of the Ottoman Empire furnished the best opportunity for Najd to rid itself of Ottoman suzerainty and drive the Ottoman troops out of Hasa. The Ottoman sultan, Ibn Sa'ud told Shakespear, was in no sense the caliph of Islam. The Turks had neglected their religion, and God had abandoned them. It was therefore obligatory on all good Wahhabis to sever contacts with the "backslider and reprobate Turks." By the end of May Hasa and Qatif were under Saudi control, and Britain had to deal with the question of its precise relations with Ibn Sa'ud.[30]

The entry of the Ottoman Empire into World War I, and its call for jihad against the Allied Powers, released Britain from its obligation to take a neutral stand toward Ibn Sa'ud's relations with the Ottomans. In December 1915 Ibn Sa'ud met Percy Cox, the British chief political agent in the Persian Gulf, and the two signed a formal agreement. Britain recognized Ibn Sa'ud's claim to territorial independence in Najd and Hasa, undertook to support him in the event of aggression from the Ottomans or other foreign powers, and presented the emir with a thousand rifles and a sum of twenty thousand pounds. Ibn Sa'ud's close connections with Britain received public confirmation in a meeting of Arab chiefs held in Kuwait in November 1916. "On that memorable occasion," wrote one British official, "three powerful Arab chiefs, the Shaykh of Muhammara, the Shaykh of Kuwait, and Ibn Sa'ud stood side by side in amity and concord and proclaimed their adherence to the British cause." In a speech Ibn Sa'ud asserted that the Turks had placed themselves outside the pale of Islam because of their mistreatment of other Muslims. He pointed out that whereas the Turks had sought to dismember and weaken the Arab nation, British policy aimed at uniting and strengthening Arab leaders. The practical outcome of this meeting was an agreement under which Ibn Sa'ud was to receive a monthly subsidy of five thousand pounds. He continued to receive British subsidies until 1924.[31] His power increased steadily during and after the war, and by 1926 he controlled all the former Ottoman territories in Arabia except Yemen.

In Saudi historiography the period between 1902 and 1918 is presented as the renaissance of the Arabs, who managed to liberate themselves from Ottoman imperialism. Ibn Sa'ud is portrayed as the leader of the movement of Arab awakening who purified Najd from the Turkish infidels and freed Arabia from Ottoman occupation. His friendly relations with the British are explained as a tactical move intended to achieve Saudi independence and assist the Arabs in gaining freedom. Saudi writers also relate that in a meeting with Percy Cox in 1915, Ibn Sa'ud rejected the suggestion that he should claim the caliphate, thus refusing to play a role in British designs in the Middle East.[32]

It was not until the Iranian Islamic Revolution of 1978–79 that Shi'is attempted to publicly challenge this official version of Saudi history. During the 1980s and early 1990s—a period marked by growing activism among a younger generation of Shi'is who rebelled against the passive attitude of their elders—Saudi Shi'is began offering their own account of Ibn Sa'ud's relations with the Ottomans and the British. Shi'i writers focused on the period between Italy's occupation of Libya in October 1911 and Ibn Sa'ud's participation in the Kuwait conference of November 1916. In their accounts, Shi'is in Hasa and Qatif emerge as advocates of Muslim unity, while Ibn Sa'ud is depicted as a separatist who betrayed the Ottomans and collaborated with the British. They point out that on 29 May 1914, just five months before the Ottoman Empire entered the war, Ibn Sa'ud added his signature to a contract that had been concluded two weeks earlier between his agent in Basra and Sulayman Shafiq ibn 'Ali Kamali, the Ottoman governor of the city. In return for Ottoman recognition of Ibn Sa'ud as the governor of Najd for life, the Saudi emir pledged to support the Ottomans in the event of war with a foreign country. A few months later, however, when the Ottoman war minister asked Ibn Sa'ud to join the Ottomans against the British landing in Basra in southern Iraq, the Saudi emir refused, saying that he was busy fighting the Rashidis, his major rivals in Najd, who were allied with the Ottomans. Shi'is took Ibn Sa'ud's contacts with Shakespear and Cox during 1913–15 as further proof that the founding father of Saudi Arabia had supported a Christian power in a campaign to destroy the Ottoman Muslim state.[33]

While pointing to Ibn Sa'ud's collaboration with Britain, Shi'i writers highlighted the loyalty of Shi'is in Hasa and Qatif to the Ottoman Empire, beginning in the sixteenth century when the people of Qatif joined Ottoman forces in defeating the Christian Portuguese who attempted to take Hasa. They argued that although the Ottomans often mistreated Shi'is, the Shi'i ulama considered it a duty to defend a state that symbolized the Islamic caliphate. The religious leaders remained loyal to the Ottomans even after receiving British offers of protection and promises of Shi'i autonomy in Hasa and Qatif. Italy's occupation of Libya generated an outcry in Hasa and Qatif, and led the mujtahid Hasan 'Ali Al Badr to compile a treatise calling for jihad. By contrast, they wrote, Ibn Sa'ud showed no sympathy toward the Ottoman Empire and instead took advantage of the occupation of Libya to prepare his attack on Hasa. During World War I, the Shi'is of Hasa and Qatif lost their religious leader, 'Abd al-Hussein al-Jum'a, who was executed on orders of Ibn Sa'ud after being charged with collaborating with the Ottoman Empire and its allies Germany and Austria. The Shi'is were forbidden to demonstrate in support of the Ottomans, or even to express their grief when the news of the British occupation of Basra reached Hasa and Qatif in November 1914.[34]

In contrast to Saudi Arabia, where the ruling family built a myth around Ibn Sa'ud as the founding father of the state, in monarchic Iraq neither the Sharifians led by King Feisal nor the ex-Ottoman officers around him could claim such a role; both groups came to Iraq from Syria in 1920–21 and owed their position and status to the British. Shi'i writers accordingly depicted Iraq's monarchic rulers as outsiders and collaborators—an image reinforced by the Qasim and the Ba'th regimes after the overthrow of the monarchy in 1958. A good example is the discussion of the role of the ex-Ottoman officers in the Arab revolt of 1916, declared by Sharif Hussein with British encouragement against the Committee of Union and Progress in Istanbul. Shi'is pointed out that Iraqi Sunni officers were a majority among those who joined the Arab revolt. They singled out Nuri Sa'id, the most powerful Iraqi politician during the 1940s and 1950s. Sa'id, we are told, deserted the Ottoman army just before the outbreak of the war and escaped to Basra. When the British occupied the city in 1914, they captured Sa'id and exiled him to India. Sa'id later volunteered to join the revolt and played an active role in persuading hesitant Iraqi officers to join the anti-Ottoman movement of Sharif Hussein.[35] By contrast, Iraqi Shi'is considered themselves "the real patriots" who not only remained loyal to the Ottomans but also led the jihad movement against the British.

The jihad movement had its origin in the first decade of the twentieth century when the Ottoman Empire lost large territories to European powers and subsequently began calling for Muslim unity. The Pan-Islamic policies of the Ottomans intensified during World War I, as the empire was nearing its collapse, allowing the Shiʻi mujtahids in Iraq to gain freedom of action and eventually to dominate the jihad movement. In April 1915 Shiʻi ulama and tribesmen joined the Ottoman forces in an attempt to recapture Basra from British hands. The Ottoman offensive included a battle with British forces near Shuʻayba, a small town ten miles southeast of Basra. From British accounts it appears that the Ottoman commander Sulayman ʻAskari assembled a formidable force of 8,000 to 12,000 soldiers in addition to 10,000 to 20,000 Arab tribesmen and religious volunteers. The battle of Shuʻayba lasted three days and claimed heavy casualties on both sides. Although the Ottoman offensive failed, British officers considered Shuʻayba a hard-fought infantry battle, referring to their success in repelling the Ottomans as the "miracle of Shuʻayba."[36]

In Iraqi Shiʻi memory the battle of Shuʻayba has become a symbol of Muslim unity and a landmark in Iraqi history. Shiʻi writers relate that following the British landing in Basra, the Shiʻi religious leaders issued edicts calling for the defense of Islam and dispatched clerics to urge the tribesmen to join the jihad to expel the British from Iraq. The Shiʻi volunteers were placed under Ottoman command and were divided into three groups sent to Qurna, Huwayza, and Shuʻayba. The group that participated in the battle of Shuʻayba was led by the mujtahid Muhammad Saʻid al-Habubi and by ʻAjmi al-Saʻdun, the paramount sheikh of the Muntafiq tribal confederation.[37] Shiʻis recognize Habubi as the hero of the battle of Shuʻayba, considering him the most fervent in his desire to fight the British. Shiʻi texts relate that Habubi left Najaf weeks before the battle in order to motivate the tribes, accompanied by the poets Muhammad Baqir al-Shabibi and ʻAli al-Sharqi. A modest, pious, and honest man, Habubi is said to have refused an Ottoman offer of five thousand Turkish pounds to cover his expenses and instead to have used his own money to buy food and equipment for the warriors. Throughout the battle Habubi remained in the front line, demonstrating unusual bravery. Habubi was among the last warriors to retreat to Nasiriyya, where a few days later he died of "the grief of defeat." Shi'is have regarded Habubi as a martyr and a national hero, resenting the fact that history books published under the monarchy did not recognize his courageous stand in defending Iraq against the British occupation.[38]

In contrast to Shi'is in Iraq, who attempted to use the events surrounding the destruction of the Ottoman Empire to prove both their commitment to Islam and their strong Iraqi national loyalties, Lebanese Shi'is were not united around a single interpretation. The question of who stood up to defend the Ottoman Empire was complicated in Lebanon by the controversy over the rise of the Arab nationalist movement from the late nineteenth century to 1916, when the Ottomans crushed the movement. Christians, and in particular the Greek Orthodox, played a leading role in the development of Arabism as a cultural and political concept beginning in 1868 when Ibrahim al-Yaziji called for an Arab national revival. Unlike the Maronites of Mount Lebanon, who were geographically concentrated and lived under a system of local autonomy between 1861 and 1915, other Christian communities, and particularly the Greek Orthodox, were intermingled with the predominantly Muslim population of Syria and Lebanon. These Christians desired new political arrangements that would give them increased control over their own affairs. They began talking about Arabism as a cultural and linguistic identity, and about Syria and Lebanon as one geographical and historical unit, attempting to appeal to Arab Muslims whose support they needed. Yet until the twentieth century, the concept of Arab nationalism did not attract Syrian and Lebanese Muslims, who for the most part accepted the Ottoman government. The turning point, according to a widespread view, was the Young Turk revolution of 1908. The Young Turks abandoned the Pan-Islamic policy of Sultan 'Abd al-Hamid II, adopted Turkish nationalism, and discriminated against Arab Muslims. This change of policy provoked a strong reaction among Arab Muslims in Syria and Lebanon, and they began to plead for administrative decentralization. In fact, Arab nationalism had few adherents in the Ottoman Empire. Yet the idea that a large movement had existed was to gain ground among Syrians and Lebanese later in the twentieth century, forcing people to take a stand for or against the Arab nationalism of late Ottoman times.[39]

Following the creation of Lebanon, Shi'is offered disparate views of the past. Some claimed a leading role for themselves in the Arab nationalist movement, others maintained that like all Muslims in Syria and Lebanon they were loyal to the Ottoman Empire until 1908, and still others denied any connection at all with this "Christian-inspired" movement. Muhammad Jabir Al Safa' was the leading Shi'i writer among those who attempted to emphasize the contribution of Shi'is to Arab nationalism. Jabir discussed the tense historical relations between Arabs and Turks in articles published in al-'Irfan between 1936 and 1939, and in a book entitled *Ta'rikh jabal 'amil* (The History of the Jabal 'Amil). He presented the Turks as a foreign element within Islam, comparing the desire of the Arabs to be rid of the Ottoman Empire to the rebellions of the Arab tribes against the 'Abbasid caliphate, which was dominated by non-Arabs. In the articles Jabir recounted the activities of the Arab nationalists in Nabatiyya between 1908 and 1915, highlighting his own role in the movement alongside Ahmad Rida and Sulayman Zahir. According to Jabir, the movement sought to incite youth to rebel against the Young Turks in support of demands for autonomy and reform in the Jabal 'Amil.[40] In his book, however, Jabir went even further, asserting that Shi'is had been involved in the Arab nationalist movement from as early as 1877. He related that in that year Shiʻi clerics and notables from the Jabal ʻAmil joined Sunni leaders in holding a secret congress in Damascus to consider the independence of greater Syria from Ottoman rule. The participants elected ʻAbd al-Qadir al-Jazaʼiri (who led the Algerian resistance to the French in the 1830s and 1840s before being forced to leave for Damascus in 1855) as the emir of independent Syria. The four Shiʻis said to have been present at that meeting were Muhammad al-Amin, ʻAli ʻUsayran, ʻAli al-Hurr al-Jubaʻi, and Shabib al-Asʻad.[41]

The story of an Arab Muslim congress in 1877 generated a controversy among Shiʻis in modern Lebanon. While some accepted Jabir's account, others considered it a fabrication. Among those who did not question the validity of the story were secular writers who were eager to document the role of Shiʻis in the Arab nationalist movement in Syria and Lebanon, and a few Islamists who pointed to it as proof of the strongly Arab character of Shiʻism in the Jabal ʻAmil.[42] Still, many Shiʻis rejected the story because it suggested that their leaders conspired with Christians to secede from the Ottoman Empire. Some held that, like other Muslims, Shiʻis in Lebanon joined the Arab movement only after 1908, in reaction to Turkish nationalism.[43] Others, most notably ʻAli al-Zayn, rejected the very notion that Shiʻis could act against the Ottomans at a time when the Muslim state was experiencing intense European pressures. The Shiʻi leaders in the Jabal ʻAmil, he argued, opposed the secular nationalism of the Christians, whom they viewed as agents of the European powers in Syria and Lebanon, and instead adopted a Pan-Islamic line as advocated by the leading Muslim thinkers of the time, Jamal al-Din al-Afghani and Muhammad ʻAbduh.[44]

The conflicting views of Lebanese Shiʻis regarding the Arab nationalist movement reveal their uncertainties about the place of the Shiʻi community within Lebanon. The Shiʻis of Lebanon would harbor these uncertainties up until the second half of the twentieth century when they emerged as a vibrant political community demanding its share of power in the state. As will be seen in each of the coming chapters, the growing activism of Lebanese Shi'is was a development experienced by Saudi, Bahraini, and Iraqi Shi'is as well. All four communities entered nationhood with an attitude of political defeat, but their members in turn became energized and challenged the existing sociopolitical order.

Chapter 2
Containment Politics in the Persian Gulf

◈

State policy toward Shiʻis varies throughout the Persian Gulf, often standing in marked contrast to the cases of Saudi Arabia and Bahrain discussed in this book. Consider the example of Kuwait. Saddam Hussein's invasion of that country in 1990 put to the test the relationship between Kuwaiti Shiʻis, a minority of some 25 percent, and the Sunni Al Sabah ruling family. While Shiʻis constituted the backbone of the Kuwaiti resistance to the Iraqi occupation, and bore the brunt of it, members of the Al Sabah family fled to Saudi Arabia. Yet with the return of the Al Sabah in the wake of the Gulf War, Shiʻis put aside their reservations against the ruling family and reaffirmed their allegiance to the emir, Jabir Al Sabah, viewing him as a symbol of national unity.

What explains the positive attitude of Shiʻis toward the ruling family in Kuwait? The sense of Kuwaiti nationalism generated by the Iraqi invasion is only one factor. Another, and no less important, has been the tolerant policy of the Al Sabah toward Kuwaiti Shiʻis during the twentieth century, a policy that did not strip them of their dignity. Although the Al Sabah occasionally discriminated against Kuwaiti Shi'is, and kept them out of the inner circle of power, the Shi'i community has played a significant role in the economy, and its members participated in parliament and held positions in the army and the police. As a result, Kuwaiti Shi'is have taken pride in their Kuwaiti identity and have felt that their destiny was tied to that of the ruling family—a fact acknowledged by both Shi'is and their adversaries, as well as by Western writers.[1]

In contrast to Kuwait, where the rulers took steps to integrate the Shi'is into the state, in Saudi Arabia and Bahrain the ruling families have often viewed the Shi'is with hostility. The problem has been especially noticeable in Saudi Arabia, where the rulers and the state clergy have considered the Shi'is as beyond the pale of Islam.

Under the Shadow of Wahhabism

We are Arabs, but
our land has become desolated
and we who live on it have become
[a people] without identity . . .
O God, give us American nationality
so that we can live with dignity
in the Arab countries.[2]

The poetry of Saudi Shi'is conveys the despair of this small minority. Almost a century after Ibn Sa'ud's conquest of Hasa in 1913, Shi'is have still not reconciled their sectarian and national identities—a problem which they attribute to the failure of the Al Sa'ud to create bonds that could unite the different communities and religious currents within the kingdom. Shi'is view the process of Saudi state formation as the victory of Najd, with its tribal culture and puritanical Wahhabi Islam, over the settled communities and more tolerant Muslim populations of the Hijaz and Hasa. They charge that Ibn Sa'ud and his successors have treated Saudi citizens as their subjects and made no serious attempt to build a state based on partnership between the diverse communities of the kingdom. Before the increase in oil revenues in the 1950s, force was the glue that held the Saudi state together. The ruling family has enjoyed a monopoly on power and economic resources, and its members have encouraged a concept of nationalism that required Saudis to put their loyalty to the king before their allegiance to the country (*al-malik, thumma al-watan*). In the absence of a "unifying nationalist project," Shi'is have argued, people in the Hijaz, 'Asir, and Hasa have flaunted their regional and communal identities. This was their reaction to the Al Sa'ud's use of sectarian, tribal, and regional origins as the criteria for determining the status of people in the state.[3]

The Al Sa'ud's adoption of Wahhabi-Hanbali Islam as the religious ideology of Saudi Arabia has had direct bearing on the inferior status of Shi'is in the state. From the Wahhabi point of view there is little to choose between the various Shi'i sects. All Shi'is, including those who adhere to the main branch of Shi'i Islam, are considered either extremists or infidels. On several occasions in the twentieth century, Wahhabi activists and ulama argued that Shi'ism contains Jewish, Christian, Zoroastrian, and Sasanid seeds, ruling out any possibility for accommodation between Shi'i and Sunni Islam. Some even went so far as to portray the Shi'is as a "virus" and a "fifth column" within Islam, urging the Saudi government to eradicate Shi'ism in order to secure the preservation of Islam.[4] The inferior status of Shi'is, below even Jews and Christians, is evident from Ibn Sa'ud's remarks to John Philby, his British confidant: "I should have no objection to taking to wife a Christian or a Jewish woman, and she would have full liberty of belief and conscience though her children would necessarily be brought up as Muslims. The Jews and Christians are both people of the book; but I would not marry a Shi'a . . . [who] have been guilty of backsliding and *shirk* [polytheism] . . . for do they not pay divine honours to Muhammad, 'Ali, Husain, and other saints and seers?"[5]

The extent of Wahhabi hostility toward the Shi'is may be appreciated from the dissemination in Saudi Arabia of an old myth to the effect that the founder of Shi'ism was a Jew named 'Abdallah ibn Saba'. Very little is known about Ibn Saba' other than his appearance after the death of the fourth caliph, 'Ali ibn Abi Talib, in 661, and his propagation of the idea that 'Ali would return one day to defeat his enemies.[6] Yet the apocryphal story associating Ibn Saba' with Shi'ism gained adherents among Sunnis as early as the medieval period. In modern times, the myth has been widely current in Saudi Arabia (and to a much lesser extent elsewhere in the Arab world), as well as in Pakistan, where Shi'is are a minority of about 20 percent and Wahhabi doctrines have a large following. The volume of publications espousing this myth increases in periods of upheaval and sectarian strife, leading to angry responses by Shi'is. In the 1920s and 1930s such publications were connected to the failure of Muslims to unite against the European presence in the Middle East—a failure that supporters of Ibn Sa'ud ascribed to the refusal of Iran and the Shi'i ulama to recognize Saudi Arabia as the power that should lead Muslim opposition to imperialism.[7] New publications of this kind appeared after the Egyptian religious university of al-Azhar recognized Shi'ism in 1959 as one of the five Islamic schools of law, and following the Iranian Islamic Revolution of 1978–79. The most recent waves were inspired by the rise of a new generation of anti-Shi'i Wahhabis in the wake of the Gulf War of 1991, as well as the 9/11 attacks and the wars in Afghanistan and Iraq. Some of these writers are ulama who enjoy the patronage of the Saudi state. All of them depicted Ibn Saba' as a malicious Yemenite Jew who caused the first breach in Islam by stirring up the rebellion against the caliph 'Uthman, and invented the doctrine that 'Ali was the divinely appointed heir of the Prophet Muhammad.[8]

In contrast to Kuwait, where the rulers have relied on Shi'i merchants both to check other groups in society and to mitigate the spread of Arab nationalism during the 1960s, the Al Sa'ud have not considered the Shi'is a partner worthy of inclusion in their system of alliances. Instead, Saudi rulers have sought to isolate the Shi'is and dissolve their identity. In 1926 the cupolas built over the tombs of Shi'i imams in the Baqi' cemetery in Medina were destroyed—an act that Shi'is regarded as a Wahhabi attempt to erase Shi'i heritage. Shi'is across the Muslim world were outraged by this desecration, but it had an especially humiliating effect on the tiny Nakhawila Shi'i community in Medina whose members were forced to destroy the cupolas themselves.[9] The condition of Shi'is in Hasa and Qatif in the eastern province was hardly any better than that of their coreligionists in Medina. Shortly after his occupation of Hasa in 1913, Ibn Sa'ud appointed his cousin 'Abdallah ibn Jiluwi as the first governor of the province. Ibn Jiluwi embarked on a campaign intended to force the conversion of Shi'is to Wahhabism, ordering Shi'i legal courts to follow Hanbali law, introducing new prayer guidelines, and prohibiting Shi'is from performing their rituals. The Jiluwi family ruled the eastern province until 1985 when King Fahd appointed his son Muhammad as governor.[10] Until the increase in oil revenues in the 1950s, the burden of taxation fell mainly on the Shi'is, who were engaged in agriculture, fishing, pearl diving, and commerce. Shi'is paid a protection tax, as well as other discriminatory taxes, including the *jizya*, a poll tax normally levied in Islam on non-Muslims, and the *jihad*, in lieu of service in the army.[11]

In dealing with the Shi'is, the Al Sa'ud have enjoyed the backing of the Wahhabi religious establishment. While the Wahhabi ulama often pushed the Al Sa'ud to impose restrictions on the Shi'is, the rulers used "the Shi'i question" both to appease the ulama on issues relating to the status of minorities and religious freedom, and as a means of reducing tension among competing Sunni groups within the kingdom. A good example of how this trilateral relationship has worked is the way Ibn Sa'ud handled the challenge posed to him by the Ikhwan in the mid-1920s. The Ikhwan were Sunni tribesmen who settled in religious-agricultural communities established by Ibn Sa'ud. Organized as a religious brotherhood whose members adopted a strict Wahhabi way of life, the Ikhwan formed the backbone of Ibn Sa'ud's forces during the period of Saudi expansion in the 1920s. In October 1926, some three years before he crushed their military power, the Ikhwan held a conference in Artawiyya. The delegates criticized Ibn Sa'ud's use of modern technology, notably motor transport, the telegraph, and the telephone, and discussed ways to combat Shi'ism. In voicing criticism against Ibn Sa'ud, the Ikhwan challenged not only the authority of the ruler but the competence of his advisers, the ulama of Riyadh. To deal with this challenge, Ibn Sa'ud invited the heads of the Ikhwan and the ulama to a congress in Riyadh in January 1927. While the ulama took a neutral stand concerning Ibn Sa'ud's use of technology, they endorsed the Ikhwan's demand that Shi'is be forced to convert to Wahhabism. Accordingly, the ulama issued a ruling in February urging Ibn Sa'ud to send instructors and teachers to Hasa and Qatif to ensure that the Shi'is accepted true Islam. The ulama also ruled that those Shi'is who refused to conform should be exiled from Muslim territory. Subsequently, a large number of Shi'is were forced to convert to Wahhabism, while many others fled to Bahrain. Among those who were forced to publicly announce their adherence to Wahhabism was Musa Bu Khamsin, the leading mujtahid of Hasa with whom Ibn Sa'ud had concluded the 1913 agreement guaranteeing security and religious freedom for Shi'is. The persecution of Shi'is stopped only in the early 1930s, by which time the decline of Shi'i cultural life in Hasa and Qatif was well under way.[12]

With the discovery of oil in 1938, the Al Sa'ud came to regard the Shi'is as a security problem. Ibn Sa'ud granted the concession to explore the eastern province for oil to Standard Oil of California. The American company operated its concession through an affiliate, the California Arabian Standard Oil Company, to which the Texas Oil Company was admitted as an equal partner in 1936. In 1944 the company renamed itself the Arabian American Oil Company (Aramco). Until the 1978–79 Iranian revolution, Shi'is constituted the backbone of the Aramco work force. The prominent role of Shi'is in the early decades of the oil industry may be attributed to their predominance among the population in Hasa, the refusal of Sunni tribesmen to accept menial positions which they viewed with disdain, and the fact that in the late 1930s and early 1940s American officials in Aramco did not consider sectarian origin as a criterion for hiring workers. But the oil strikes of 1944, 1953, 1956, and 1967 changed hiring patterns. In all these strikes workers demanded better economic and working conditions, and in 1956 and 1967 they were clearly influenced by the Arab nationalist and socialist ideas of Gamal 'Abd al-Nasser. The strike of June 1956 coincided with the Egyptian president's visit to Saudi Arabia and his meeting with King Sa'ud in Dammam in the eastern province. On that occasion protesters threw stones at the king's car and chanted anti-American slogans. Workers demanded the expulsion of all foreign workers employed by Aramco and the removal of Sa'ud ibn Jiluwi, the governor of the province. Several hundred Shi'is also signed a petition against the government's decision to continue leasing the Dhahran base to American forces. Shi'is claim that Aramco officials subsequently gave preference to Sunnis in hiring. This trend intensified after the Iranian revolution, when the company laid off many of its Shi'i workers.[13]

Whereas in Kuwait some Shi'is in the oil industry grew immensely rich, and a Shi'i even held the post of oil minister in the mid-1970s, in Saudi Arabia Shi'is benefited little from the oil boom of the second half of the twentieth century. This reality shaped the political identity of Saudi Shi'is and their view of the ruling family. In their publications, Shi'is took pride in their prominent role in the oil industry, which they viewed as the lifeblood of Saudi Arabia. Yet they charged that Ibn Sa'ud had acted negligently in granting the oil concession to Standard Oil of California in return for a paltry sum of money. Shi'is deemed the concession a capitulation that enabled foreigners to control the country's oil wealth and undermine the government's ability to set oil prices according to Saudi national interests. They came to regard Aramco as a symbol of American imperialism—a view reinforced by the fact that until the 1970s the senior staff in the company were mainly Americans.

Saudi Shi'is likewise resented the medical tests that they had to pass as a condition for employment, a humiliating experience which they compared to the inspection of animals in the marketplace. They were annoyed by the race and class barriers, and by the segregation of Saudi and foreign workers in the company; they protested against the disparity between the low wages and inferior living conditions of the Shi'is and the high salaries and modern housing of the foreigners. Much of the Shi'is' anger stemmed from the requirement that they work during Muslim religious holidays and take their vacation at Christmas instead. Shi'is compared Aramco to a "flood" that threatened to "wash Shi'i identity away." While some depicted the American company as a state within the Saudi state, others portrayed it as a pillar of the Saudi state, which, like Wahhabism, was designed to guarantee the Al Sa'ud's survival.[14]

Saudi Shi'is thus came to view themselves as the disinherited. Referring to themselves as the indigenous population of Hasa and Qatif, they charged that the Al Sa'ud had exploited the resources of the region ever since the eighteenth century. Before the discovery of oil, Shi'is related, the oases of Hasa and Qatif were the agricultural core of inner Arabia, while the ports of Qatif, Jubayl, and 'Uqayr served as commercial gateways to the Persian Gulf. The discovery of oil enriched the Al Sa'ud but dealt a blow to agriculture—the time-honored occupation of Shi'is in the eastern province. They attributed the abandonment of agriculture to the lure of cash payments in the oil industry, the lack of government investment, the transfer of large tracts of land into the hands of a few princes, and the development of a construction industry, which inflated the value of landed property. The increase in oil revenues, Shi'is charged, benefited mainly the Sunni population of the province, while the Shi'i areas remained neglected. The government settled Sunni tribesmen in new cities and constructed large ports in Khobar and Dammam that eclipsed those of Qatif, Jubayl, and 'Uqayr. In 1950 the administrative center of the eastern province was moved from Hufuf to Dammam, where Sunnis formed a majority.[15] The decline of their cities and villages has sharpened the Shi'i sense of exclusion from the state.

Saudi Shi'is regard the decade following the Iranian revolution of 1978–79 as one of the worst in their modern history. The tension between Saudi Arabia and Iran led to an increase in Wahhabi attacks on Shi'ism as a belief system. The Saudi government restricted the names that Shi'i parents could choose for their children. Names like Muhammad Hasan, Muhammad 'Ali, or Muhammad al-Baqir, as well as the use of the title Sayyid to designate individuals claiming descent from the Prophet Muhammad, were forbidden. At the same time, Wahhabi ulama, led by the chief state cleric 'Abd al-'Aziz ibn Baz (d. 1999), issued new rulings against the Shi'is, reaffirming that they were infidels and prohibiting Muslims from dealings with them.[16]

The Iranian revolution had a strong impact on the Shi'i minority in Saudi Arabia, inspiring the mass demonstrations of 1979–80. On 28 November 1979 Shi'is took to the streets of cities and villages in the eastern province, defying a government ban on the rituals of Muharram in commemoration of the martyrdom of imam Hussein at Karbala. During the ten-day commemoration period, Shi'is chanted slogans critical of the royal family, and called on the government to stop supplying oil to the United States and to support the Iranian revolution under Ayatollah Ruhollah Khomeini. The demonstrations continued intermittently for about four months, ending only after government forces arrested hundreds of protesters and Saudi officials pledged to improve Shi'i living conditions. The demonstrators were young men between the ages of twenty and thirty, mostly workers in the oil industry. They were led by a few clerics and by students from the University of Minerals and Petroleum in Dammam. Most of the leadership went into exile in Iran in the early 1980s, and some later moved to Lebanon and England. Interestingly, the outbreak of the Shi'i demonstrations on 28 November followed the occupation of the Meccan sanctuary a few days earlier by a group of Sunni radicals led by Juhayman ibn Muhammad al-'Utaybi and Muhammad ibn 'Abdallah al-Qahtani, who protested the religious and moral laxity in the kingdom and demanded the removal of the Saudi ruling family. The overlap between the two movements indicated mounting tensions within very different segments of Saudi society. Yet while 'Utaybi and Qahtani (like the Ikhwan in 1927) protested against the ills of modernity, Shi'is were driven primarily by a sense that they had been deprived of the fruits of modernization.[17]

The Muharram demonstrations marked a departure from the quietist behavior of the Saudi Shi'i minority throughout much of the twentieth century. The shift from quietism to activism among Saudi Shi'is is evident from the development of a memory around the demonstrations, which became known as "the uprising (*intifada*) of the eastern province." The various accounts, written in the 1980s and 1990s, reveal the transformation of the community, as well as the tension between the older and younger generations. The first attempt to give meaning to the demonstrations was a book published in 1981 by Saudi members of the Organization for Islamic Revolution in the Arabian Peninsula, based in Iran. It chronicled the ten-day demonstration period, fusing it with the rituals in commemoration of imam Hussein. Both this account, and later publications that built on it, presented the uprising as an event that ushered in a period of renewal within the Shi'i minority and as a turning point in its relations with the Saudi government. The uprising, we are told, was spontaneous, nonsectarian, and Islamic in nature; it was directed against a tribal regime that sought to erase the identity of Shi'is and deny them freedom, justice, economic benefits, and equality in the state. Inspired by the experience of Hussein and his followers, who confronted a superior Umayyad force at the battle of Karbala, the authors compared the Saudi Shi'i protesters to David, who defeated Goliath with only a stone as his weapon. The uprising, Shi'is relate, culminated on the tenth day of Muharram when both men and women clashed with armed government forces, thus breaking "the barrier of fear" that had held back the Saudi Shi'i community and ending its isolation.[18]

The tense relations between the elders of the Shi'i community, who were guided by caution and by a desire to mend fences with the government, and the younger generation, whose members adopted a defiant approach, was built into the accounts of the uprising. Written mostly by young Shi'is in exile, they questioned the right of notables, landowners, and merchants to lead the community and speak for it. These writers portrayed the elders as driven by fear and by personal and material interests, and viewed their attempts to stop the demonstrations as an act of betrayal. By contrast, they related, the uprising saw the emergence of a new generation of grassroots leaders, who fought to end the status of Shi'is as second-class citizens in the kingdom and assumed responsibility for the future of the community.[19]

The desire of a small minority to attach itself to movements that transcended the confines of the eastern province is evident in the Saudi Shi'i view of the Iranian revolution as an alternative to the tyranny of the Al Sa'ud. The revolution preached freedom, justice, and equality, and as such it tapped the grievances of Saudi Shi'is. Khomeini was the new Saladin. He was the reformer who carried the torch of the movement for Islamic revival—the great hope of Saudi Shi'is and all the other disinherited groups (al-mustad'a-fun).[20] The Iranian revolution had thus succeeded in emboldening Saudi Shi'is, giving them the courage to challenge the Saudi ruling family. Nevertheless, by the 1990s, a growing number of activists had come to recognize the limits of this revolution. Khomeini was dead, and his followers were losing fervor. But the Saudi ruling family was still in power. These realities had a sobering effect on Shi'is, who began to seek accommodation with the government as a way to improve Shi'i life in the kingdom.[21]

Yet the Saudi government was slow to respond to this changed attitude within the Shi'i community. At the same time, Saudi Shi'is came under a new wave of verbal attacks from Wahhabis, who viewed the presence of Western troops in Saudi Arabia in the wake of the Gulf War as proof that a new order was being established in the Middle East with Shi'is at its core. Two prominent examples of these attacks are the memoranda sent to the association of the leading Saudi ulama by Safar al-Hawali (who was then dean of the Islamic College at Umm al-Qura University in Mecca) and Nasir ibn Sulayman al-'Umar (a professor of Koranic studies at Imam Muhammad ibn Sa'ud University in Riyadh). Hawali warned that a block of Shi'i states could emerge, one that would include Iran, Syria (under the 'Alawis), and Iraq, as well as the Shi'is of Saudi Arabia and other monarchies in the Persian Gulf. 'Umar outlined a comprehensive program for eradicating Shi'ism in the kingdom.[22] Seeking to neutralize this Wahhabi critique, the government in 1992 imprisoned and executed a number of Shi'is and razed four Shi'i mosques—a move reminiscent of Ibn Sa'ud's response to the Ikhwan threat to his rule in 1927.[23] The attacks of the early 1990s led Shi'is to conclude that Wahhabism had developed into a political order that did not tolerate any degree of religious pluralism or intellectual dissent, prompting them to seek closer alliances with other minority and opposition groups in the kingdom.[24]

The attacks on Shi'ism abated only after a reconciliation in 1993 between the Al Sa'ud and leaders of the Shi'i opposition—a development that I will discuss in chapter 5 in the context of Saudi Shi'i demands for minority rights. The Al Sa'ud's decision to appease the Shi'is coincided with the improvement of relations between Saudi Arabia and Iran from the mid-1990s; this was mirrored in Saudi newspaper articles that questioned the myth that 'Abdallah ibn Saba' was the founder of Shi'ism and caused the first breach within Islam.[25] Nevertheless, the Al Sa'ud stopped short of recognizing Shi'ism as a legitimate form of Islam, and did not grant Shi'is the status of full-fledged citizens—a problem they would find increasingly difficult to ignore in the face of the assertion of Shi'i power in post-Ba'th Iraq.

The problem of rights of citizenship has not been unique to the Shi'is of Saudi Arabia; it has also influenced the strained relations between Shi'is and the ruling family in neighboring Bahrain.

Tensions in the Bahrain Archipelago

The Al Khalifa's time-honored practice of relying on foreign powers to preserve their authority, and their tendency to rule the islands as their private estate, accounted for many of Bahrain's sociopolitical problems. Bahrain's precarious position as a tiny country between Iran and Saudi Arabia has shaped the Al Khalifa's strategy for survival and their treatment of the Shi'is. After their conquest of the islands in 1783, the Al Khalifa made several token submissions, and simultaneous offers of submission, to a variety of pretenders to sovereignty over Bahrain, hoping that one submission would cancel the other. This strategy worked well in the case of Oman and the Ottoman Empire, but proved less effective in coping with the challenges posed by Iran and Saudi Arabia. During the nineteenth and twentieth centuries Iranian rulers made several claims to Bahrain on the basis of the periodic submission of the islands to provincial governors in southern Iran from 1602 to 1783. Under Muhammad Reza Shah, Bahrain was listed in official publications as a province of Iran. Although the shah knew that he had neither a strong legal basis nor the military force to make good on Iran's claim to Bahrain (which was a British protectorate until 1971), he kept the claim alive, trying to make some political gains from it. In 1970, however, Iran officially dropped its claim to Bahrain. This Iranian act followed a UN-administered referendum in Bahrain earlier that year in which the vast majority of Bahrainis, irrespective of their sectarian affiliation, had expressed a desire for an independent Arab state in Bahrain. The shah's announcement that he accepted "the will of the people of Bahrain" enabled Saudi Arabia to increase its leverage in the islands.[26]

Saudi Arabia's interference in Bahrain reflected the geographical proximity of the two countries, the close contacts between Shi'is on the islands and those on the Saudi mainland, and the Al Sa'ud's desire to spread their Wahhabi ideology outside Arabia. The Al Khalifa had first succumbed to the Al Sa'ud in 1801. Under the first Saudi state the Al Khalifa for a time paid tribute to the Al Saʿud and accepted religious instructors sent to the islands to convert Bahrainis to Wahhabi doctrines. When in 1810–11 the Al Khalifa stopped paying tribute and obstructed the propagation efforts, the Al Saʿud imprisoned their leaders for about a year in the Saudi capital Dirʿiyya. In 1831, after the Saudis established their second state, the Al Khalifa were again forced to acknowledge their supremacy until the Egyptians reduced the power of the Wahhabis in 1838. After Ibn Saʿud captured Hasa province in 1913, he made claims to Bahrain on the ground that his forefathers had once controlled that territory. The Saudi ruler appointed ʿAbd al-ʿAziz al-Qusaybi as his agent in the islands and supported the Sunni Dawasir tribe, whose leaders objected to British attempts to give Shiʿis equal rights with Sunnis. The pressures that Ibn Saʿud exerted over Bahrain led the British political resident in the Persian Gulf to observe in 1927 that Iran did not pose a significant threat to Bahrain, and that the real danger lay in the growth of Saudi power.[27] It was the British presence in Bahrain that kept Saudi influence in the islands at bay until the 1970s.

After Bahrain gained independence in 1971, the Al Khalifa grew dependent on the Al Saʿud for their survival. As Britain prepared to withdraw its forces from the Persian Gulf, King Feisal of Saudi Arabia reached an understanding with the shah of Iran whereby the latter recognized the Arab emirates and sheikhdoms of the Gulf as falling within the Saudi sphere of influence, while Saudi Arabia acknowledged Iran's role as guardian of the Gulf waters. Feisal also persuaded the British to grant Bahrain and Qatar independence as separate states, thus detaching them from the original plan for a federation of nine emirates that Britain had proposed. Following the Iranian revolution, Bahrain became embroiled in the tension between Saudi Arabia and Iran. Both the Al Khalifa and the Al Saʿud feared that the revolution would lend weight to the grievances of Shiʿis, but the former were also anxious that the Islamic Republic might revive Iran's claim to Bahrain. During the Iran-Iraq War of 1980–88, the Al Khalifa publicly acknowledged the Al

Sa'ud as their guardians and encouraged publications that high-lighted the ties between the two families as descendants of the 'Anaza tribal confederation of Najd. The opening in 1986 of the King Fahd Causeway connecting the Bahrain islands with the Saudi mainland brought the two countries closer together. When in 1996 Bahrain's oil fields began drying out and its revenues decreased, its welfare became dependent on the aid that it received from Saudi Arabia, most notably the right to the income from oil production in the Abu Safa offshore field that the two countries had previously shared. By the end of the twentieth century, Saudi aid amounted to about 45 percent of Bahrain's annual budget.[28] Saudi Arabia's leverage on Bahrain has influenced the way the Al Khalifa have dealt with the Shi'i majority in the islands.

Following their conquest of Bahrain in 1783, the Al Khalifa in-vited Sunni tribes to settle in the islands, thus altering the sectarian balance between Shi'is and Sunnis on the islands. While the Al Bu Falasa and the Bin Jawdar tribes were already present in Bahrain at the time of the conquest, the bulk of Bahrain's Sunni tribes, in-cluding the Dawasir and the Na'im, arrived either with the Al Kha-lifa or during the nineteenth century. Like the 'Utub tribe of the Al Khalifa, most of these tribes were Maliki Sunnis. The sheikhs of the tribes became part of a new Bahraini upper class that developed during the nineteenth century. Acting as landowners and as boat captains and dealers in the pearl industry, they were usually loyal to the Al Khalifa, with whom they shared a tribal past and vested economic interests. A clear social and cultural divide separated the Sunni tribes from the Shi'is. The newcomers regarded social stand-ing as a matter of tribal lineage. Although by the twentieth century the Sunni tribes had settled, they continued to refer to themselves as tribes and looked down on the Shi'i cultivators, pearl divers, and fishermen as a nontribal population. The Sunni tribesmen were often exempted from taxation, the burden of which fell on the Shi'is. Until the fiscal reform of 1923, Bahraini Shi'is, like their coreligionists in Saudi Arabia, were subject to various discriminatory taxes, including a poll tax alongside water, date gardening, and fish taxes.[29]

The case of the Dawasir shows the preferred status enjoyed by Sunni tribes in Bahrain. The Dawasir originated in southern Najd. They migrated to Bahrain around 1845 at the encouragement of the Al Khalifa, settling mainly in Budayyi' and Zallaq in the northwestern part of the country on land granted to them by the ruling family. By the twentieth century the tribe included several thousand people and had become the second largest and most powerful tribe after the 'Utub. So powerful were the Dawasir that their members recognized Sheikh 'Isa Al Khalifa as ruler in name only and considered themselves immune from taxation. They gained wealth from the pearl trade, owning a fleet of pearling boats and employing many divers under conditions of near servitude. The tribe played an important role in Bahraini politics. Its leaders opposed the British deposition of Sheikh 'Isa Al Khalifa (who was replaced in May 1923 by his son Hamad as the deputy ruler), as well as the proposed reforms of the tax system and the pearl industry aimed at putting Shi'is and Sunnis on an equal footing. When in November 1923 the Dawasir leaders realized that Sheikh Hamad, with British support, was determined to enforce their submission, almost the entire tribe took to their boats and crossed to Dammam in Saudi Arabia. Acting under British pressure, Sheikh Hamad ordered the seizure of Dawasir property and the release of their divers from contractual obligations and any debts that they owed the tribe.[30]

The events surrounding the subsequent return of the Dawasir to Bahrain reveal the leverage exercised by the Al Sa'ud on the Al Khalifa, as well as the dependence of the Bahraini ruling family on Sunni tribes to preserve its rule. Once in Saudi Arabia, the leaders of the Dawasir received the backing of Ibn Sa'ud. They set out conditions for their return to Bahrain, demanding restoration of their property and government compensation for both the rents collected from their property during their absence and the cash that their divers owed them. The British political agent in Bahrain opposed this settlement since it would be construed by the tribe as a sign of government weakness and would enable its leaders to regain their former privileged status. However, Sheikh Hamad spoke of the "disgrace" that he had suffered on account of the confiscation of Dawasir property in his name. The sheikh was anxious to see the return of the Dawasir, and in a goodwill gesture toward Ibn Saʿud, he decided to accept all their demands. He explained to British officials that Ibn Saʿud "was the one big Arab ruler and it was natural for all smaller Shaikhs such as himself to look up to him and try to please him." The Dawasir were accordingly allowed to return to Bahrain in April 1927, recovering their property and gaining one-third of the rents collected during their absence. In explaining the return of the Dawasir, British officials noted that the Al Khalifa were a Sunni people governing a Shiʿi population, and that they did not desire to weaken their position by expelling a powerful Sunni group. The British saw no point in opposing the return of the Dawasir against the wishes of the ruler.[31]

The Al Khalifa's conquest of Bahrain altered the class structure on the islands, reducing the Shiʿi owners of the land to something little better than serfdom. Because Bahrain did not submit peacefully to the Al Khalifa, the ruling family under Islamic law considered all property on the islands as booty, confiscating most of the agricultural land and leasing it back to Bahraini Shiʿis. By the twentieth century the ruling family had become the largest owner of property and date gardens in Bahrain, controlling as much as 80 percent of the agricultural land. Under the new government system that the Al Khalifa introduced, family members acted as feudal lords, each controlling several villages and deriving income from the taxes extracted from the population in his domain. As the ruling family increased in size, reaching some two hundred members in 1935, competition intensified among its male members for property in Shiʿi villages. The livelihood of Shiʿi cultivators, who until 1783 owned their land outright, now became dependent upon their securing tenancy of a garden. Since the demand for gardens exceeded supply, the new landlords were able to charge inflated rates. When tenants defaulted on their rent, which was common, their houses were confiscated and their belongings auctioned. Thus the Shi'i cultivators, in the words of British officials, became a "shame-fully rack-rented peasantry" and "helots," who could call no land or produce their own. The status of Shi'i cultivators changed little before the development of the oil and construction industries in the 1940s and 1950s, which reduced the amount of agricultural land and put an end to date growing as a significant economic activity in Bahrain.[32]

The position of Shi'is in the pearl industry was hardly any better than that of the Shi'i cultivators. Before the production of oil in commercial quantities in 1934, Bahrain's prosperity depended on the pearl trade. A successful season meant that more money was in the hands of the diving community, raising demand for imported goods. This, in turn, increased government revenues that derived mainly from customs. Shi'is were a majority of the pearl industry workforce, estimated in 1930 at fifteen thousand men. The Shi'is were employed mainly as divers and were hired by a captain to work on his boat during the catch seasons, the longest of which was between mid-May and the end of September. The majority of boat captains were Sunnis of tribal descent and were allied with the Al Khalifa. Most divers were not paid wages, but shared in the profits from the sale of the catch and also received a small allow-ance during the season to buy their food. They were attracted to the industry by a cash advance paid by the captain at the beginning of the season, and another during the off-season. Having taken an advance, the divers were compelled to work for the captain in the following season. Because of occasional poor catches, and the abuses that crept into the industry, many divers became virtual slaves of the captains. Their patrons charged high rates of interest on the advances (a practice forbidden under Islamic law) and forced the divers to work for them as unpaid servants in the off-season. Divers could be transferred without their consent from one captain to another, or handed over to a shopkeeper in payment of a debt and forced to pay a proportion of their earnings to the shopkeeper every season. When a diver died, his debt passed to his sons, who, as soon as they were old enough, had to dive for the captain to whom their father owed money. If there was no son to take the deceased's place, his belongings were seized by the captain. The condition of the divers remained unchanged until Sheikh Hamad, under pressures from the British political agent, introduced new diving laws in 1924, much to the chagrin of the Sunni tribal leaders. The world recession, followed by the Japanese development of cultured pearls in the 1930s, dealt the pearl industry in Bahrain a blow from which it never recovered. Bahrain's pearl diving fleet, which in its heyday in the 1920s had numbered 2,000 sailing craft, dropped sharply to 192 in 1945.[33]

The decline of agriculture and the pearl industry coincided with the discovery of oil and the development of a modern administration in Bahrain. This, in turn, led the Al Khalifa to employ a large number of foreign workers in the economy and the bureaucracy, as well as in the army and the security services, thereby attempting to prevent the rise of political organizations and labor unions that cut across regional and sectarian lines. The proportion of expatriates in the workforce in Bahrain, which in 1935 was 20 percent, had climbed to about 41 percent in 1956. It reached 60 percent in 1995 and was as high as 65 percent in 2002. Between the 1930s and 1950s, Indians were the main group among the foreign workers in Bahrain, followed by Iranians. Indians played a prominent role in the oil industry, the banking system, customs, the post office, and the police. Iranians dominated commercial activity in Manama during much of the twentieth century, but their number decreased significantly following the Iranian revolution. At the turn of the twenty-first century, Indians continued to form a substantial part of the foreign workforce in Bahrain, followed by Pakistanis, Bangladeshis, and Filipinos. The large number of foreign workers has led to a substantial cash flow from Bahrain in the form of remittances. It also caused high unemployment among the native population; the rate was put at 15 percent by the government in 1997 but was estimated by Shi'i opposition groups to be as high as 30 percent.[34]

As the case of the oil industry demonstrates, the demand of Bahrainis for job opportunities and improved working conditions has been a bone of contention between Shi'is and the ruling family. Oil was first discovered in Bahrain in 1932 by the Bahrain Petroleum Company (Bapco), a subsidiary of Standard Oil of California. Although the discovery of oil in Bahrain preceded that in other monarchies in the Persian Gulf, the country's oil reserves proved to be small, and Bahrain became the poor relation among the oil monarchies. The sheikh took one-third of the oil revenue for the privy purse and used part of it to pay the allowances of his innumerable relatives. The other two-thirds was invested in British banks and used for administration and development.[35] Between the mid-1930s and the 1950s Bapco was the largest employer in Bahrain. The majority of its workers were foreigners, and the rest were mostly Shi'is, who were hired from a pool of unemployed cultivators and pearl divers. These Shi'is formed the nucleus of the working class in Bahrain.

Bapco's decision to reduce its local workforce from 3,350 in 1937 to 1,569 in 1938 sparked off protests among Bahrainis. They demanded the right to form a representative body to defend their interests, preference in job hiring in all cases where Bahrainis and foreigners had equal qualifications, an increase in wages to reduce the gap between their pay and that of foreign workers, improved housing for Bahrainis who lived in huts, free transport to work like that provided for foreign workers, compensation for workers who became disabled on the job, annual paid leave of twenty days, training courses, and the building of two mosques. Company officials rejected most of these demands, particularly the request for a wage increase, arguing that Indians were more efficient than Bahrainis. A new wave of protests erupted in 1943. Bahraini workers in the refinery on the island of Sitra went on strike, and this spread to other sectors in the economy in what amounted to the first industrial strike in the Persian Gulf. Workers again demanded a pay increase (above the maximum of one rupee a day earned by Bahrainis), improved working conditions, and training courses.

Backed by the government and the British administration, Bapco rejected most of these demands, including the request that Friday be designated as the weekly day of rest with pay. Seeking to downplay the social significance of the protest, Sheikh Salman ibn Hamad put the blame on Bahraini Shi'is and Iranians, whom he portrayed as the strike's instigators.[36]

With the decline in oil reserves, Bapco lost its position as the largest employer in Bahrain, retaining only 10 percent of the local workforce in 1971. This development coincided with the Al Khalifa's attempt to position Bahrain as a banking and communications hub for the Persian Gulf and the larger Middle East. By 1982 Bahrain had more than 120 banks. The islands had become a service center for the Saudi economy, capitalizing on the decline of Beirut, which experienced a setback to its position as the financial center of the Arab world during the Lebanese civil war of 1975–90. This transformation spurred the growth of a foreign-based bureaucracy in the latter part of the twentieth century and pushed Shi'is into the service and distribution sectors of the economy. The increase in foreign workers caused resentment among Bahrainis and was a major factor behind the strikes of 1965, 1967, 1970, and 1972, as well as the uprising of 1994–99.[37]

The presence of a large number of foreigners holding positions in the security services, and dominating important sectors of the economy, has had an impact on Bahraini nationalism and the Shi'i view of the state. This point is evident from the rise and fall of Charles Belgrave, the British adviser to both Sheikh Hamad and his successor Sheikh Salman between 1926 and 1957. An Oxford graduate and a former administrative officer in the British Colonial Service, Belgrave was recruited by the British political agent in Bahrain for Sheikh Hamad, who wished to employ an Englishman as his adviser. The sheikh, as Belgrave wrote in his memoirs, "could not depend permanently on the sole advice of the Political Agents . . . [and] wanted someone belonging to him, whom he could trust and rely upon."[38] Belgrave's official designation by the India Office was that of financial adviser to the sheikh. But over time the sheikh came to rely on his advice in political and personal matters, and delegated numerous responsibilities to him, making Belgrave one of the most powerful figures in Bahrain.

As financial adviser, Belgrave produced a first budget of seventy-five thousand pounds for Bahrain in 1926. He saw the economy as in transition from one dependent on agriculture and the pearl trade to one relying on the production and refining of oil. Belgrave "kept a tight hold of the purse strings," and by the time he left the country in 1957, he controlled a budget reaching almost five and half million pounds. During World War II, he introduced price controls and food rationing, setting up a Food Control Department that continued to function for several years after the end of the war. In 1953 he replaced the Islamic with the Gregorian calendar as the basis for all fiscal and government operations. Belgrave held judicial responsibilities as well, acting as the first judge of the civil court in Bahrain together with Sheikh Salman, who would become ruler in 1942. In 1938 Belgrave established the Minors' Department, which protected the interests of minors, widows, and orphans. Together with his wife Marjorie, Belgrave left his mark on the field of education. While she supervised the establishment of the first girls' school in Bahrain, he controlled for many years the development of education, assisted by a Lebanese inspector and by Sheikh 'Abdallah, who acted as the "minister." In 1928 Belgrave persuaded Sheikh Hamad to build a school for Shi'is in Manama, arguing that they would not attend a school in which all the teachers were Sunnis. Belgrave also oversaw the development of the medical system in Bahrain, setting up the Public Works Department, which was responsible for building hospitals. As the commander of the police, Belgrave introduced a system of passport control. He recruited a British national to serve as chief police officer and built a force that by 1957 relied heavily on Baluchis, Omanis, Yemenis, and Iraqis. Belgrave continued to oversee police operations in Bahrain even after the appointment of Sheikh Khalifa as director of public security in 1954.[39]

By the late 1940s, Shi'is, as well as Sunnis, had come to regard Belgrave as the symbol of colonialism in Bahrain. Among the local population he was known simply by his designation as "the adviser." Bahrainis associated Belgrave with the Al Khalifa as the source of their poverty and suffering. They resented the power that he wielded, as well as his position as a confidant of the ruler. In a petition to the British minister of colonies in July 1947, the writers complained that in the absence of a constitution, Belgrave had become "the main source of regulation" in the country and the person responsible for the wage gap between Bahrainis and foreign workers in Bapco. In various publications Bahrainis noted that Belgrave's power exceeded the influence of most of the British political agents who served in Bahrain between 1926 and 1957. They took the employment of his son James in various government positions as proof that Belgrave was grooming his son to succeed him upon his retirement. The campaign for Belgrave's dismissal was shaped by the growing influence of Arab nationalism in Bahrain. It intensified in 1956 after the nationalization of the Suez Canal by Gamal 'Abd al-Nasser and the dismissal of John Glubb Pasha, the British commander of the Arab Legion in Jordan. In organizing their campaign, Bahrainis took advantage of the competition between Belgrave and the political agents, who considered him a liability for the British government and suggested ways to hasten his retirement. In August 1956, the Bahraini government announced Belgrave's resignation, but no date was set for the termination of his position. Belgrave left Bahrain in April of the following year, only after being diagnosed with cancer, which required treatment in England.[40]

The Al Khalifa have grown yet more dependent on foreign workers, as well as on foreign powers, in the years following Belgrave's departure and the coming of independence in 1971. On the eve of its withdrawal from Bahrain, Britain ceded part of its sphere of influence in the islands to the United States. While ex-British officers were hired to run the Bahraini security services, the U.S. Navy negotiated an agreement with the Al Khalifa to lease British bases on the islands. Bahrain thus became the home port of the U.S. Fifth Fleet in the Persian Gulf. Its importance to U.S. strategic interests was evident in the aftermath of the Iranian revolution and during the Gulf War of 1991, when Bahrain became an advance U.S. military outpost in the campaign against Saddam Hussein. In the wake of the 9/11 attacks, the U.S. administration designated Bahrain a major non-NATO ally (a status reserved for a handful of countries), a move followed by the signing of a free trade agreement between the two countries in September 2004. These developments signaled both the effort of the administration to assert U.S. supremacy in the Persian Gulf and an attempt on the part of the Al Khalifa to draw closer to the United States in order to reduce their dependency on Saudi Arabia. The growing U.S. military presence in Bahrain, however, has influenced domestic politics in the country and exacerbated tensions between Shi'is and the Al Khalifa.[41]

The tensions had already come to a head in the late 1970s. In 1975 the emir dissolved parliament and suspended the constitution that he had granted two years earlier. Four years after this act the Islamic Revolution brought Shi'i clerics to power in neighboring Iran. I will discuss the dissolution of parliament in chapter 5 in the context of the constitutional movement in Bahrain. Here it is important to highlight the struggle for leadership that erupted within the Bahraini Shi'i community following the revolution, and the eventual success of Shi'is in isolating the radicals in their midst—an outcome reminiscent of the one that took place in Saudi Arabia in the 1990s, and which carries important implications for the political reconstruction of post-Ba'th Iraq. In 1981, the Bahraini government foiled a Shi'i coup attempt by the Islamic Front for the Liberation of Bahrain, which sought to establish an Islamic government in the country and called for the departure of American forces from the islands. More than seventy Islamic Front members received long sentences and scores were deported, but it remained the most vocal Bahraini Shi'i group throughout the 1980s. The Islamic Front was led by foreign clerics, most notably the Iraqi-born Hadi al-Mudarressi and the Iranian Sadiq Ruhani,

Khomeini's representative in Bahrain, who challenged the position of the more established Shi'i clerics in the country. Initially, the Islamic Front recruited young urban Shi'is, but over time its influence extended to villages—the power base of native ulama such as 'Abd al-Amir al-Jamri, a member of the dissolved parliament who envisaged reforming, not dismantling, the Al Khalifa's rule. As it turned out, the call for an Islamic state failed in its appeal to the majority of Shi'is. But the struggle for leadership, and for the political direction of the community, took its toll and led Shi'is to refer to the 1980s as one of the "darkest" decades in Bahrain's modern history.[42]

The Islamic Front was isolated during the uprising of 1994–99, which revealed a tangible degree of cooperation among the Bahrain Freedom Movement (which attracted primarily Shi'is of rural background), the National Liberation Front (consisting of Marxists and Arab nationalists, both Shi'is and Sunnis), and the Popular Front (which had support among workers, students, and intellectuals from both sides of the sectarian divide). The willingness of members of the Sunni minority to side with the Shi'i majority reflected primarily their frustration with the ruling family's tight control of legislative powers since the 1975 dissolution of parliament. The reluctance of the Islamic Front to fully cooperate with this alliance enabled the Bahrain Freedom Movement to emerge as the leading Shi'i opposition force. The 1994–99 uprising grew out of the Gulf War of 1991. There had been talk then about a new world order led by the United States, and the Al Khalifa, like other ruling families in the Persian Gulf, embarked on a campaign promising human rights and political openness. Encouraged by these signs, Bahrainis submitted a petition to the emir in November 1992. It was signed by some three hundred people and called for elections to a restored parliament, the release of political prisoners, and the return of exiles. The petition was sponsored by a committee of six. Its Shi'i members were the clerics 'Abd al-Amir al-Jamri and 'Abd al-Wahhab Hussein, as well as Hamid Sangur, a professional. The Sunni members included two clerics, 'Isa al-Jawdar and 'Abd al-Latif al-

Mahmud, and a nationalist, Muhammad Jabir al-Sabah. The petition, though polite in tone and expressing respect for the Al Khalifa, went unanswered. Meanwhile, the government announced in December the formation of a nonelected consultative council composed of an equal number of Shi'is and Sunnis. This development led to demonstrations in 1993–94 that grew into a protest movement. In October 1994 leaders from both sects submitted a new petition to the emir signed by twenty-three thousand people. It called for the return of exiles, a reduction in the number of foreign workers, freedom of expression, and the restoration of the constitution and parliament. The organizers asked to present the petition to the emir in person, but this request was turned down.[43]

A few weeks later, the government deported three Shi'i clerics—'Ali Salman, Hamza al-Dayri, and Haydar al-Sitri—on charges of organizing the petition. This move triggered large demonstrations in December 1994, marking the beginning of the uprising. In its first stage the uprising lasted about a year, leaving more than thirty people dead and hundreds wounded. Between three thousand and five thousand Bahrainis, including women and children, were arrested during that time. Hardly any Sunnis were arrested at this stage because the government strategy was to co-opt the Sunnis and deal firmly with the Shi'is. Among those arrested was the cleric 'Abd al-Amir al-Jamri, who would emerge as a national leader recognized by both Shi'i and Sunni opponents of the government. Jamri was inspired by India's leader Mahatma Gandhi. He advocated passive resistance—a strategy that according to British officials had generally been preferred by Shi'is in Bahrain in the twentieth century.[44] In his sermons, Jamri portrayed the uprising as an indigenous movement of all Bahrainis, irrespective of sectarian affiliation and ideological preference, urging the government to introduce reforms for the benefit of the entire people. Jamri was first arrested in April 1995, but he was released four months later as part of an agreement between opposition leaders and the government. While the opposition agreed to end the demonstrations, the government promised to start a dialogue with the opposition. A period of relative calm followed Jamri's release, but the demonstrations resumed in December after the government had refused to make any serious concessions. Jamri was arrested again in January 1996 and sentenced to ten years' imprisonment on charges of spying for a foreign country, running an illegal group, and fanning unrest in the country.[45]

In dealing with this second stage of the uprising, the Bahraini government attempted to divide the opposition along sectarian lines by accusing Shi'is of collaboration with Iran. Accordingly, the minister of information announced in June 1996 the arrest of forty-four Bahrainis on charges of plotting to topple the ruling family and replace the government with one modeled on the Islamic Republic of Iran. State television broadcast the confessions of six people who said that they belonged to the military wing of an organization called Hizballah al-Bahrain, established on the instructions of the Iranian Islamic Revolutionary Guard and with its financial support. Unlike the aborted coup of the Islamic Front in 1981, however, there was little evidence to support the government claim of a coup attempt in 1996. Yet the Al Khalifa won some support from the U.S. administration because of the latter's fear that political reforms and free elections would lead to a pro-Iranian parliament opposed to U.S. military bases in Bahrain. All three Bahraini opposition groups denied the reality of the alleged plot. Their members pointed out that on various occasions in the twentieth century the Al Khalifa had attempted to deflect attention from their domestic problems by accusing foreign countries of supporting coup attempts in Bahrain. Thus in the mid-1950s the Al Khalifa put the blame on Egypt, in the 1970s on South Yemen, and since the 1980s mainly on Iran. Bahraini Shi'is argued that the Al Khalifa invoked Iran in order to undermine the nationalist credentials of Shi'is, to pose as "the guardian of the Sunnis," and to undercut the demands for job opportunities and political reforms.[46]

The tension between the Shi'is and the ruling family intensified as the Al Khalifa sought to alter the sectarian balance to the advantage of the Sunnis, as they had done during the nineteenth century.

Shi'is charged that in the mid- and late 1990s the Al Khalifa had invited new sections of the Dawasir from the Saudi mainland, as well as distantly related Shammar tribesmen from the Syrian desert, to settle in Bahrain. The newcomers were granted citizenship and housing, and their children were enrolled in special schools. Some of these tribesmen were recruited to military units responsible for protecting the regime. Shi'is also denounced the existence of a tight junta of British intelligence officers led by Ian Henderson, a Scot who had been recruited in 1966 and acted as head of Special Branch in Bahrain. In Shi'i memory, Henderson symbolized the repression of Bahrainis by foreigners—a metaphor once reserved exclusively for Charles Belgrave.[47] What is more, Shi'is drew attention to the problem of citizenship, and to the existence of some fifteen thousand people born in Bahrain whose parents and great-grandparents were of Iranian origin, both Persian speakers from the interior of Iran and ethnic Arabs from the northern shore of the Persian Gulf. Known as the *bidun* ("without" citizenship), they were denied any citizenship rights and ranked at the bottom of the social scale in Bahrain. Shi'is resented the government's classification of Bahrainis according to such categories, the most prestigious of which was that designating the Al Khalifa as Bahrainis by descent. Like their coreligionists in Saudi Arabia, Bahraini Shi'is demanded full citizenship as well as the right to serve in the army.[48]

The role of Shi'is in leading an uprising that cut across sectarian lines constituted a novelty in Bahrain's modern history. This development reflected the increase in the share of Shi'is from around 50 percent in 1941 to some 70 percent in 1996 out of a native population of some 400,000. Shi'is were the main group affected by the influx of foreign workers to Bahrain, and hence the most strongly motivated to take to the streets in protest. The role of Shi'i ulama in leading the uprising reflected the rise of Islam as the most viable political force in the Arab world at the expense of Arab nationalism and communism, and the reluctance of the Sunni Muslim Brothers, organized in the Islah Society led by Sheikh 'Isa ibn Muhammad Al Khalifa, to join the opposition. One may appreciate the changes in the nature of opposition leadership in Bahrain by comparing the 1954–56 and the 1994–99 protest movements. On both occasions the leaders opposed the sectarian policies of the government and the role of foreigners in running the country, and advocated a constitution and an elected parliament. Yet whereas the first movement was dominated by Arab nationalists of Sunni origin whose demands included the establishment of labor unions, the second was led mainly by Shi'is of religious background whose demands involved an end to Christian missionary activities and to public displays offensive to the Islamic religion. In 1956 the government dealt a blow to the movement by imprisoning and deporting its Sunni leaders and encouraging Shi'i leaders to organize independently, thus undercutting the national dimension of the movement. By contrast, the arrest and deportation of Shi'i opposition leaders during the mid-1990s failed to split the movement and led the exiles to mount a public relations campaign, winning support from international human rights groups, members of the British Parliament, and even the European Parliament.[49]

Only in late 1999, after the death of Sheikh 'Isa, did the Bahraini government declare national reconciliation and open a dialogue with the opposition. This development coincided with publications that urged the Al Khalifa and the Shi'is not to let the past stand as a barrier between the ruling family and the people. While pleading with the Al Khalifa not to assert themselves as "the conquerors and liberators" of Bahrain, the writers called on Shi'is to stop referring to themselves as "the original inhabitants" of the islands.[50] The opening of a dialogue between the government and Bahraini Shi'is in 1999 was reminiscent of the Saudi government's reconciliation with its Shi'is in 1993. Yet the political reforms introduced by the new emir, Sheikh Hamad, were more daring than the concessions made by King Fahd of Saudi Arabia, reflecting international pressures, the absence of a Wahhabi clerical institution, and the clout of the Bahraini opposition. In a widely publicized campaign, the government released political prisoners (including 'Abd al-Amir al-Jamri), permitted the return of exiles, and licensed independent newspapers, as well as civil society organizations and trade unions. It also issued a new passport describing its holder as a citizen of the state of Bahrain, granted citizenship to Bahrain's *bidun* residents, modified the state security law of 1975, abolished the state security court of 1995, and settled issues relating to human rights. Moreover, Ian Henderson, head of Special Branch, left Bahrain in 1998—a move recalling the retirement of Charles Belgrave in 1957.[51]

The reconciliation of 1999 has reduced tension between the Al Khalifa and the Shi'is. Yet, as will be shown in chapter 5, the political reforms turned out to be limited in scope. One reason for this was the government's refusal to reinstate the 1973 constitution and allow a strong parliamentary system in the country. Another was the crackdown on the reformers in the wake of the 9/11 attacks and the subsequent U.S.-led war on terrorism.

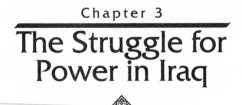

Chapter 3
The Struggle for Power in Iraq

The U.S. invasion of Iraq in 2003 ended eighty-two years of Sunni minority rule in the country. To appreciate the events that followed the war, and the causes behind the ambivalence of Iraqi Shiʻis toward America, we need to explore the struggle between the Sunni ruling elite and the Shiʻi majority over the right to rule and to define the meaning of nationalism in prewar Iraq.

Unlike the rulers of Saudi Arabia, who acted as the guardians of "true Islam," Iraq's rulers adopted a secular ideology and declared themselves to be the standard-bearers of Arabism. Whereas officials and ulama in Saudi Arabia expressed their hostility toward Shiʻism in religious terms, successive Sunni governments in Iraq questioned the Arab origin of the Shiʻis and associated Iraqi Shiʻism with Persian culture and Iranian history. Iraq's rulers thus pursued a strategy similar to that adopted by the Al Khalifa in Bahrain: both tried to legitimize their right to rule by portraying the Shiʻi majority as people with inferior Arab credentials in comparison with the Sunnis. Yet the ruling minority in Iraq went to greater lengths than its Bahraini counterpart in claiming the right to judge who was a patriot and who was a traitor, who was a nationalist and who undermined Arabism. Here the struggle between Shi'is and the Sunni ruling elite manifested itself in many ways, including the debate over the 1920 revolt that preceded the establishment of modern Iraq.

In the three years between the completion of the British occupation of Iraq in 1918 and the formation of the Iraqi monarchy in 1921, two conflicting movements competed in the country, each of them calling for Iraq's independence. The first movement was led by the Sharifians, then based in Syria; they appealed to London requesting that Iraq be included within the administrative province of Sharif Hussein of Mecca. The second was led by the Shi'i religious leaders, who had organized the jihad movement in Iraq against the British in 1914–15, and whose aim was to establish an Islamic government in the country. Despite their fundamentally different aspirations, the Sunni Sharifians and the Shi'i clerics agreed to work together under a vague formula, advocating an Arab-Islamic state ruled by an Arab emir bound by a legislative assembly. While the Sharifians considered this formula an opening for their rule of Iraq through the nomination of one of the sons of Sharif Hussein as king, several Shi'i clerics, led by Mirza Muhammad Taqi Shirazi, hoped that this system of government would enable them to oversee the legislative process and the affairs of Iraq once British control of the country was ended. The Shi'i tribes rose, but after a substantial struggle they were crushed by superior British arms. And then, to the dismay of Shi'is, the British brought the Sharifians to power, even though their role in fomenting the rebellion was not less than that of the Shi'is.[1]

The British formation of the Iraqi monarchy under King Feisal was a blow to the Shi'is. In the new state, power rested in the hands of a Sunni minority led by the Sharifians and the ex-Ottoman officers, while the Shi'i majority was by and large excluded. One way in which the Sharifians and ex-Ottoman officers sought to discredit the nationalist credentials of the Shi'is was to play down the importance of the 1920 revolt and the role of Shi'is in it. The reluctance of the Sunni monarchic elite to turn the revolt into the foundation myth of modern Iraq stands in sharp contrast to Shi'i writings on the revolt, which began appearing in significant numbers in the 1950s. The stream of publications increased between the first Ba'th seizure of power in 1963 and the Iran-Iraq War of 1980–88, leading to the development of a memory of the revolt that emphasized unity among Iraqis against foreign occupation. While the Ba'th attempted to use the episode of the revolt to create political cohesion in the country, the development of a memory among Shi'is was their response to the growing divisions within Iraqi society and to the Ba'th attempt to deny them access to power in the second half of the twentieth century. Shi'is attempted to use the 1920 revolt both to establish their Iraqi national credentials and as a basis for their claim to rule.

A Memorable Moment of Unity

The 1920 revolt reflected the different motivations of the individuals, groups, tribes, and cities that took part in it, and it is therefore not surprising to find a variety of Shi'i interpretations of its nature and origins. Some writers highlighted the central role of the southern Euphrate region and the importance of the Shi'i tribes in fighting the actual battles against the British. The account of Fariq al-Muzhir Al Fir'awn, the sheikh of a section of the Al Fatla tribe settled in Abu Sukhayr, is the most notable example of this type of writing. Fir'awn not only stressed the role of the tribes but went so far as to argue that those Shi'i tribal sheikhs and clerics who participated in the revolt were the true representatives of Arab nationalism in Iraq.[2] Shi'is in Najaf and Karbala vied in attempting to emphasize the role of their city in the revolt. Highlighting the importance of Karbala as the hometown of Mirza Muhammad Taqi Shirazi, Salman Hadi Al Tu'ma wrote that the city was the stronghold of the rebels, commanding the attention of all other Iraqis who joined the revolt. Shirazi, who was of Iranian origin and who issued the main rulings calling for the revolt, was depicted as the guiding spirit of an authentic Iraqi national movement that sprang from Karbala.[3] Najafis also attempted to portray their city as the center of the revolt. But they went further than Tu'ma, arguing that the revolt was both the culmination of a renaissance that had begun earlier in the twentieth century and an extension of a smaller rebellion in Najaf two years earlier.[4]

The 1918 rebellion had been led by the sheikhs of two tribal factions who controlled Najaf's four quarters against the British attempt to reduce their power. And as such, it bears some resemblance in its motivations to the rebellions of Muqtada al-Sadr against the U.S.-led coalition during 2004—both demonstrating the resistance of Iraqi Shi'i groups to a foreign occupier seeking to strip them of power. Before Iraq's occupation was completed, the British permitted the sheikhs to maintain order in the city, and they were each paid a monthly allowance. But in February 1918, Captain Marshall was put in charge of Najaf. Marshall attempted to organize a police force and sought to regulate the payment of municipal taxes. At his suggestion the allowance that had been paid to the sheikhs was discontinued. Faced with this threat to their authority, they rebelled and dispatched a group that killed Marshall in his residence outside the city's walls. The rebels were probably influenced by the Islamic Rebellion Committee, whose members were drawn from among the lesser ulama. Yet the leading mujtahids in the city did not support the rebellion. Najaf was put under siege for six weeks and its freshwater supply cut off. The blockade was raised in early May only after the rebels had given up. The British executed 11 people considered to be the ringleaders of the rebellion and deported 123 to India.[5]

Shi'i writers described the 1918 rebellion as part of Najaf's continuing struggle on behalf of Islam, Arabism, and the Iraqi national cause. This theme was particularly evident in publications that appeared on the eve of the Iran-Iraq War, when the Ba'th sought to mobilize Iraqi Shi'is against Iran and permitted them to publish their works on the rebellion. Both the prose and poetry highlighted the strongly Arab and tribal character of Najafi society. We are told that Najafis have always valued their honor and freedom, and that in 1918 they demonstrated their bravery by standing up against a superior British enemy that symbolized despotism, tyranny, and oppression. Two figures received special attention: Najm al-Baqqal, a man in his sixties and the owner of a grocery, and Fadil, a young man in his twenties who emerged as the hero of a novel by Zuhayr Sadiq Rida. Baqqal is depicted as an honest and respected merchant. He was born a Sunni in Dulaym north of Baghdad and had impeccable Arab tribal credentials on the side of both his parents. When he was twelve, Baqqal's family migrated from Dulaym to Hilla in southern Iraq; they later settled in Najaf and espoused the Shi'i creed. Baqqal's conversion to Shi'ism was said to have transformed his life and personality, turning him into a man who valued freedom and independence. Shi'i accounts portrayed Baqqal as a major architect of the 1918 rebellion and as the person who planned Marshall's killing. In contrast to the elderly Baqqal, Fadil is young, physically strong, and in the prime of his life. His character evokes the image of 'Abbas (Abu al-Fadil), the son of imam 'Ali, who is famous among Iraqi Shi'is on account of his masculinity and his fight against tyranny as exemplified at the battle of Karbala. In Rida's novel, Fadil appears as the leader of the group sent by Baqqal to kill Marshall. His noble character is evident, however, when he allows the British officer to pull his gun first so as not to murder him in cold blood. Baqqal and Fadil are described as men motivated by a strong nationalist zeal and by a desire to free their homeland from the foreign invader. Fadil died fighting the British expedition sent to subdue Najaf after Marshall's killing, while Baqqal was among the rebels executed by the British after Najaf capitulated. Both, we are told, died as martyrs for the sake of Iraq and its people, and for Arabism and the Islamic cause.[6]

A recurring theme in the literature on the 1918 rebellion is the British forces' harshness in dealing with Iraqis—a complaint that Iraqis would sound repeatedly against the Americans in 2003–5. In Rida's novel, Iraq is compared to a beautiful woman named

Huda (meaning right guidance); she craves freedom for her country and an end to the British occupation. Huda is coveted by Balfour, the British officer investigating Marshall's murder, who orders his soldiers to kidnap her and bring her to his room. Balfour attempts to rape her, but she struggles and succeeds in keeping her honor intact until she is saved by Fadil.[7] The 1918 rebellion, Shi'is asserted, reinforced religious and nationalist feelings among Najafis, as well as a strong sense of resentment against the British. It was the event that inspired the revolt of 1920 and the struggle of all Iraqis for independence.[8]

The 1920 revolt has been recorded in Iraqi Shi'i memory as a symbol of Iraqi unity—a view which dominates the large majority of studies that deal with the revolt, irrespective of the ideological inclinations of the writers. It is claimed that the revolt spread to all parts of the country, but took a different shape in urban and rural areas in southern, central, and northern Iraq. Najaf, Karbala, Kazimain, Baghdad, and Mosul were the main cities that participated in the revolt. While the cities were the scene of much of the planning for the revolt, as well as the subsequent demonstrations, the main fighters were Shi'i tribesmen in the rural south. Shi'i poets and preachers encouraged Muslim unity and whipped up anti-British feelings during demonstrations and religious gatherings in the mixed cities of Kazimain and Baghdad. Hadi Zuwayn, Ja'far Abu Timman, and Muhammad al-Sadr, as well as the two brothers Muhammad Rida and Muhammad Baqir al-Shabibi, were depicted as the links between the Sharifians and the mujtahids. Among the mujtahids, Muhammad Mirza Taqi Shirazi of Karbala, Sheikh al-Shari'a Isfahani of Najaf, and Mahdi al-Khalisi of Kazimain emerged as the outspoken clerics whose actions unified Shi'is and Sunnis in a struggle for Islam and Arabism and for an Iraq free of foreign control.[9]

Shi'is offered conflicting accounts, however, regarding the extent of Baghdad's participation in the revolt and the role of religion and nationalism in shaping its nature. Both 'Ali al-Sharqi and Muhammad Mahdi al-Basir, who participated in the revolt, as well as

Hibat al-Din al-Shahrastani and Muhammad Mahdi Kubba, who held ministerial positions under the monarchy, emphasized the national dimension of the revolt and the role of Najaf and Karbala in leading it together with Baghdad. Shi'i communists, as evidenced by 'Adnan 'Ali's account, depicted the revolt as a struggle of the Iraqi masses against foreign imperialist rule.[10] By contrast, various religious figures stressed the Islamic dimension of the revolt and the role of the mujtahids in providing leadership and ideological direction to it.[11] The precedence of the religious over the nationalist factor was also noted by 'Abdallah al-Fayyad and by the sociologist 'Ali al-Wardi, whose work may be regarded as constituting the most balanced Iraqi Shi'i account on the revolt to date. The 1920 revolt, Wardi wrote, was one of the most important events in modern Iraqi history in increasing the political consciousness of ordinary people. Unlike the 1918 rebellion, which was confined to Najaf, the 1920 revolt was a national affair that taught Iraqis the meaning of freedom, independence, and nationalism.[12]

The 1920 revolt laid the foundations for the establishment of modern Iraq. Yet those Shi'is who participated in the revolt viewed themselves as its chief losers, whose rising against the British enabled the Sharifian intruders to enjoy all the fruits of office. The feeling of Shi'is that they were robbed of power explains their ambivalence toward Feisal, whom the British chose for the throne in Iraq. Feisal came to Basra by ship in June 1921 and made the journey to Baghdad through the Shi'i south. He stopped in several cities, trying to shore up support for his installation as king. While some Shi'is received him with enthusiasm, others were cautious and reserved. Feisal spoke Arabic with a Hijazi accent, which Iraqi Shi'is liked. They also liked the reverence that he showed toward the Shi'i imams, to whom he referred as his ancestors, as well as his visit to 'Ali's shrine in Najaf. Nevertheless, Feisal failed to win the hearts of important Shi'i leaders in the city. During a welcome dinner in the house of Hadi al-Naqib, the custodian of the shrine, Feisal made a speech linking the 1920 revolt to the Arab revolt of 1916 led by Feisal's father, the Sharif Hussein. In his reply Muhammad Baqir al-Shabibi reminded Feisal that he was "a guest of Iraq." Shabibi spoke passionately about the sacrifices that Iraqis had made in revolting against the British and stressed that they would entrust the fruits of their revolt only to a faithful man committed to fighting for Iraq's independence and safeguarding its national interests. Feisal also encountered difficulties in gaining the support of the leading mujtahids. Thus, for example, Mahdi al-Khalisi agreed to pledge allegiance to Feisal on condition that his rule should be free of foreign interference and that he would agree to be bound by a parliament. Shi'is viewed the British preparations for Feisal's installation with suspicion and noted that during the ceremony in August 1921 the king was flanked by Percy Cox, the British high commissioner, and by Lieutenant-General Aylmer Haldane, the commander of British forces in Iraq. Until his death in 1933, Feisal remained in the British embrace, which, according to 'Ali al-Sharqi, undermined the nationalist credentials of the king in the eye of Iraqis.[13]

In reflecting on the 1920 revolt, many of its Shi'i participants concluded that it ended before achieving its goals. They claimed that the British formation of modern Iraq undermined the unity of Iraqis generated by the revolt and reinforced sectarian divisions between Shi'is and Sunnis. Sharqi compared the new state to a building resting on foreign foundations and decorated with a national facade. He and other writers argued that a wide gap separated the government from the people, and that power rested in the hands of a Sunni minority elite whose members collaborated with the British. Shi'is pointed out that after 1921 Britain retained its paramount influence in the country by simply replacing the military officers with political advisers, who dominated the ministries. Moreover, Shi'is were deeply offended by the Iraqi government's ill-treatment of those rebels whom the British deported to the island of Hanjam in the Persian Gulf in the wake of the revolt, and who were nevertheless not welcomed as national heroes upon their return to Iraq. There were only a few references to the revolt in the nationalist educational curriculum under the monarchy, and this became a sore point for Shi'is. Both those who had participated in the revolt and Shi'is of later generations lamented that it was like a legend left out of history. In playing down the revolt's historical importance, Shi'is charged, Iraq's monarchic rulers falsified history and marginalized the Shi'is—the real nationalists. Much of the Shi'i anger was directed against Sati' al-Husri, director general of education between 1923 and 1927. Pointing to his Turkish descent, Shi'is asserted that Husri sought to erase the memory of the revolt from Iraqi consciousness, and to discourage the development of a national history that built on Iraq's heritage and on the struggle of Iraqis for independence from foreign rule.[14] The feeling of Shi'is that Iraq was born in sin remained strong throughout the period leading up to the U.S. invasion of 2003, shaping their suspicion of the American presence in the country as well as their view of the Iraqi Governing Council and the interim government appointed by the Coalition Provisional Authority led by L. Paul Bremer III.

To varying degrees, however, Sunni governments did acknowledge the historical importance of the 1920 revolt. But they highlighted the wider Arab nationalist character of the revolt and the role of Baghdad, thus countering the claim of Shi'is to have played the leading role in the revolt. Iraq's monarchic rulers made little effort to integrate the revolt into the official nationalist narrative because the Sharifians and the majority of the ex-Ottoman officers were outside Iraq in the period leading up to the revolt. Only a few accounts appeared between 1921 and 1958, most notably a government-inspired drama that highlighted the Iraqis' desire for a Sharifian ruler, as well as a book first published in 1954 by 'Ali al-Bazirgan, who stressed the importance of Baghdad in preparing the ground for the revolt and encouraging the Shi'i tribes to rebel.[15]

In contrast to Iraq's monarchic rulers, the Ba'thists emerged from within Iraq, and they made a conscious effort to control the meaning of the revolt and transmit its memory to younger generations of Iraqis. Under the Ba'th, the revolt became a tool in the hands of the regime in serving the needs of the moment. Thus Salim Taha and Kamal Muzhir Ahmad stressed the role of the revolt in

uniting all Iraqis, including Arabs and Kurds, against British imperialism. Taha criticized any attempt to assign greater weight to one
Iraqi group over another in leading the revolt, arguing that the
revolt transcended the borders of Iraq and inspired the wider struggle of the Arab people against imperialism.[16] The Ba'th used the
memory of the revolt to both reward and punish Shi'is. The surge
of publications between 1963 and the Iran-Iraq War of 1980–88
(which included the works of 'Abdallah al-Fayyad, Ibrahim al-
Wa'ili, Muhammad 'Ali Kamal al-Din, and 'Ali al-Wardi, as well
as reproductions of articles by 'Ali al-Sharqi) signaled the Ba'th
attempt to mobilize the Shi'is by acknowledging their major role
in the revolt. By contrast, the republication of Bazirgan's book in
the wake of the 1991 Iraqi Shi'i uprising against Saddam Hussein
was intended to stress the role of Sunnis and the importance of
Baghdad in leading the revolt. In their annotations to the new edi-
tion, the editors attacked all previous works that highlighted the
role of Shi'is. One of them was Bazirgan's son, who depicted these
works as a "falsification of history" and described their authors as
"neo-*shu'ubi*s," a term we will come back to later in this chapter,
and which refers to followers of the Persians who undermined
Iraq's unity and sowed discord among its people.[17] However, the
Ba'th reversed course a few weeks before the U.S. invasion. Thus,
in February 2003, Saddam Hussein drew parallels between the Iraq
the British occupied in 1920 and the country the United States was
about to encounter: "We hope," he said in a televised meeting with
his military commanders, "that the British will tell the Americans
about their experience in 1920. . . . The Iraqis were poor, [but] they
fought the superior British army with axes and shovels. . . . The
Iraqis defended their country and forced the occupying army to
meet [their] demands for national rule."[18]

As will be shown below, the debate around the 1920 revolt
was part of a larger controversy that has been absorbing Iraqis,
namely, who belongs to Iraqi society and the Arab nation and who
does not.

Who Is an Iraqi?

The disagreement over this question between Shi'is and the ruling Sunni elite reflected the different ideological inclinations of the two groups. Whereas the majority of Shi'is preferred a specifically Iraqi nationalism, which stresses the tribal and Islamic values of Iraqi society, Iraq's Sunni rulers adopted a wider Arab nationalism as their main ideology and took Shi'i preference of Iraqi nationalism as proof that the Shi'is did not share their commitment to the ultimate goal of an Arab state extending far beyond the borders of Iraq.

For King Feisal and his Hashemite successors Arab unity was not a vague conception but a mission nourished by a family ambition that went back to the 1916 Arab revolt led by Feisal's father, the Sharif Hussein of Mecca. Iraqi government ideologues, beginning with Sati' al-Husri in the 1920s, were among the first in the Arab world to preach Arab unity. Arab nationalist ideas were further spread in Iraq by Syrian and Palestinian teachers, who were employed in the education system during the monarchy, and the concept of Pan-Arabism became part of the political climate that led to Rashid 'Ali al-Gaylani's coup in 1941. Those few Shi'i politicians who espoused Pan-Arabism did not represent their community, which feared the prospect of losing its majority status in the pan-Arab state that Iraq's rulers envisaged. The various proposals for unity between Iraq and other Arab countries that were floated in the 1930s, and again in the 1940s and 1950s, did not materialize. But the propagation of Arab unity under the monarchy helped defuse the calls of Shi'i clerics for Muslim unity and enabled the ruling Sunni minority to deter the Shi'is from pressing a claim to political representation in accordance with their numbers among the population.[19]

Arab nationalism took a more radical form following the coming to power of the Ba'th in 1968 and the establishment of a one-party system in Iraq. Although Shi'is were among the founders of the

Iraqi Ba'th in 1952, by 1968 the ruling members of the party had become almost exclusively Sunni. The early stages of this process are described by Hani al-Fukayki, who was among the first Shi'is to join the Ba'th. His book sheds light on the attempt of Shi'is to reconcile their sectarian identity with the secular political ideology adopted by the Ba'th Party. It also illuminates the rivalry between the Iraqi Shi'i Fu'ad al-Rikabi and the Syrian Christian ideologue Michel 'Aflaq. Whereas the former sought to distinguish the Ba'th in Iraq from its Syrian counterpart, the latter in 1958 urged Iraqi Ba'thists not to delay their declaration of support for the United Arab Republic of Egypt and Syria.[20] While in subsequent years party officials occasionally emphasized Iraqi nationalism as well as the ancient Mesopotamian past of Iraq, Pan-Arabism remained the core of Ba'th nationalist ideology. Ba'thi writers often spoke of the mission that Iraq took upon itself to protect the Arab nation, presenting their country as a sanctuary for Arab nationalists and as the object of hope for all Arabs. The provisional constitution of 1970 declared the establishment of a single Arab state to be "the central aim" of the Iraqi Republic. Party officials urged mergers between Arab countries throughout the 1970s, causing apprehension among the oil monarchies in the Persian Gulf. During the Iran-Iraq War, the Ba'th toned down its calls for mergers and instead emphasized the mutual responsibility that binds Arab countries together. Yet this ambiguity ended with Saddam Hussein's invasion of Kuwait in 1990—a move that the Iraqi propaganda machine described as an act of unification and as a great achievement of the Arab army.[21]

The struggle between Shi'is and the Sunni ruling elite over the meaning of Iraqi and Arab nationalism dates back to the early years of the monarchy. The Shi'i literature includes a series of thirty-two articles published between April 1927 and March 1928 in the newspaper *al-Nahda* by the literary figure 'Ali al-Sharqi, who gives a moving description of the success of Baghdad in dominating the Shi'i south, isolating Najaf, and preventing it from playing a role in national politics. Sharqi's ideas on nationalism, expressed between the 1920s and the early 1960s, reflect the feelings of a generation of Iraqi Shi'is who participated in the 1920 revolt and became disillusioned with its outcome. Members of that generation rejected the government's attempt to promote a model of a secular modern Arab, viewing it as an invention of Sharifian and ex-Ottoman officials (whom the poet Muhammad Mahdi al-Jawahiri compared to swarms of locusts descending on Iraq after the 1920 revolt). Alarmed by the assault on their Iraqi identity and Arab tribal attributes, Shi'is maintained that they were the "pure" Arabs in Iraq. Sharqi offered a vision of Iraqi nationalism that built on the strong tribal character of Iraqi society and the historical role of Iraq's tribes in preserving the "true" spirit of Arabism in the country. He advocated the development of an Iraqi national history, arguing that Iraq needed a nationalist ideology that combined Eastern and Arab elements with Iraqi values and heritage. Sharqi attempted to articulate a concept of Iraqi nationalism that was clearly inspired by the effort of Egyptians to preserve their past. He argued that only an authentic Iraqi nationalism, free of foreign contents, would yield a legitimate government that served its people.[22]

Sharqi died in Iraq in 1964. He and many of his generation lived at a time when Iraqi governments tolerated a degree of opposition and intellectual dissent. Unlike Sharqi, who published his works in Iraq, later Iraqi Shi'i writers ended up in exile and, at least until 2003, had to publish their books outside Iraq. Two of the most prolific writers have been Hasan al-'Alawi, who worked for the Ba'th before breaking ranks with the party in the early 1980s, and Salim Matar, whose book *al-Dhat al-jariha* (The Wounded Soul), published in 1997, is the most serious attempt yet by an Iraqi Shi'i to offer a concept of Iraqi nationalism that builds on Sharqi's ideas and incorporates the various pre-Islamic civilizations of Iraq. Both 'Alawi and Matar argued that the use of Pan-Arabism by Iraqi rulers as their main ideology denied Iraqis the knowledge of their distinct historical past, and blocked the development of an Iraqi national identity that could unify the various sectarian and ethnic groups in the country. Together with other writers, they highlighted the Hijazi and Syrian origins of the officials who accompanied Feisal to Iraq, as well as the Turkish origin of leading politicians under the monarchy. Shi'is charged that although Iraq's Sunni politicians claimed to rule in the name of Arabism, they had no familial links to the Arab tribes in Iraq and did not share in the life of the Iraqi people. They singled out Sati' al-Husri, who built an educational program in Iraq inspired by German concepts of nationalism, as well as the Ba'th ideologue Michel 'Aflaq, arguing that both were disconnected from the Arab Islamic heritage. Moreover, Shi'is pointed out that Iraqi governments emptied the word "Arab" of its old meaning (which connoted tribal origin and identity) and infused the word "Arabism" ('uruba) with a new, Western meaning. Iraqi Shi'is had understood 'uruba as a quality derived from a person's descent, but 'uruba became associated with the word "nation," and in modern Iraq it has been used interchangeably with the term qawmiyya, which refers to Arab nationalism. 'Alawi further observed that the rise of Arab nationalism coincided with the emergence of Iraqi politicians who attempted to emulate Bismarck as a grand national leader. While under the monarchy Yasin al-Hashimi, Hikmat Sulayman, and Rashid 'Ali al-Gaylani vied for the role of an Arab Bismarck, after 1968 Saddam Hussein took on the mantle of the great leader. All four, argued 'Alawi, attempted to project themselves as the protectors of Arab nationalism while depicting Iraqi Shi'is as separatists.[23]

The government portrayal of Iraqi Shi'is as separatists stemmed from their objection to Iraq's inclusion in a confederation of Arab states. Shi'is perceived the possibility of unification between Iraq and other Arab states as a threat to their majority position in the country, fearing that if Iraq joined an Arab confederation, they would become a politically marginal sectarian group. It is that fear which explains the objection of Shi'is to Arab unity as advocated by Gamal 'Abd al-Nasser and espoused by Sunni Ba'thists and other Arab nationalists in Iraq, notably President 'Abd al-Salam 'Arif during his rule between 1963 and 1966. 'Ali al-Sharqi portrayed Nasser as an opportunist who rode the wave of Pan-Arabism, asserting that he did not grasp the social conditions of Iraq. And in a manifesto submitted to the Iraqi premier in 1965, Muhammad Rida al-Shabibi advocated that all plans for unification should first be put before the people of Iraq in a national referendum.[24]

The struggle for power between Shi'is and the government found embodiment in the Iraqi nationality law, first introduced in 1924. This law distinguished between Iraqis who held Ottoman nationality before 1924 and those who carried Iranian nationality, including many Arab Shi'is who were seeking to escape taxation or conscription into the Ottoman army. The guiding principles of the law were put to the test soon after the establishment of the monarchy. In 1922 a struggle erupted between the government and the Shi'i mujtahids, who led the opposition to the proposed Anglo-Iraqi treaty. Noting that the great majority of the mujtahids were Iranian subjects, the government of 'Abd al-Muhsin al-Sa'dun introduced an amendment to the existing law of immigration permitting the deportation of foreigners engaging in antigovernment activity. Under this provision, the government in June 1923 deported to Iran the Arab mujtahid Mahdi al-Khalisi, who held Iranian nationality. Yet the deportation of Arab Shi'is was limited in scope under the monarchy. It gained momentum after the Ba'th first came to power in 1963. Both the nationality law of that year and the provisional constitution introduced by 'Abd al-Salam 'Arif in 1964 dealt a blow to the legal status of many Shi'is in Iraq. The law referred to those who held Ottoman nationality before 1924 as indigenous Iraqis (asliyyun), stipulating that all others had to apply for Iraqi citizenship. It also granted permission to the minister of interior to strip citizenship from any person who was found to be disloyal to the Iraqi Republic. Article 41 of the 1964 constitution stated that the president of Iraq must be an individual born to Iraqi parents of Ottoman nationality who had resided in Iraq since 1900. Under this article, a large number of Shi'is were blocked from access to high office in the state. After its second accession to power in 1968, the Ba'th used the nationality law (which was amended in 1972, 1977, and 1980) to deny a great number of Shi'is, including Fayli Kurds, Iraqi nationality, citing their Iranian origins. The Ba'th deported Iraqis to Iran in 1963 and again in 1969–71. The waves of deportation increased in the course of the Iran-Iraq War of 1980–88, when as many as 300,000 Iraqis were forced to leave their country.[25]

In reacting to the Iraqi nationality law, Shi'is highlighted the Turkish and otherwise obscure origins of government politicians under the monarchy, most notably Hikmat Sulayman, Ja'far al-'Askari, 'Abd al-Muhsin al-Sa'dun, Yasin al-Hashimi, and Nuri Sa'id. They often cited the example of 'Abd al-Muhsin al-Sa'dun, who committed suicide in 1929, leaving a will written in Turkish for his wife. In his book on the Ba'th, Hani al-Fukayki recounted that several Sunni members of his party cell in Baghdad were of Turkish origin. Other writers pointed to the government's distinction between Iraqis of "sacred" Ottoman origin and those of "despicable" Iranian origin, charging that Iraqis should not take pride in an Ottoman nationality associated with a foreign occupation of Iraq. The deportations, they said, split families and caused severe hardship to Arab Shi'is as well as to Shi'is of Iranian origin who had resided in Iraq for centuries and become thoroughly assimilated to Iraqi society. These acts led many Iraqis to question their national identity and sense of belonging to the Iraqi people.[26] The nationality law remained in force until the collapse of the Ba'th in 2003. A year later, the Governing Council approved a provision within the interim Iraqi constitution that reinstated those who had been stripped of their citizenship under the law—an act that signaled the first attempt by Iraqis to confront the devastating consequences of the nationality law for the country and its people.

As part of an effort to discredit the nationalist credentials of the Shi'is, Iraqi rulers invoked the memory of the *shu'ubiyya* movement that appeared within Islam in the eighth century. The term *shu'ubiyya* is derived from the Arabic word *shu'ub*, which means "peoples." The majority of those who joined the movement during the eighth and ninth centuries were Persians and the Aramaeans of Iraq who protested the privileged position of the Arabs within Islam and demanded equality between all Muslims. The appearance of the *shu'ubiyya* alarmed Arab historians and literary figures of the time, most notably al-Jahiz (d. 868) who considered the movement a threat to Islam and to the supreme position of the Arabs among all nations. The term *shu'ubiyya* fell out of use in the medieval period, and its reappearance in modern times was connected to the rise of Arab nationalism.[27]

The first explicit Iraqi government attempt to depict Shi'is as a threat to Arabism may date from 1923, when the Shi'i mujtahids led an opposition to the proposed elections to the constituent assembly. Seeking to discredit the mujtahids, the government encouraged the publication of articles in Baghdad's newspaper *al-'Asima* portraying them as "aliens" whose "intention was to undermine the blessed Arab movement . . . and serve a foreign people [the Persians] who were one of the major causes of the termination of the Arab Empire."[28] A few years later, a confrontation took place between Sati' al-Husri, the director general of education, and the Shi'i poet Muhammad Mahdi al-Jawahiri, one of Iraq's leading literary figures in the twentieth century. Asked by the Shi'i education minister to appoint Jawahiri as an Arabic-language schoolteacher in Baghdad, Husri objected on the ground that Jawahiri held Iranian nationality. His objection was overruled and Jawahiri got the job. A few days later, however, the poet published a sarcastic ode in one of Baghdad's newspapers that praised Iran's natural beauties. Furious, Husri asked another leading Iraqi poet, the Sunni Ma'ruf al-Rusafi, to examine the piece, which, according to Husri, was found to be anti-Arab (*shu'ubi*).[29]

The Ba'thists had begun using the word *shu'ubi* to attack their opponents long before they came to power. Between the mid-1940s and early 1970s, *shu'ubi* was used as a curse word directed mainly against Iraqi communists, the majority of whom were Shi'is. Ba'thi writers highlighted the opposition that the Iraqi Communist Party voiced to the idea of unification between Iraq and other Arab states, taking its contacts with the Iranian Tudeh communist party as evidence that Iraqi communists were not Arabs. They portrayed Iraqi communists as a fifth column within Iraq whose goal was to split the Arabs, destroy their values, and cut them off from their heritage and civilization. 'Abd al-'Aziz al-Duri (who became president of Baghdad University in 1963) and Khayrallah Tulfah (Saddam Hussein's uncle and father-in-law) are representative of that anticommunist type of writing. Both stressed Iraq's position as the historical battlefield between the Arabs and their *shu'ubi* and communist enemies in Iraq and Iran, thus creating a link between early and modern enemies of the Arab people.[30]

'Abd al-Karim Qasim, who ruled Iraq for five years after the 1958 collapse of the monarchy, became a prime target of the Ba'thists, who depicted him as a separatist and a *shu'ubi* despot. The son of a Kurdish-Fayli Shi'i mother and a Sunni Arab father, Qasim advocated Iraqi nationalism and declared the achievement of unity within Iraq as his main goal. In Shi'i literature, Qasim appears as a modest man who did not seek to establish his own political party or build a power base that relied on family members. Instead, he derived his power from popular support, counting on soldiers (the majority of whom were Shi'is) and on Shi'i immigrants in the Thawra slum neighborhood of Baghdad, renamed Saddam City in the 1980s and today known as Sadr City. Qasim found the Iraqi Communist Party a useful ally in resisting the attempts of Iraqi and Syrian Ba'thists and Gamal 'Abd al-Nasser of Egypt to get him to join the United Arab Republic. In an interview with the Lebanese journalist Muhammad Baqir Shirri, Qasim articulated his view of Arabism—a view shared by many Iraqi Shi'is. "For us," Qasim said, "Arabism is not a means for achieving political ends (*siyasa*), but a quality derived from our noble social origin and standing (*nasab* and *hasab*)."[31] In opting for Iraqism as their framework of identity, Qasim and the majority of Iraqi Shi'is adopted a line similar to that advocated by the Egyptian nationalist Lutfi al-Sayyid, who maintained that Egyptians should insist on preserving their Egyptian identity and not seek affiliation with any other state.

Qasim was assassinated by Ba'thi officers who led the 1963 coup, on the charge that he was an enemy of Arabism. He has been remembered by Shi'is as the single nationalist leader who attempted to break the mold of an Iraqi state built on sectarian divisions and ruled by a Sunni minority elite.[32]

The rise of the Ba'th coincided with the decline of communism and the success of Islamic ideology in gaining ground among lay Shi'is in Iraq, beginning in the 1960s. Subsequently, the Ba'th began using the word *shu'ubi* to describe Shi'i Islamists. At the same time, it tied the issue of *shu'ubiyya* to Shi'i protests against discrimination on the part of the government and presented Shi'i grievances as acts that promoted sectarian divisions (*ta'ifiyya*) in the state. The Ba'th held that sectarianism had deep roots in history, and that there were groups within Iraq that sought to promote civil strife in order to fragment society. Although Sunnis and Kurds were at times blamed for sowing domestic discord, it was Shi'i opponents of the Ba'th whom the regime labeled most frequently as *ta'ifis*. The exact meaning of the word was left somewhat vague until the late 1970s, but it assumed a clear meaning following the rise of the Islamic Republic of Iran in 1979. Those accused of promoting divisions were individuals and groups who were seen as placing their Shi'i sectarian identity above their loyalty to Iraq and the Arab cause, a choice that was tantamount to an act of treason.[33]

During the Iran-Iraq War the Ba'th tied the themes of *shu'ubiyya* and *ta'ifiyya* to the critical question of who belongs to Iraqi society and the Arab nation and who does not. Declaring itself the defender of the Arab nation against its Persian and Zoroastrian enemy, the Ba'th launched a campaign to discredit Iraqi Shi'i opposition groups by linking them to the Islamic Republic of Iran. The war was called *Qadisiyyat Saddam*, a name that evoked the historic Arab victory against the Persians at Qadisiyya in southern Iraq in A.D. 636. The Ba'th propaganda machine presented the war as a cultural and national struggle between Arabs and Persians—an experience that was supposed to enable the Arabs to rediscover themselves and their historical roots. Saddam Hussein was the leader chosen by modern Arab history to fight Iran and establish one Arab nation. Iran and its people, led by Ruhollah Khomeini, were *shu-'ubis* whose goal was to destroy Arab culture and replace the Arab rulers with Persians. The Ba'th drew a line between "bad" and "good" Shi'is. The Iranians who fought Iraq were depicted as extremists and descendants of the Jew 'Abdallah ibn Saba', the Ba'th thus evoking an image of Shi'ism that was widespread among the Wahhabis in Saudi Arabia. By contrast, those Iraqi Shi'is who were not swayed by the Islamic Revolution and did not join the opposition to the Ba'th were declared followers of imam 'Ali, who fought extremism.[34]

The Ba'th found the work of the ninth-century thinker and satirist al-Jahiz useful in its attempt to put Iraqi Shi'is on the defensive. Jahiz, as we saw earlier, was a fervent defender of the Arabs and Arab cultural tradition against all latecomers to Islam, especially the Persians. One of his works that the Ba'th published with annotations was *al-Bukhala'* (The Misers), in which Jahiz used a wide variety of anecdotes to describe the character, lifestyle, and ethos of the misers of 'Abbasid Baghdad. The main theme of this work is generosity (a core principle of the Arab value system), and the reader cannot escape the impression that the misers and those who exalt the virtues of miserliness are mostly Persians, with the admixture of a few Arabs who are portrayed as corrupt and despicable. The Ba'th thus conveyed the message that those who did not support the regime in its war with Iran were descendants of the misers—that is, people of disputed Arab origin who could not be trusted.[35]

The language used by the Ba'th to distinguish between nationalists and traitors became bolder following the Iraqi Shi'i uprising in the wake of the Gulf War of 1991. Fighting for survival, the Ba'th attempted to drive a wedge between the Shi'is who rebelled in southern Iraq and the residents of Baghdad, who did not join the uprising. At a time when army units loyal to Saddam Hussein were still trying to regain control of the south, the Ba'th published a series of articles in the newspaper *al-Thawra al-'Iraqiyya* attacking the identity and origins of Iraqi Shi'is, particularly the marsh Arabs. The writers presented the Shi'i rebels as a foreign people within Iraq. While some were of Iranian or Indian origins, others were Arabs who had lost their identity because they had lived for so long close to the border with Iran. The marsh-dwellers were depicted as barbarians whose value system was primitive in comparison with that of the people of Baghdad. The backwardness of the marsh people stood in contrast to the progress achieved by other segments of Iraqi society under the Ba'th, and hindered the attempt to build a unified state. The writers also attacked the Shi'i religious seminaries in Najaf and Karbala, arguing that the students there were exposed to a foreign religion spread by Iran, and were the enemies of Iraq and the Arab nation. Highlighting the difficult mission that the Ba'th leadership took upon itself in trying to restore Iraq to its 'Abbasid glory, the writers reminded Iraqis that they themselves had agreed to make sacrifices in order to achieve that goal. The uprising, they asserted, was an act of betrayal by those who attempted to undermine that mission and steal Iraq from its people.[36]

Shi'is viewed the government's use of charges of *shu'ubiyya* and *ta'ifiyya* as a strategy of the Sunni minority elite to retain power by undermining the nationalist credentials of the Shi'i majority. They argued that the debate over the *shu'ubiyya* movement of the eighth and ninth centuries should have been confined to academia. In introducing the issue of *shu'ubiyya* into political life, Iraq's rulers risked creating a rift among Arabs in modern times similar to the strife that divided the Muslim community over the question of succession to the Prophet Muhammad. Shi'is highlighted the Arab roots of Shi'ism and defended Shi'i poets of the 'Abbasid period whom Sunni writers depicted as *shu'ubis*. Ahmad al-Wa'ili dedicated an entire book to the topic, denying the Persian origin of Shi'ism and arguing that Shi'i poets had led the opposition to the *shu'ubiyya* movement during the 'Abbasid period. In addressing the issue of *ta'ifiyya*, Shi'is noted that sectarianism assumed a distinct character in Iraq. The problem was not simply a matter of the religious differences between Iraqis who adhered to the Sunni creed and those who espoused Shi'ism. *Ta'ifiyya* was seen as a modern creation of secular Sunni rulers, who adopted policies of discrimination against the Shi'i majority in all areas of public life. The degree of discrimination, Shi'is noted, escalated following the Ba'th assassination of Qasim in 1963, as Iraqi regimes grew increasingly dictatorial. Moreover, during the 1960s *ta'ifiyya* spread rapidly even within the Iraqi military, where Shi'is constituted 70 percent of the common soldiers but barely 20 percent of the officer corps. While several Iraqi Kurds, as well as Sunnis of Turkish origin, had occupied the position of chief-of-staff in Iraq, not a single Shi'i was ever appointed to that position, although a good number of Shi'i officers had the qualifications.[37]

As sectarianism spread in Iraq, Shi'is found themselves trapped in a situation whereby they had to prove their Arab identity to Sunni officials and politicians whose own Arab origins were in doubt. "A Shi'i," wrote Hasan al-'Alawi, "will bear any accusation, but the charge that he is a *ta'ifi*." 'Alawi's statement is echoed in the example of Hani al-Fukayki. The latter related that after his father's death in 1970, he decided to donate his collection of books to the Ministry of Endowments and not to a Shi'i library, which would have benefited more from the collection, fearing that he might be accused of promoting sectarian divisions. Sa'id al-Samarra'i, a Sunni who espoused Shi'ism in his twenties, wrote after the Gulf War that sectarianism had come to dominate political relations between Sunnis and Shi'is in Iraq and to shape their view of one another. *Ta'ifiyya* became so woven into the fabric of Iraqi society that many Iraqis could not transcend the sectarian barriers separating them and acknowledge that Saddam Hussein was a *ta'ifi* ruler who thrived on the splits within society. Indeed, during much of the twentieth century the majority of Iraqis denied the existence of a sectarian problem in the country, and those few who acknowledged it usually described it as a legacy of the Ottoman past or a result of British imperialism. It was only following the Iran-Iraq War, and increasingly in the decade that preceded the collapse of the Ba'th in 2003, that Iraqis began debating the consequences of sectarianism for Iraqi society. Many compared *ta'ifiyya* to a disease that blocked pluralism and just government. Dealing with the problem, they argued, was a life-or-death matter for Iraq and for its people.[38]

The Ba'th Legacy

During its thirty-five years in power, the Ba'th took advantage of the divisions among Shi'is between secularists and Islamists, between rural- and urban-dwellers, and between Shi'is in exile and those inside the country. These divisions help explain the difficulty of developing a Shi'i political leadership that could unite the community and at the same time appeal to non-Shi'is in Iraq. The lack of a credible secular Shi'i leader was evident in the case of Salih Jabir, the first Shi'i to hold the position of prime minister in monarchic Iraq.[39] The problem of leadership became more pressing in the years following the death in 1965 of Muhammad Rida al-Shabibi—a man whose role as a link between Shi'is and Sunnis has been widely acknowledged in modern Iraq.[40] By the time of Shabibi's death, Islamic ideology was already encroaching on communist influences in Iraq and attracting lay Shi'is who considered Islam a vehicle for political change that might succeed where communism had failed. These Shi'is had given up on the secular politicians and were looking for an Arab cleric attuned to their specific Iraqi aspirations.

Against this background Muhammad Baqir al-Sadr emerged in the 1970s as a cleric who commanded support among young Shi'is affiliated with the Islamic Da'wa Party. Sadr distinguished between two types of religious leaders: *al-marja' al-dhati*, the preeminent cleric who gains recognition by consensus, or a majority, among ulama and followers in the Shi'i world, and *al-marja' al-salih* (also known as *al-rashid* or *al-mawdu'i*), who is not necessarily the most learned cleric, but springs from within his milieu and responds to the needs of his local constituency. Sadr envisaged *al-marja' al-salih* as a politically minded cleric involved in all areas of life. Acting as one, he focused on Iraq and on the Iraqi people, attempting to appeal to Arab Shi'is and Sunnis as well as to Kurds. His activism, however, was a threat to the Ba'th and eventually led to his execution in 1980.[41] Subsequently, Iraqi Shi'i leadership became divided among several opposition groups. Whereas the Da'wa and its off-shoots, as well as the Supreme Council for the Islamic Revolution in Iraq (SCIRI), became the largest Islamist groups in exile, the movement of Muhammad Sadiq al-Sadr (a cousin of Baqir al-Sadr known among Shi'is as Sadr II) evolved into the most organized Shi'i opposition within Iraq in the period leading up to the U.S. invasion.

Sadr II emerged as a dominant figure after his release from prison in the wake of the 1991 Shi'i uprising. Initially, the Ba'th tolerated, probably even encouraged, his rise, seeking to use him both to placate Iraqi Shi'is and as an alternative to the preeminent and aloof religious leadership in Najaf led by Abu al-Qasim Khoei (until his death in 1992) and 'Ali Sistani. Yet if the Ba'th expected Sadr II to show acquiescence toward the regime, it was proven wrong. During the 1990s, this energetic figure succeeded in reconnecting the Najaf world of clerics and seminaries (the *hawza*) with the rural communities of southern Iraq as well as with the Shi'i urban poor in Baghdad. Sadr II sought to implement Muhammad Baqir al-Sadr's ideas regarding clerical involvement in all areas of life. His strategy built on grassroots politics and on the function of the religious leader as a field commander (*marja'iyyat al-maydan*). Sadr II disapproved of the quietist approach of the leading clerics in Najaf, who abstained from politics, arguing that clerics should be outspoken or lose the right to lead. Accordingly, he instituted the Friday prayer as a link between the *hawza* and Shi'i believers, using a simple colloquial language in sermons delivered in the Kufa mosque that appealed to his followers. Most Shi'i clerics in Iraq have traditionally considered the Friday prayer as in abeyance, but during the 1990s the practice was said to attract thousands of worshipers in as many as seventy localities. In an effort to reach out to followers, Sadr II also adapted Shi'i law to tribal custom, opened religious courts, and established a network of deputies and charities in cities and villages, filling a void left by the state during the twelve years of sanctions and contracting government welfare services. In his sermons he lashed out against the United States, viewing it as a power seeking to dominate the world. At the same time, he pursued a policy of indirect confrontation with the Ba'th, refusing to bestow political legitimacy on the regime in exchange for freedom of religious activities. Yet his path to becoming an independent cleric commanding popular support was cut short when unidentified gunmen shot him to death in Najaf in 1999. His movement, made up mainly of Shi'is of poor background, many of whom were veterans of the 1991 uprising, remained intact under his son Muqtada, who went underground. The Sadr movement would reemerge with vigor in the power vacuum that followed the collapse of the Ba'th in 2003.[42]

Still, the Ba'th did not hold power for thirty-five years simply by using violence and instilling fear among Iraqi Shi'is. In an attempt to consolidate power in the 1960s, Ba'th leaders courted the Shi'i mujtahids, who then viewed communism as the main threat to Islam. The Ba'thists took advantage of the mujtahids' opposition to the personal status law introduced under Qasim in December 1959, a law that accorded women equal rights with men in matters of intestate succession and thus undermined the legal authority of Shi'i clerics. 'Abd al-Salam 'Arif rewarded the mujtahids for their opposition to Qasim, as evidenced by the provisional constitution of 1964, which stated that inheritance was to be guaranteed in accordance with Islamic family law.[43] The Ba'th attempted to appeal to Shi'is again during the war with Iran and following the Gulf War. In order to mobilize Shi'is in the war with Iran, a biographer of Saddam Hussein in 1980 constructed a family tree showing that the Iraqi leader, a member of the Al Bu Nasir tribe, was a descendant of imam 'Ali. This claim was repeated during and after the war.[44] In addition, various writers highlighted Saddam Hussein's tribal origin and portrayed him as a great leader who took his people to war with Iran in order to redeem the honor of Iraq's tribes. Invoking the Arab value system (*muruwwa*), these writers emphasized the bravery of the Iraqi soldiers, who were portrayed as descendants of the great Arab tribes of Iraq.[45] Ba'th propaganda gave special attention to the largely Shi'i city of Basra and to the province of 'Amara (renamed Maysan in the 1970s) because of their proximity to the Iranian front. It depicted Basra as the symbol of Arab and Iraqi opposition to the Persian enemy, and highlighted the historical role of the tribes of 'Amara in preserving the Arab character of the province.[46]

Saddam Hussein's revival of tribal values and institutions—a policy that started in the 1980s and accelerated following the Gulf War—was both a strategy for survival and an attempt to use tribalism as a common denominator of Arab Sunnis and Shi'is. Tribalism as a framework of identity, formerly denounced by the Ba'th, became an important component of the state's national ideology after 1991. Like the British in Iraq in the 1920s, Saddam bolstered the position of those tribal sheikhs whom he considered loyal, trying to turn them into a medium through which the countryside could be administered. The revival of tribalism coincided with the Ba'th policy of attempting to regulate the rise of religion in public life, among both Shi'is and Sunnis. For several years the Ba'th tolerated the activities of Muhammad Sadiq al-Sadr as a way to absorb the religious energy of Shi'is and direct it away from the regime. At the same time, it allowed the organization of Sunni Islamist groups, including the Muslim Brothers and Salafis with Wahhabi inclinations, seeking to use them to counterbalance the Shi'is. In the final days of his rule, Saddam sanctioned the formation of Islamic fedayeen groups as well as the Army of Muhammad led by an officer of the Republican Guard, turning them into part of the military wing of the Ba'th Party.[47] The Ba'th regime thus set the stage for the emergence of tribalism and Islam as potent forces following the U.S. invasion.

The period of Sunni minority rule between 1921 and 2003 was a setback to the position of Shi'i Islam in Iraq. This repression stood in contrast to the surge of Shi'ism in Lebanon in the second half of the twentieth century, the focus of the next chapter.

The Revival of Shi'ism in Lebanon

◈

Question: Why doesn't the Jabal 'Amil push for unity [between Lebanon and Syria]? Why are its leaders in constant disagreement with one another and why are they not following a course that will benefit their community? And why don't the ulama of the Jabal 'Amil rise in action?

Answer: It's not up to the Jabal 'Amil to decide whether to pursue unity or not. The matter is in the hands of the French; they do not want unification and use the disunity among the people as a pretext. The leaders of the Jabal 'Amil are in disagreement because of their competition for office and influence and because of the envy that embitters their hearts. There is no unified community in the Jabal 'Amil that could demand the return of its abrogated rights, but only those who make trivial demands from the leaders for their own personal interests. And the ulama don't rise because most of them are asleep; they will take action, God willing, when they wake up from their sleep.[1]

In October 1918, French forces landed in Beirut and were greeted by Maronites and other Christians who cheered their arrival. Proud of their long historical connection with France, the Maronites did not hesitate to collaborate with this Western power, which they perceived as their savior. The French terminated the short-lived Arab government of King Feisal in Beirut and Damascus and created Greater Lebanon as a mandate (1920–1943) separate from Syria and dominated by the Maronites. In the census of 1932 the Maronites were the largest single sect, about 30 percent of the population in Lebanon, followed by Sunnis and Shi'is, who constituted 22 and 20 percent, respectively. Sunni Muslims had difficulty in recognizing Lebanon as a state independent of Syria—an attitude that was most noticeable among Sunnis in the coastal cities. In contrast to Shi'i leaders, who supported the idea of an independent Lebanon, Sunni leaders with few exceptions boycotted the Lebanese state until the mid-1930s, making it easier for the Maronites to secure most of the key government and administrative positions and ultimately the presidency of the republic.[2]

Did Lebanon constitute a final state (*watan niha'i*) for its people or did it lack national validity as long as it was separated from Syria? That question has stood at the heart of the political debate in modern Lebanon. The Maronites and many other Christians conceived of Lebanon as a final state, advocating a Lebanese national identity. But the Maronites did not frame Lebanese nationality within the broader context of Arabism, presenting it instead in terms of their own communal particularism. To them, the Lebanese were not Arabs but a distinct people whose heritage was a combination of ancient Phoenicia and the broader Mediterranean culture. This version of history and civilization had little attraction to those Muslims in Lebanon who questioned the national validity of the state. The Sunnis, much more than Shi'is, articulated their identity in terms of Arab nationalism, regarding their incorporation into a Lebanese state under Christian domination as a separation from the Arab world. They held the Maronites accountable for pushing France to split Syria and Lebanon, refusing to forget the humiliation of the battle of Maysalun in July 1920 when Maronite volunteers joined the French force that defeated the Arab army of King Feisal and occupied Damascus. From the Sunni Muslim point of view, the Maronites were isolationists who had to be persuaded, and if necessary coerced, to rejoin the Arab national ranks. Thus in Lebanon, a force called Lebanonism has stood face-to-face with another force called Arabism. The state could prevail only so long as these two forces were kept in balance, so long as Christians and Muslims did not push their conflicting visions of Lebanon's nationality too far and settled instead for pragmatism and compromise.[3]

Unlike the Sunnis, who viewed themselves as the heirs of the Ottoman Empire and had the support of their coreligionists in the larger Arab world in resisting an independent Lebanon dominated by Christians, the Shi'is lacked a patron in the Arab world and were unsure about their political allegiance. The desire of Shi'i notable leaders and ulama to protect their socioeconomic interests and gain official recognition as a distinct sect thus led them to recognize independent Lebanon ahead of their Sunni counterparts.[4]

The Road to Independence

The backing that Shi'i leaders gave to the establishment of independent Lebanon became clear between 1918 and 1936. In the two years preceding the creation of the French mandate, Feisal attempted to shore up support among Shi'is to his accession as king of a Syria united with Lebanon. His task was easier in the Bekaa, which had historically looked to Damascus. Shi'i leaders from this region held positions in Feisal's government, and they expressed a clearer opinion in favor of unity than did their counterparts in the Jabal 'Amil, who sought rather an arrangement that would allow them to run their own affairs. Politics in the Jabal 'Amil were dominated by the rivalry between Kamil al-As'ad, the most powerful Shi'i leader in the region, and Riyad al-Sulh of Sidon, an ardent Sunni supporter of unity between Syria and Lebanon who attempted to establish the city as the administrative center of the Jabal 'Amil. Feisal, who recognized the importance of enlisting As'ad's support for his rule, promised him in 1919 the position of governor of the Jabal 'Amil after independence. But As'ad, who had also been courted by the French, was not reassured by this promise and remained ambivalent about the idea of unity. Fearful that he would lose power unless he secured a special status for the Jabal 'Amil under his leadership, As'ad exerted pressures on Shi'i ulama to advocate administrative autonomy for the Jabal 'Amil within Syria. Thus when the clerics 'Abd al-Hussein Sharaf al-Din and Hussein Mughniyya met in the summer of 1919 with the King-Crane Commission (appointed by the mandate commission of the Varsaille peace conference to ascertain national sentiments among the people of Syria and Lebanon), they asked for a decentralized government in Syria and Lebanon. Shi'i leaders made a similar demand in a conference held in the Hujayr Valley in April 1920, calling for autonomy for the Jabal 'Amil within Syria under King Feisal. Yet the French move to terminate Feisal's government during May–July 1920, and the breaking of the power of Shi'i bands in the Jabal 'Amil, persuaded Shi'i leaders to accept Lebanon as an independent state under a French mandate. By the time the French high commissioner presented the Légion d'Honneur to As'ad in April 1921, Shi'is in the Jabal 'Amil were already competing for positions in the French administration, seeking equality with Christians in taxation and educational opportunities.[5]

The contrasting attitude of Shi'i and Sunni notable leaders toward the Lebanese state became apparent during the Druze revolt of 1925–27, when the French succeeded in enlisting Shi'i support for the Lebanese constitution. In the summer of 1925 a revolt broke out in the Jabal Druze, southeast of Damascus. The revolt, which acquired a nationalist dimension after a group of Syrian nationalists joined the rebels, spread from Syria into Lebanon at a time when the French were attempting to have a constitution for Lebanon passed in the Lebanese Representative Council. In the Jabal 'Amil, the revolt reignited the struggle for power between

Riyad al-Sulh and the As'ad family. While Sulh attempted to mobilize Shi'is in support of unity between Syria and Lebanon and against the constitution, Mahmud al-As'ad (who replaced his brother Kamil as head of the family after the latter's death in 1924), together with other Shi'i leaders, declared his support for the French mandate in Lebanon and persuaded the Shi'is of the Jabal 'Amil not to join the revolt. In the Bekaa, however, the majority of Shi'is (led by the Haydar family) supported the Druze revolt and demanded annexation to Syria. The French therefore acted to reduce the power of the Haydars; they began relying on the Hamadeh family of Hirmil (previously known as the Himada), which competed with the Haydars for influence in the Bekaa, convincing their leaders to stop Shi'i support of the rebels. Moreover, in a move intended to woo Shi'is, and encourage their representatives in the Lebanese Council to support the constitution, the French in January 1926 recognized the Shi'is as an independent sect separate from the Sunnis in matters relating to personal status. The French decision to authorize the opening of Shi'i legal courts was a break with the Ottoman past, when Shi'is had to settle issues relating to personal status either before Sunni judges or before Shi'i judges who often had to follow the Sunni Hanafi law. This concession to the Shi'i community produced the desired results. The constitution was approved on 23 May 1926, paving the way for the declaration of the Lebanese Republic. Most Shi'i leaders supported the constitution, both in the Representative Council and in questionnaires sent by the drafting committee to dignitaries in various localities. By contrast, Sunni leaders refused to participate in drafting the constitution and nearly all Sunni dignitaries returned their questionnaires unanswered.[6]

Shi'i recognition of Lebanon as a state independent of Syria became even more pronounced in the decade between the approval of the constitution in 1926 and the signing of the French-Lebanese treaty of 1936. In 1928 Shi'i notables and religious figures in Baalbek gave a welcoming reception to President Charles Dabbas on his visit to the Bekaa region, proclaiming their allegiance to the Lebanese state and thus following the lead of their coreligionists in the Jabal 'Amil. Shi'is in both regions subsequently began competing for government funds, with those of the Jabal 'Amil on occasion complaining of the preference given to the Bekaa. The backing given by Shi'i leaders to the Lebanese state manifested itself again in the negotiations leading to the signing of the French-Lebanese treaty on 23 November 1936. In July, Sunni leaders in Sidon attempted to rally support in the Jabal 'Amil for unity between Syria and Lebanon. Although at a meeting attended by both Sunnis and Shi'is the organizers succeeded in passing a resolution in favor of unity, Shi'i notable leaders in a countermove staged demonstrations and circulated petitions in support of the Lebanese state. Sunni leaders again tried to organize opposition to the proposed treaty in a meeting in Beirut in late October, but they failed to attract many Shi'is. In response, Shi'i notables and religious leaders held a large rally in Nabatiyya in early November, backing the Lebanese state. Shi'is also sent delegates and petitions to the French high commissioner and the Lebanese president Emile Eddé, affirming their community's support of the treaty. As in 1926, when they broke ranks with their Sunni counterparts and participated in drafting the Lebanese constitution, in 1936 Shi'i leaders backed the French-Lebanese treaty, helping clear Lebanon's road to independence.[7]

The vital support extended by Shi'i leaders to independent Lebanon has been acknowledged by various writers, including the Maronite journalist Iskandar al-Riyashi, who noted that by the mid-1930s Shi'i deputies in parliament had formed a political block independent of the Sunnis and in favor of Emile Eddé. It was the Shi'i block, wrote Riyashi, "which played the most important role in firmly establishing Lebanon as a state after the French had left."[8] Nevertheless, the Shi'i community did not receive a share of resources from the state commensurate with its size, and Shi'i religious and cultural life continued to decline in the first half of the twentieth century.

On the Margin of Lebanese Politics

The demarcation of borders in the Middle East undermined the position of the Shi'i community in Lebanon. The French and the British agreement on the border between Lebanon and mandatory Palestine in the early 1920s reduced the size of the Jabal 'Amil. Among Shi'is, the Jabal 'Amil was historically known as the area extending from the Awali River in the north down to Acre, Tarshiha, and Safad in the south, and from the Mediterranean in the west to the Hula Lake and up to the Taym and the Bekaa Valley in the east. In 1924 an area of about 250,000 dunams, including several villages and the Hula Lake, was detached from the Jabal 'Amil and added to mandatory Palestine—an act that disrupted socioeconomic life, particularly around Marja'yun. Shi'i anger over the loss of land was reinforced by the fact that in modern Lebanon the Jabal 'Amil became known simply as "the South," which Shi'is took as an insult to their historical heritage.[9] Government neglect of their regions further alienated Shi'is from the state.

In twentieth-century Lebanon, Shi'is were the most economically disadvantaged group among the country's seventeen sects. Shi'is often complained that residents in the Jabal 'Amil and the Bekaa paid more taxes but received fewer government resources than people elsewhere in the country. The two regions lagged behind other parts of Lebanon in economic development as well as in education and income levels. There was not a single hospital in the Jabal 'Amil as late as 1943 and only health offices in Sidon, Tyre, and Nabatiyya. The Jabal 'Amil had very few paved roads. Most of its three hundred predominantly Shi'i villages had no electricity, and there was a chronic shortage of freshwater. In the absence of sufficient government funds, Shi'is in the Jabal 'Amil relied on contributions from Shi'i émigrés, particularly those in West Africa, who sponsored the building of schools and mosques as well as social services and cultural projects, including the publication of the famous journal *al-'Irfan*. Until the 1960s, the Shi'is in Lebanon were mainly peasants, the community lacking a sizable urban middle class. Shi'i politics were dominated by notable leaders. While the As'ad, the Zein, the 'Usayran, the 'Abdallah, the Bazzi, the Baydun, the Fadil, and the Khalil constituted the prominent families in the Jabal 'Amil, the Haydar, the Hamadeh, and the Husseini families played a leading role in the Bekaa. Members of these families were elected to parliament and dispensed favors; they acted as brokers between individuals and the state, arranging jobs, loans, and businesses for their clients. Nevertheless, none of the Shi'i notables could claim to represent the community as a whole.[10]

Shi'i religious institutions declined in the first half of the twentieth century—part of a pattern of contracting religious activities in most of the Middle East, as both governing elites and individual families gave preference to secular education and modern professions. It is estimated that between the late 1930s and early 1940s there were only forty-two Shi'i ulama in Lebanon for the roughly 155,000 Shi'is spread over 450 to 500 villages. Many of these ulama were not qualified to hold their positions as religious teachers and judges. Of the forty-two, only fifteen had received their training in Najaf, the center for advanced Shi'i religious training at the time. The decreasing number of Shi'i clerics reflected changes in attitudes toward religious occupations among families that traditionally generated ulama in Lebanon. Young members of famous families like the Amin, Sharaf al-Din, Sadr al-Din, Muruwwa, and Sharara did not complete their religious studies or opted to study medicine, engineering, law, and literature. Many young Shi'is, influenced by socialism and Arab nationalism, espoused secular politics, joining the Ba'th Party, the Syrian Social Nationalist Party, or the Progressive Socialist Party. Others, like Hashim al-Amin, Muhammad Sharara, and Hussein Muruwwa, joined the Communist Party. Until the establishment of the Higher Islamic Shi'i Council in 1969, there was no institution that oversaw Shi'i national affairs. The ulama lacked esteem among the people and were overshadowed by notable leaders. 'Abd al-Hussein Sharaf al-Din (d. 1958) and Muhammad Jawad Mughniyya (d. 1979) were the exceptions, but they lacked the seniority of the prominent mujtahids of Najaf and Qum. It was the absence of a suitable figure in the country that led Sharaf al-Din shortly before his death to invite the Iranian-born Musa Sadr to lead the Shi'i community in Lebanon.[11]

In the course of the twentieth century, several Shi'i writers accused the notable leaders of neglecting their duty to support religious institutions and fight for the socioeconomic and political rights of the community. The criticism, which was muted during the mandatory period, became more pronounced after independence as a new generation of Shi'is sought an alternative to the politics of notables and joined the political parties of the Left. It intensified during and after the civil war of 1975–90 when Shi'is began rewriting their national history. One of the early critics was Muhammad Jawad Mughniyya, who complained that the notables had become distant from Islam, channeling very little money into the upkeep of religion. The notables' pursuit of personal wealth and power, lamented Mughniyya, weakened the Shi'i community and corrupted its values. Mughniyya accused the notables of complacency with regard to the Maronite elite, pointing out that unlike the Druze deputies in parliament, who were united in fighting for the rights of their community, the Shi'i deputies put their personal interests ahead of those of their community.[12] In fact, it is evident from the proceedings of parliamentary sessions between 1923 and 1989 that Shi'i deputies repeatedly complained about discrimination against the Shi'i community, demanding socioeconomic justice, better education, and more appointments of Shi'is to state positions.[13] Most Shi'i writers interpreted these complaints as the notables' way of placating their voters and avoiding a real struggle for the rights of the community. Yet the cleric Hani Fahs has argued persuasively that the first generation of Shi'i leaders achieved as much as they could given their limited political power.[14]

Indeed, there was little the Shi'i notable leaders could do to improve the position of their community, mainly because of the decision of Sunni leaders in the mid-1930s to enter the political game. As Lebanon moved toward independence, the Maronites increasingly needed the goodwill of Sunni leaders because of their links with the wider Arab world. And once they shared power with Sunni leaders, the Maronites lost the incentive to form alliances with Shi'i notable leaders and invest resources in the Shi'i areas. The Sunni entry into Lebanese politics thus diminished the political clout of Shi'i leaders and set the Shi'i community back; between the mid-1940s and the late 1960s it was pushed to the side and viewed as part of the larger Muslim community represented by the Sunni mufti of the republic.

Maronite and Sunni leaders concluded a deal in 1943 with the termination of the French mandate. While the former agreed to pay homage to Arabism, the latter were persuaded to view Lebanon as a link between the Arab world and the West. This understanding, known as the National Pact, represented an unwritten agreement between the Maronite president Bishara al-Khuri and his Sunni prime minister Riyad al-Sulh. The brain behind the pact was Michel Chiha, a Chaldean Christian banker, who envisaged Lebanon as the natural bridge between Islamic and Western civilizations and as the financial center of the Arab world. Under this pact, Lebanon was declared an independent and sovereign state within the Arab world. Its guiding principles built on article 95 of the 1926 constitution, which stipulated that for a transition period all sects should be represented proportionally in government and administrative positions. In 1943 it was agreed that the Maronites would keep the presidency of the republic, while the office of prime minister would become the preserve of the Sunnis. After 1947 the speakership of the parliament came to be reserved for the Shi'is. Other government and public positions were distributed proportionally among the various Lebanese communities. The representation of Christians and Muslims in parliament was fixed at a ratio of six to five. The architects of the National Pact left no record of the manner in which they negotiated their deal. What amounted to a gentlemen's agreement became the formula under which power was shared in modern Lebanon.[15]

The National Pact both acknowledged and fostered a Lebanese political system based on confessionalism (*ta'ifiyya*). We encountered the term *ta'ifiyya* in the previous chapter in dealing with Iraq. Yet this term has assumed different meanings in Lebanon and Iraq. When used by Iraqis, at least until 2003, the term had strong derogatory connotations, with the government often labeling its opponents as *ta'ifis*, in other words, people who promoted sectarian divisions in the country. In Lebanon, by contrast, the Maronite elite and the leaders of other communities recognized confessionalism as a fact of life, arguing that political representation along communal lines served the interests of all Lebanese and fostered stability in the country. The difference in attitude toward *ta'ifiyya* in the two countries has accounted for the rise in Lebanon of parties overtly organized along sectarian lines, like the Kata'ib of the Maronites, the Sunni Najjada Party, the predominantly Druze Progressive Socialist Party, the Shi'i Nahda and Talai' Parties of Ahmad al-As'ad and Rashid Baydun, respectively, as well as Amal and Hizballah—an idea inconceivable in Iraq before the U.S. invasion.[16]

Until the Iran-Iraq War of 1980–88, Iraqis by and large did not publicly acknowledge the existence of a sectarian problem in their country. The Lebanese, by contrast, have debated the advantages and drawbacks of confessionalism ever since the establishment of Mount Lebanon as an autonomous district in 1861. Some Lebanese writers have regarded confessionalism as a disease, and as the basic problem of Lebanon, arguing that the National Pact of 1943 and the preservation of the laws of personal status governing each sect exacerbated religious, political, and class tensions in the country. Others, however, have viewed the pact favorably, as the unwritten constitution of Lebanon, contending that confessionalism was the essence of Lebanese society and therefore could not be abolished by law.[17] The Maronite writer Kamal Yusuf al-Hajj was a most enthusiastic advocate of "positive confessionalism." Hajj argued that confessionalism was both a condition stemming from the lack of a clear concept of Lebanese nationalism and a mechanism acting to reduce sectarian tension within society. Confessionalism, according to Hajj, has historical roots in Lebanon and a legal basis in the constitution and the National Pact. He explained that the importance of the pact lay in its turning Lebanon into a national state that demands recognition and loyalty from all segments of society. The balance of confessional representation stipulated in the pact amounted to a set of national values that were as important as religion in holding people together, and without which the Lebanese state would collapse. Therefore, concluded Hajj, anyone who attempted to abolish the system of confessional representation was conspiring against the notion of Lebanon as a final state.[18]

During the 1950s and 1960s, confessionalism gained ground in Lebanese public life. At the same time, the Maronites succeeded in creating some sense of a common Lebanese history while bolstering their political hegemony in the country. Maronite and other Christian writers argued that for many centuries Lebanon had preserved the true heritage of Syria. Building on the work of Henri Lammens (a Jesuit priest and professor of Oriental studies at the Saint-Joseph University who died in 1937), they depicted Mount Lebanon as the historical place of refuge for all the persecuted communities of Syria, who valued their freedom and escaped there after the Arab Islamic conquest in the seventh century. Yet the Maronites, who generally viewed themselves as a non-Arab Christian minority living in a tiny corner of the vast Arab and Islamic sphere, also used the refuge idea to justify their political dominance in Lebanon. Arguing that the Muslims in Lebanon could not be trusted, the Maronites claimed the key security and military positions, and instituted Sunday as the official day of rest in Lebanon. All this was necessary to allay the Maronite fear of what might happen to Lebanon if the Muslims took over.[19] The logic used by the Maronites to justify their political dominance in Lebanon bears resemblance to the arguments used by the Sunni minorities in Iraq (until 2003) and in Bahrain to support their monopoly on power. While the Christian Maronites cited the close relations between Lebanese Muslims and their coreligionists in the Arab world as proof that the Muslim majority was not truly loyal to Lebanon, the Sunni ruling elites in Iraq and Bahrain disputed the national credentials of Iraqi and Bahraini Shi'is by pointing to their links with Iran. Yet unlike the Sunni rulers of Iraq and Bahrain, who had the backing of other Sunni states in dealing with the Shi'is, the Maronites were a Christian minority within the Muslim Arab world and therefore had to concede some power to Sunnis in Lebanon.

The ideas upon which pre–civil war Lebanon was based left little room for the Shi'is. Neither the Sunni conviction that Lebanon was a fragment of the larger Arab world nor the Maronite concept of Lebanon's Christian identity appealed to the Shi'is. Before the revival of Shi'ism in the second half of the twentieth century, Sunnis often took the Shi'is for granted. Cultural, class, and doctrinal gaps separated the Sunni merchants of the coastal cities from the rural Shi'i population of the Jabal 'Amil and the Bekaa, as well as from the Shi'i migrants, who began arriving in Beirut in great numbers starting in the 1950s. While Sunnis agreed to share power with the Maronites, they did not accept the Shi'is as a community in their own right and objected to the establishment of an independent Shi'i religious institution separate from the Supreme Islamic Legislative Council led by the Sunni mufti. Shi'i restiveness in the Jabal 'Amil between 1918 and 1936 was given an Arab nationalist interpretation by the Sunnis, but this was accepted by only some Shi'is. Indeed, Arab nationalism primarily attracted Sunnis in modern Lebanon because the majority of Shi'is, like Christians, did not wish to be dominated by Sunnis in the name of Arabism.[20]

Shi'is and Maronites did not have easy relations either. As we saw in chapter 1, the Maronite migration from northern to southern Lebanon between the seventeenth and nineteenth centuries reduced the size of the Shi'i communities. The struggle over territory created tensions between Shi'is and Maronites that intensified when the latter gained autonomy in Mount Lebanon between 1861 and 1915. Although the Maronites constituted a majority in Mount Lebanon, they lost this status after the inclusion of the Shi'i areas and the predominantly Sunni coastal cities in modern Lebanon. Subsequently, the Maronite share of Lebanon's population has decreased while the number of Shi'is has grown steadily, mainly because of their higher birthrates. Whereas in 1932 the Maronites constituted the largest sect in Lebanon, they later lost this position to the Shi'is, who by the turn of the twenty-first century constituted 40 percent of the population. Demography had caught up with the Maronites and continues to work to the benefit of the Shi'is.[21]

Aware of the declining proportion of their community among the population, Maronite leaders explored various ways to reestablish Christians as a majority in Lebanon, beginning in the mandatory period. One solution proposed in August 1932 by Emile Eddé (who would serve as Lebanon's president between 1936 and 1941) was to detach the area of Tripoli and the Jabal 'Amil from the country, a move that would have left the Christians 80 percent of the population. Eddé sought to persuade the French authorities to turn the Jabal 'Amil, with its large Shi'i population, into an autonomous unit under French control along the model of Alexandretta, which the French had established in 1920 as an autonomous 'Alawi-populated district within the province of Aleppo in Syria.[22] Having failed to persuade the French to accept the idea, Eddé and other Maronite leaders turned to Jewish leaders for help. In August 1941 Eliahu Sasson, director of the Arab section in the Jewish Agency, met in Beirut with Bishara al-Khuri, Lebanon's first president after independence. Khuri had his own idea of how to increase the share of Christians in the population of Lebanon. He drew Sasson's attention to the Jabal 'Amil, which stood as a dangerous Shi'i barrier between the Christians in Lebanon and the Jews in mandatory Palestine. Khuri proposed to empty the area of its Shi'is and settle it with members of the Maronite diaspora who had emigrated to the United States, suggesting that the Jews advance a loan to the Maronite patriarch for that purpose. This move, said Khuri, would bring Maronites and Jews together as close neighbors who could stand against the Arab Islamic tide in the region. Sasson did not mention where Khuri sought to resettle the Shi'is, but he cited a conversation with a Muslim businessman who assured Sasson that it would be possible in the course of ten years to purchase all the lands of the Jabal 'Amil and resettle its Shi'is in Iraq.[23]

The schemes of Maronite leaders for turning Lebanon into a state with a Christian majority did not materialize, and so they turned again to the Shi'is to counterbalance the Sunnis. Noting the increase in the influence of Nasserism among Muslims in Lebanon during the 1960s, Maronite leaders and intellectuals argued that the Shi'is should be embraced more closely by the country's political system. The Maronites took a special interest in Musa Sadr, who at the time was emerging as the leader of the Shi'i community in Lebanon. As will be seen below, however, the Maronites did not foresee either the Shi'i bid for power or the setback to their own political hegemony in the wake of the Lebanese civil war.[24]

The Revolt of the Oppressed

Conditions became ripe for Shi'i mass politics in Lebanon only in the second half of the twentieth century. At the core of this development was the great increase in the number of Shi'is in Beirut, a result of a migration from the Jabal 'Amil and the Bekaa beginning in the 1950s. The Shi'is in Beirut, whose number in 1920 was about 1,500, and who did not have their own mosque until the 1940s, had established themselves by 1975 as the single largest community in the capital. Shi'is were driven from their native regions because of changes in land ownership and the decline of agriculture, and because of security problems resulting from the war between Israelis and Palestinians in southern Lebanon in the 1970s and early 1980s. Unlike Christians and Sunni Muslims who lived mainly in the affluent eastern and western sections of Beirut, the Shi'i immigrants, estimated at 800,000 in the mid-1990s, were crammed into an area of twenty-eight square kilometers in the southern suburbs known as "the belt of misery." The depressed living conditions of these Shi'is have resembled those of their coreligionists in Sadr City in Iraq today. In Lebanon, Shi'is constituted some 80 to 90 percent of the workforce in Beirut's factories, and 50 to 60 percent of the service workers in the predominantly Christian eastern section. The Shi'i migration to Beirut not only established the capital as the largest place of concentration of Shi'is in Lebanon, but also enabled Shi'is from the Jabal 'Amil and the Bekaa to interact on a large scale, at first in political parties of the secular Left that championed socioeconomic reform. The influx of Shi'is from rural areas to the capital coincided with the rise of a Shi'i intelligentsia and the return to Lebanon of Shi'i émigrés with money earned overseas. These two groups established themselves in the 1960s and 1970s as a new Shi'i middle class. Their members felt entitled to play a role in Lebanese politics, but they were shunted aside by a Lebanese establishment dominated by Maronites and Sunnis, as well as by Shi'i notable leaders who feared the new challenge to their authority. It was Musa Sadr who tapped the various grievances of the Shi'i urban poor and the middle class and who succeeded in mobilizing Lebanese Shi'is as a national group.[25]

The rise of Musa Sadr as the charismatic leader of Lebanese Shi'is was part of a larger trend within Shi'ism in the Middle East beginning in the 1960s toward activism among the clergy. While in Iran Shi'i clerics led by Ruhollah Khomeini succeeded in establishing an Islamic government in 1978–79, in the Arab world the gains had been much more modest largely because of the lack of the sociopolitical preconditions for a Shi'i theocracy. Yet Lebanon was different from other Arab countries with Shi'i communities for two important reasons. First, Lebanon's system of confessional politics and the relative freedom of publication in the country enabled Sadr to openly push for a Shi'i sociopolitical agenda. Second, unlike Iraq, Saudi Arabia, and Bahrain, where the ruling Sunni elites did not hesitate to use force to check the tide of Shi'i upheaval, the Lebanese state led by its Christian Maronite elite was far weaker, and its eventual collapse with the outbreak of civil war in 1975 facilitated the upsurge of the Shi'is during the war and in its wake.

Sadr set out in the 1960s and 1970s to create a new and self-confident Lebanese Shi'i individual and to redefine relations between Shi'is and the state. The Shi'is of Lebanon, he noted, had a handicap in dealing with the state that stemmed from the weakness of the community. Its inability to display its full energies and shield its people, Sadr argued, undermined its morale as well as people's trust in their religious and political leaders. Consequently, Shi'is were unable to act in unison and to assume full responsibilities in the state. Sadr attempted to reconcile the sectarian and national identity of Lebanese Shi'is. He urged Shi'is to love Lebanon, declaring that it was their ultimate state. While advocating that Shi'is should place their national loyalty above their sectarian interests, he demanded that the state should care for its Shi'i citizens and treat them with respect. In his speeches Sadr talked about the historical bonds connecting Shi'is with the state. He reminded his audience that for more than a thousand years the Shi'i seminaries had preserved the Lebanese heritage, and that Shi'is had always taken a lead in defending Lebanon against foreign invaders, starting with the Crusaders. The Shi'is, he said, did not demand government money and political favors immediately after Lebanon gained independence; instead, they accepted discrimination in the allocation of funds and in political appointments, viewing it as a necessary sacrifice during the state's formative period and anticipating better times once the state stood firmly on its feet. Yet, Sadr lamented, Shi'i hopes of gaining a fair share of power and spoils were not fulfilled. During the 1950s and 1960s, the government continued to discriminate against Shi'is and tarnished their honor, forcing them to flaunt their sectarian identity and fall back on their community, convinced that it could do more for them than the state could.[26]

In establishing the Higher Islamic Shi'i Council in 1969, Sadr sought to turn this institution into the focal point of a Shi'i community independent of its Sunni counterpart. Unlike the Sunnis, who had formed the Supreme Islamic Legislative Council in 1955, and the Druze, who since 1962 had their own council, the Shi'is lacked a corporate body that could oversee their interests. Until 1969 the Sunni Council ran Shi'i religious affairs and endowment property, and appointed Shi'i religious functionaries. Although in the mid-1950s Shi'is attempted to establish forums for voicing their social concerns, these either lacked strong leadership or were undermined by the state. The idea of a Higher Shi'i Council generated opposition both from Shi'i clerics, who feared that their incorporation into the council would render them financially dependent on the state, and from members of the Sunni establishment, who claimed that a Shi'i council would divide the Islamic front in Lebanon. In making his case, Sadr argued that the Shi'i community needed an institution to oversee its religious affairs and endowment property, and to unite the community and save it from its crisis. Sadr enjoyed the support of Maronite leaders, as well as the backing of middle-class Shi'i professionals and a few notable leaders, including Sabri Hamadeh, the speaker of parliament. Money came mainly from those Shi'i émigrés who had returned home and sought ways to influence Lebanese politics. In turning the council into an independent body, Sadr enabled the Shi'i community to break free from Sunni control. It was a move intended to increase the clout of the community in a state in which resources were distributed according to sectarian affiliation and the relative political weight of the various sects. In May 1969, Sadr was elected the first chairman of the council, establishing himself as the head of the Shi'a of Lebanon.[27]

Sadr transformed the Shi'is of Lebanon from a sect characterized by an attitude of political defeatism into a community that challenged the entire system of government. A religious reformer, Sadr gave the Shi'is a new identity. He reinterpreted Shi'i history and used religious occasions as vehicles for building political consciousness among Lebanese Shi'is. Thus, for example, he presented imam Hussein's bid for the caliphate at the battle of Karbala in 680, in confrontation with the army of the Umayyad caliph Yazid, as a revolt against injustice. Sadr bridged the gap between the seventh and the twentieth centuries, enabling Shi'is to label their enemy in daily life a Yazid. Moreover, Sadr recognized the enormous task of community building, working to bring people in the Jabal 'Amil and the Bekaa closer together. Seeking to infuse the role of clerics within the Shi'i community with new meaning, he worked to tear down the age-old perception of clerical parochialism, arguing that the ulama had a duty to lead the people. At the same time, he took advantage of the failure of Arab socialism to improve the economic conditions of Shi'is and acted to break the monopoly of the secular Left as the champion of social justice in Lebanon. His language of Shi'i disinheritance proved more appealing to the poor and the returning émigrés than the language of class conflict used by the Left. By 1975 the influence of the secular Left among Shi'is had diminished significantly, as is evident from the fact that several of the Higher Shi'i Council executive committee members had formerly belonged to or identified with parties of the Left. As Lebanon neared civil war, Sadr's strategies of mobilization grew even bolder, building on agitation and assertion. After the breakdown in negotiations with the government of Suleiman Frangié for more senior Shi'i appointments in the administration, the foreign service, and the army, and for more government investments in Shi'i areas and better security arrangements in the south, Sadr began organizing mass rallies. In a speech in the Bekaa in February 1975 he proclaimed a new beginning for the Shi'i community, urging its members to shed the term *matawila* (followers of 'Ali ibn Abi Talib), by which the Shi'is in Lebanon had been known since the seventeenth century, and adopt the term *rafidun*, in the sense of men of refusal and vengeance who revolt against oppression and tyranny. In another rally in March, he launched the "movement of the oppressed," vowing to struggle until the government addressed Shi'i grievances. Several months later, Sadr revealed the existence of a Shi'i militia called Amal (literally, hope), an adjunct to the movement of the oppressed. With these moves, the Shi'is of Lebanon were prepared to participate in their country's militia politics.[28]

The fragile partnership that the National Pact had created between Christians and Muslims collapsed with the outbreak of civil war in 1975. Among the Sunnis, a new generation of Arab nationalists had emerged in the 1950s, strongly influenced by Nasserism and Ba'thism. That generation did not accept the pact as reasonable, as many of the older generation had. Meanwhile, within the Maronite community a new force emerged, the Phalanges (also known as the Kata'ib Party), originally founded as a paramilitary organization in 1936 under the leadership of Pierre Jumayyil. Renamed the Social Democratic Party in 1949, it did not enjoy wide following in the 1950s and 1960s and was dismissed by most Christians as an authoritarian organization. The rise of the Phalanges as the dominant voice of the Maronite community in the 1970s, however, signaled the passing of power from leaders who had made their peace with Arabism to those who sought a full break with the Arab world. Party officials and ideologues portrayed modern Lebanon as the incarnation of ancient Phoenicia. They positioned Phoenicianism as a counter to Arab nationalism, which they regarded as a force undermining the freedom of Christians and threatening to absorb Lebanon into the Arab world. The Maronites under Pierre and his son Bashir Jumayyil opted for the unthinkable: an alliance with Israel and a full commitment to partition Lebanon.[29]

The events surrounding the civil war of 1975–90 radicalized Lebanese Shi'is. In the mid-1970s the Higher Islamic Shi'i Council collapsed along with other institutions of the Lebanese state. In 1978 Musa Sadr disappeared during a trip to Libya. His disappearance left the Shi'is without their preeminent national figure—a man who combined political and religious leadership, who advocated power sharing between Lebanon's main sects, and who acted during the first years of the war as an important intermediary between Syria's president, Hafiz Assad, and the Maronite and Sunni establishment in Lebanon. The interference of both Syria and Israel in Lebanon brought large Shi'i areas under occupation and, in turn, increased Shi'i militancy. In 1976 Syrian forces invaded the Bekaa. Two years later, Israel launched its first major operation against Palestinian strongholds in southern Lebanon; this was followed by a larger excursion in 1982, which brought Israeli forces to the outskirts of Beirut. Both operations were intended to destroy what amounted to a PLO mini-state in Lebanon, and the second also sought to restore Maronite hegemony in the country. The departure of the PLO from Lebanon in the wake of the 1982 Israeli invasion helped Shi'is overcome their inferiority complex vis-à-vis Palestinian fighters and push their cause. Yet at the same time, the Shi'is in the Jabal 'Amil had become the main victims of the fighting between Israel and the Palestinians, neither of whom offered an apology to the Shi'is for the disruption of their lives.[30] Moreover, eighteen years of Israeli occupation of southern Lebanon gave rise to a powerful myth among Lebanese Shi'is, who depicted themselves as the vanguard of a resistance movement fighting to rescue Lebanon from a foreign invader. The myth shaped both the political development of Lebanese Shi'is and the struggle for leadership that erupted within the community following Sadr's disappearance.

In the early 1980s Amal emerged as the main Shi'i movement. But it soon faced a bold challenge from Hizballah, the Party of God. Amal and Hizballah differed in their social composition and organizational form, and offered different visions of society and state in Lebanon. Amal, as we noted earlier, was created by Musa Sadr as the militia of the Shi'i community. Some of its members were young professionals. Others were newly urbanized and less-educated youth. Still others were former activists in Palestinian and leftist groups who became disillusioned with both the Palestinians and the Left and wanted to belong to a movement of their own sect. Under Nabih Berri, who led the movement from April 1980, Amal evolved from a militia into a political party articulating Shi'i middle-class politics in Lebanon. A lawyer and graduate of the Lebanese University who spent several of his adult years in West Africa, Berri became a model for members of the Shi'i middle class who sought a political place in the state. Nevertheless, Amal's largely secular program and the willingness of its leadership to cooperate with Christians and join the national salvation committee, formed by President Ilyas Sarkis in 1982, were rejected by a new generation of Shi'i Islamists. These Islamists were influenced by the Islamic Revolution in Iran and questioned Amal's authenticity as a Shi'i movement. The main challenge to Amal came from Hizballah, which emerged in 1982 as a conglomeration of several Islamic groups. Some of Hizballah's affiliates were Shi'is who returned to Lebanon after studying in Najaf, including the Iraqi-born cleric Muhammad Hussein Fadlallah, who for a short period acted as a mentor to the movement, although he denied any formal ties to it. Others were former members of the Lebanese branch of the Iraqi Da'wa Party and the association of Muslim students in Lebanon. Still others had splintered from Amal, most notably Hussein al-Musawi, who established Islamic Amal after his expulsion from Amal in 1982, and Hasan Nasrallah, who would become Hizballah's secretary-general in 1992. Unlike Amal, which did not have a foreign patron and relied mainly on contributions from Shi'i individuals, Hizballah was founded with Iran's backing; its fighters were better paid than those of Amal, and they received training from a contingent of Iranian revolutionary guards based in the Bekaa under Syrian supervision.[31]

Hizballah is only one aspect of the revival of Shi'ism in Lebanon—a complex process that began in the second half of the twentieth century and still continues vigorously today. The rise of Hizballah coincided with the increase in the number of Shi'i clerics in Lebanon during the 1970s and 1980s, which stood in contrast to the decrease in their numbers in the first half of the twentieth century. The new generation of Lebanese clerics, who numbered about 420 early in the 1980s, was drawn from about 220 families, many of whom did not historically produce ulama in Lebanon. While some of these clerics originated in the Bekaa, an area not previously known for a tradition of religious scholarship, others were born in the Shi'i slums of Beirut. These ulama became part of a new Shi'i religious elite whose members controlled resources and thereby gained power and respect. Some received part of their training at the Islamic Law Institute established by Muhammad Hussein Fadlallah after his move from Najaf to Beirut in 1966. Fadlallah did not join the Higher Islamic Shi'i Council formed by Musa Sadr, seeking rather to establish himself as a senior cleric independent of the council, which he perceived as a state institution. Fadlallah's institute emphasized the role of clerics as community leaders who should be in tune with the needs of their society—a goal that Hizballah leaders set out to accomplish. Hizballah's top leadership consisted of a group of ulama guided by the principle of mutual consultation (*shura*). In the early and mid-1980s the movement advocated the establishment of an Islamic government in the country. Its ideology was strongly influenced by Iran's attempt to shape Lebanese Shi'ism, as evident in Hizballah's adoption of the flag of the Iranian Islamic Republic. Over time, Hizballah has emerged as a powerful socioreligious movement, controlling a large budget, an independent court system, a network of mosques and welfare institutions, and sophisticated media that include magazines and a television channel. The organization, in the words of its head of social services, has grown into "something larger than a party, yet smaller than a state."[32]

Hizballah's drive to create a society of members guided by strict Islamic values clashed with Amal's attempt to establish itself as the sole sociopolitical movement of Lebanese Shi'is. Their rivalry divided the Shi'i community between supporters and opponents of the two movements, creating splits even among members of the same family. During 1982–83 Hizballah spread from the Bekaa into the southern suburbs of Beirut and later also to southern Lebanon, the stronghold of Amal until the mid-1980s. Hizballah took advantage of the departure of Palestinian fighters from southern Lebanon and the Israeli withdrawal to a narrow strip in the south, capitalizing on Amal's restrained policy in confronting the Israeli presence in Lebanon. Hizballah's success in mobilizing Shi'is undermined Amal's stature and led to fighting between the two movements in southern Lebanon and in Beirut during 1987–89. The fighting took place as Lebanon was nearing the end of its civil war—a period when Amal and Hizballah paid growing attention to national politics and vied for control of the Shi'i Council, which began resuming its activities. Attempting to portray itself as the movement of mainstream Shi'ism in Lebanon, Amal depicted Hizballah's followers as dissidents (khawarij), thereby invoking the memory of this small group of uncompromising purists who had been defeated by the caliph 'Ali ibn Abi Talib. In likening Hizballah to the khawarij, Amal implied that Hizballah had broken with the consensus of the Shi'i community and with the decision to reach political accommodation with other sects in Lebanon.[33] Hizballah countered by blaming Amal for downplaying the heroic role of the Shi'i resistance to the presence of Israel and Western powers in Lebanon. Hizballah contended that the Shi'i Council had failed to achieve the purpose for which it had been established, and had neglected its duty to fight for the rights of the oppressed—a duty now assumed by Hizballah. Its objection to the council as a state institution also reflected Hizballah's fear that the council would reinforce separation between religion and politics and undermine the position of Shi'i clerics in Lebanon.[34] The fighting between Amal and Hizballah, which pitted Shi'i against Shi'i and left a thousand dead, was described by Lebanese Shi'is as communal strife. It ended in 1990 after Syria and Iran negotiated a truce between the two movements and as the various sects of Lebanon sought national reconciliation.[35]

The Lebanese fought a lengthy and costly civil war, which lasted fifteen years and claimed some 100,000 lives, only to return to a confessional system and witness the emergence of Syria as the power broker in Lebanon, at least until April 2005. In August 1990 the Lebanese parliament endorsed the Ta'if accord as the basis for rebuilding Lebanon. Unlike the National Pact of 1943, which recognized Lebanon as a link between the Arab world and the West, the Ta'if accord emphasized Lebanon's Arab identity. It envisaged the abolition of confessionalism in stages, but it set no timetable for achieving that goal. The Lebanese preserved article 95 of the 1926 constitution, which called for a transition period when all sects would be represented proportionally in government. More important, however, the accord changed the balance of power in

Lebanon. In contrast to the arrangement of 1943 whereby Christians and Muslims were represented in parliament at a ratio of six to five, after 1990 parliamentary seats were split evenly. The re-arrangement of the constituencies has worked to the disadvantage of the Maronite deputies, many of whom became dependent on Muslim votes. Under the new accord the Maronites lost their former privileged political status. While the powers of the Maronite presidency were reduced, those of the Sunni prime minister and the Shi'i speaker of parliament were increased.

The Ta'if accord thus created a triumvirate regime in which the president, the prime minister, and the speaker of parliament each have a veto power over the other two. This newly calibrated system has turned the business of government into an endless game of rivalries and negotiations in which the likely winner in any impasse is the person commanding the most powerful skills and enjoying the best access to Syria—the final arbiter of Lebanese politics. The accord sanctioned the presence of Syrian forces in Lebanon and placed restrictions on the country's sovereignty. Syria's dominant position in Lebanon received confirmation in a treaty of brotherhood and a defense pact signed between the two countries in 1991, and following Israel's withdrawal from southern Lebanon in May 2000. Its hegemony in the country manifested itself in September 2004, when Syria forced the Lebanese parliament to pass an amendment to the constitution, extending the six-year term of President Émile Lahoud for three more years, to the displeasure of large segments of Lebanese society. Syria retained the upper hand in Lebanon at least until April 2005, when under pressure from the U.S. and French governments it withdrew its troops from the country and increased its reliance on proxies to retain its leverage on Lebanese politics.[36]

The history of the Lebanese Shi'is in the period following the Ta'if accord demonstrates the fierce competition inside the community for loyalties and resources. In the wake of the civil war, the Higher Islamic Shi'i Council reemerged as the main institution overseeing Shi'i religious and cultural affairs in Lebanon, and in

March 1994 Muhammad Mahdi Shams al-Din was elected its head. Unlike Musa Sadr, who had embodied religious and political leadership, Shams al-Din was a cleric who recognized Amal under Nabih Berri as the principal political movement of Lebanese Shi'is. Despite some competition between Shams al-Din and Berri in the early 1990s, when the relationship between the council and Amal was still not defined, the former's main rival was not Nabih Berri but Muhammad Hussein Fadlallah, an innovative cleric who commanded a considerable following both inside and outside of Lebanon. The rivalry between Shams al-Din and Fadlallah over religious leadership manifested itself in their competition for Shi'i funds as well as in the controversy over who should lead the Friday prayer in Beirut. Shams al-Din's effort to attract Shi'is inside Lebanon was apparent in the distinction he made (not unlike that articulated by Muhammad Baqir al-Sadr in Iraq before him) between two types of religious leadership: a universal leadership held by the most learned jurist (*al-marja'iyya al-fiqhiyya*) and a political leadership (*al-marja'iyya al-siyasiyya*) held by the local figure most qualified to lead his community—namely, Shams al-Din in his capacity as head of the Shi'i Council.[37] The rivalry between the two lasted until Shams al-Din's death in 2001, which enabled Fadlallah to establish himself firmly as the undisputed senior cleric in Lebanon. Meanwhile, 'Abd al-Amir Qabalan, a staunch ally of Nabih Berri, replaced Shams al-Din as acting head of the Shi'i Council, bringing this institution and Amal closer together.

The struggle for the leadership of the community was reinforced by the competition between Amal and Hizballah after the latter announced in 1992 its openness toward all political currents and religious sects and its decision to participate in the elections for parliament. Hizballah thereby made its peace with the Lebanese state. In return, the movement won recognition as the vanguard of Lebanese resistance to Israeli occupation in southern Lebanon and was allowed to keep its arms. The increasing "Lebanonization" of Hizballah coincided with the decision of Iranian leaders to cut back their aid to the organization and the growing leverage of Syria over the movement. Initially, Hizballah had been opposed to the Ta'if accord, but its leaders soon realized that unless they adapted themselves to the changing political scene, they risked isolation and perhaps even a fate similar to that of General 'Awn, the Maronite army officer whose opposition to the accord was crushed by the Syrian army in October 1990. A struggle erupted between Subhi Tufayli (a founder of Hizballah and one of its most influential members), who was not fully supportive of the movement's decision to participate in elections for parliament, and Hasan Nasrallah, Hizballah's secretary-general, who supported the move. The struggle exposed internal debates between radical and pragmatic strands within the movement, as well as persistent regional divisions among Lebanese Shi'is. Tufayli had a large following in the Bekaa, and in mid-1977 he attempted to use his "Movement of the Hungry" to foment civil resistance and thus challenge both Hizballah's pragmatic leadership and the Lebanese government. Acting with the agreement of Hizballah leaders, the Lebanese army put an end to the civil disobedience in the Bekaa. Tufayli was subsequently isolated, and in 1998 he was expelled from Hizballah. This development coincided with the increase in the importance of midlevel leadership members supportive of Syria (most notably, ex-members of the Iraqi Da'wa Party's Lebanese branch) at the expense of those who supported Iran. Under Nasrallah, Hizballah emphasized its Lebanese identity—a turnaround backed by Muhammad Hussein Fadlallah. In 1996 Hizballah engaged in a dialogue with Muhammad Mahdi Shams al-Din on the role of the Shi'i Council and the relations between Shi'is and the state in Lebanon. Hizballah even began raising the Lebanese flag and playing the national anthem on official occasions, thus signaling its willingness to reach accommodation with the state.[38]

Over the course of a decade, Hizballah evolved from a revolutionary movement into a political party that vied not only for the votes of Shi'is, but also for those of Sunnis and Christians in mixed areas. Hizballah's decision to participate in the 1992 parliamentary elections was intended to ensure its political survival. The party has come to view parliament as the state institution to which it can address socioeconomic and political demands on behalf of its constituency. In 1992 Hizballah won 8 of the 128 parliamentary seats, and together with 4 additional seats won by non-Shi'is affiliated with its electoral list, the party had the largest bloc in parliament. In the 1996 elections Hizballah won 10 seats, 3 of which were occupied by its affiliates. In the 2000 elections, it won 12 seats including 3 held by affiliates. In the 2005 elections that followed the withdrawal of Syrian troops from Lebanon, Hizballah increased its share to 14 parliamentary seats—a result that underscored its position as a formidable force in Lebanese politics. Between 1992 and 2005 Hizballah shrewdly exploited its resistance record and its welfare services, using them as vital components of its campaign strategy. The organization reached out to Christian and other non-Shi'i groups. It relied on democratic procedures to counter challenges from its rivals and used the election machine in ways that could not be matched by any other party or any coalition of rivals. Until 2005 Hizballah ruled out participation in the government, preferring to influence Lebanese politics as a mainstream opposition party. Yet in 2005 Hizballah joined Amal in negotiating with the prime minister over the composition of the government and the number of Shi'i ministers in it. The government formed in July 2005 had 5 Shi'i ministers, including the foreign minister. What is more, Muhammad Funaysh, a founding member of Hizballah, was appointed minister of energy—a development that signaled the organization's desire to become increasingly involved in national politics.[39]

The armed conflict of the late 1980s between Amal and Hizballah gave way to political battles and, occasionally, even to cooperation between the two movements. In their election campaigns Amal and Hizballah debated socioeconomic issues, as well as the meaning of Shi'i resistance, distinguishing between armed resistance to Israel and social resistance to the neglect of Shi'i areas by the Lebanese state. Since the 1990s, Hizballah has capitalized on the salience of these issues in Lebanese politics to expand its constituency, steadily chipping away at Amal's electoral base. Hizballah's success in attracting Amal supporters, including members of the middle class, reflects the sense of some Lebanese Shi'is that Amal has lost its original values. Amal evolved from a dynamic populist movement to a full-blown patronage system characterized by inefficiency and corruption. Those former supporters of Amal who have shifted their political loyalty to Hizballah because of its perceived integrity have exerted a moderating influence on the movement and forced it to respond to their particular needs. The success of Hizballah in becoming the largest political player on the Shi'i scene manifested itself in the municipal elections of 1998 and the gains of 2004, when its candidates won overwhelmingly in the Bekaa and in the Shi'i districts of southern Beirut. While in 1998 Hizballah's candidates won fewer than half the municipal council seats in southern Lebanon, in 2004 they won a majority of them, dealing a blow to Amal's candidates. Still, under pressure from Syria, which did not allow Hizballah to eclipse Amal, the two movements ran consensual lists during the parliamentary elections of 1992, 1996, and 2000. The two ran a consensual list in the 2005 elections as well; this policy reduced competition between Hizballah and Amal and assured the movements an almost equal number of deputies. Hizballah and Amal candidates won most of the votes in the Bekaa and in southern Lebanon—a sign of the declining influence of notable families and the transformation of power relations within the Shi'i community.[40]

Over the course of half a century a profound change has taken place in the fortunes of the Shi'is of Lebanon, who have emerged as the country's principal sect. The Shi'is have shed their political quietism, revolting against Maronite and Sunni ascendancy and demanding their share of the spoils. Their bid for power has been restrained, however, by Lebanon's system of proportional representation and by Syria's military presence in the country until April 2005, which ensured that Shi'is could not sweep to a national victory. Nevertheless, the Shi'is are likely to remain a major player in

Lebanese politics that no other sect would be able to ignore, especially in the wake of the Syrian withdrawal from Lebanon.

The Lebanese Shi'i experience has direct relevance to post-Ba'th Iraq, where members of the Shi'i majority will need to adjust their political expectations to the social realities of the country and redefine their relations with the U.S. occupying power. The connection between the Lebanese and the Iraqi cases will become clearer in the next chapter, which takes up the attempts of Iraqi Shi'is to articulate the meaning of just governance.

Chapter 5

Between Aspirations
and Reality

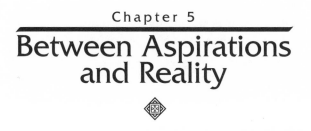

By the time a group of Sunni militants connected with al-Qaeda had carried out the 9/11 attacks in New York and Washington, the trend within Shi'ism away from violence and toward accommodation was well under way. In the Arab world, Shi'is have sought to mend fences not only with the West, but also with their governments and with other members of society at home. The cases of Saudi Arabia, Bahrain, Lebanon, and Iraq (after 2003) all underscore this point. What is more, they illuminate the distinct sociopolitical aspirations of each community, as well as the high stakes, risks and possibilities, that arise from the remaking of Iraq as a state strongly influenced, if not dominated, by Shi'is.

The Quest for Minority Rights in Saudi Arabia

The severe restrictions imposed on the Shi'i minority in Saudi Arabia explain the attraction of its members to movements promising sweeping change. In the 1950s and 1960s, Shi'is were influenced by communism and by Nasserite and Ba'thi ideas of Pan-Arabism. Shi'is constituted a majority in both the Saudi Labor Socialist Party and the Communist Party, and took part in the abortive coup attempt of 1969 in Dhahran, inspired by the Iraqi Ba'th. By contrast, in the late 1970s and 1980s Shi'is espoused Islamic ideology, most notably the small group Hizballah al-Hijaz backed by the Islamic Republic of Iran. With the U.S.-initiated talk about a new world order in the early 1990s, Saudi Shi'is flaunted the regional component of their identity. Some advocated a unification of the Persian Gulf monarchies, hoping thereby to gain greater freedom and even a degree of autonomy.[1]

Shi'is seized on the upheaval generated by the Gulf War of 1991 to wage an information campaign that both undermined the Saudi government's media monopoly and constituted a bold attempt to redraw the social contract between the Shi'is and the state. As evident from *al-Jazira al-'Arabiyya*, a monthly published in London for nearly three years between 1991 and 1993, Shi'is demanded recognition as a minority enjoying a social and national status equal to that of other groups in the kingdom. They argued that Saudi Arabia would not prosper so long as the ruling family did not espouse pluralism and continued to treat Shi'is as second- and third-class citizens. Shi'is felt humiliated by the experience of the Gulf War when the Al Sa'ud invited foreigners, including women and non-Muslims, to defend Saudi Arabia while ignoring the pleas of Shi'is to join the army. They called on the government to institute mandatory military service for Saudis and to transform the army from an instrument of social control into an institution for the defense of the homeland. Moreover, Shi'is demanded first-class citizenship (*jinsiyya wataniyya*), religious freedom, improved job opportunities, and uninterrupted access to higher education. They urged the Al Sa'ud to create a sense of partnership between the government and the people, and to build a national identity based on people's desire to preserve the territorial integrity of Saudi Arabia. Shi'is argued that national unity could be achieved in Saudi

Arabia because all citizens in the kingdom were Arab Muslims with shared ethnic and religious attributes.[2]

The Shi'i campaign of 1991–93 was part of a larger movement for reform among Saudis that intensified following 9/11 and the U.S. invasion of Iraq. In 1993 the Saudi government responded to the Shi'i challenge by announcing a reconciliation with their leaders. In a move reminiscent of its dealings with secular opposition groups in 1975, the government invited members of the Shi'i Islamic opposition in exile to return to Saudi Arabia, thus seeking to co-opt the moderates and isolate the radical group Hizballah al-Hijaz, which rejected the deal. While Saudi Shi'is pledged to stop their information campaign, the government promised to improve socioeconomic and educational opportunities for Shi'is, relax the rules regarding the building of Shi'i mosques, and allow Shi'is to observe their rituals in public.[3] The 1993 reconciliation was a gesture on the part of the government toward the Shi'i minority, but it did not alter the basic relationship between the Al Sa'ud and the Shi'is. Indeed, in the decade leading up to the 2003 war in Iraq, the ruling family, as well as the U.S. administration, continued to view the Shi'is as a security problem even though the real threat to the Saudi government came from al-Qaeda and its sympathizers in the kingdom. The government's attempt to use the Shi'i minority as a scapegoat and to deflect attention from the growing threat of Sunni radicalism manifested itself in the controversy over the 1996 truck bombing of the Khobar Towers in the eastern province that killed nineteen American servicemen. Thus, in June 2001, U.S. officials blamed Hizballah al-Hijaz and Iran for the attack, and a year later Saudi Arabia announced the sentencing of several members of the organization who were allegedly sponsored and aided by Iranian intelligence agencies. Yet in May 2003, after the United States declared war on terrorism, Saudi officials took a different view, saying that they had become increasingly convinced that the Khobar bombing could have been the work of al-Qaeda or one of the groups affiliated with it.[4]

The shocks of the 9/11 terrorist attacks and the U.S. invasion of Iraq made it difficult for the government to sideline the Shiʿi minority as it had done in the past. Saudi Shiʿis felt vindicated by 9/11, which underscored the danger of Sunni radicalism not only to the international community, but to the Saudi ruling family as well. As in the wake of the Gulf War, Shiʿis sided with other reform groups, including liberals, Islamists, and nationalists, in advocating minority rights and broader sociopolitical change in the kingdom. Already in 2002, the indefatigable Shiʿi writer Hamza al-Hasan appealed to the royal family to break the Wahhabi hold over politics and renegotiate its contract with the people. He warned that Wahhabism blocked the forging of a unifying Saudi national identity, and urged the Al Saʿud to recognize that they could not face the Wahhabi challenge alone. Hasan advocated a reform process in stages, including the establishment of an elected consultative assembly made up of men and women; reorganization of the state administration with a view to delegating more power to the provinces; reform of the court system; support for civil society organizations; a specification of the share that the royal family deserved from state income; and redefinition of Saudi relations with the West. Hasan's writings illustrate the attempt of Saudi Shiʿis to play a politically responsible role, in line with other advocates of reform in the kingdom. This was apparent in April 2003, when amid the fall of the Baʿth regime Saudi Shiʿi leaders issued a statement urging Shiʿis in Iraq to adopt a course of forgiveness and dialogue in dealing with Iraqi Sunnis. At the same time, Shiʿis petitioned Crown Prince ʿAbdallah, requesting an end to religious discrimination, the establishment of a Shiʿi religious authority to oversee community affairs, and the employment of Saudi Shiʿis in the military and in the state diplomatic corps. Their push for reforms continued throughout 2003 despite fierce verbal attacks on Shiʿism by Wahhabis.[5]

Under pressure at home and from the United States, ʿAbdallah announced a "national dialogue." Between January and May 2003 the crown prince invited advocates of reform for discussions, taking the unusual step of including Shi'is and women among the participants. Virtually all the reformers agreed that Saudi Arabia should retain its Islamic orientation, but they urged the crown prince to curb the powers of the Wahhabi clerics. They also suggested that the government take steps toward modernizing Saudi Arabia and turning it into a constitutional monarchy based on electoral institutions, separation of powers, and freedom of speech. In response, the government expanded the role of citizens in local affairs through elections—designed to fill half the seats in municipal councils—held between February and April 2005, and which included the eastern province where Shi'is form a majority of the population. Still, women were excluded from these elections, and the municipal councils were intended to serve largely as advisory boards to the mayors appointed by the government. At the same time, the Al Sa'ud have resisted any other suggestions for serious political reform, citing their fear that change might spin out of control. The suspicion with which the Al Sa'ud have viewed the reformers manifested itself in March 2004 when, on the eve of Secretary of State Colin Powell's visit to Saudi Arabia, the government arrested a dozen outspoken reformers, accusing them of dissension at a time when Saudi Arabia was facing a terrorist threat. This crackdown was a message to the reformers and the Americans to back off, and enabled the Saudi ruling family to buy some time and resist pressures for meaningful reforms. Nevertheless, in the long run the Saudi government will not be able to ignore the assertion of Shi'i power in Iraq and claim that it must capture those fomenting terrorism before opening up the political process in the kingdom. The signs of change are already evident in Saudi Arabia. Both Wahhabism and the adverse consequences of the Saudi government's ill-treatment of Shi'is and other groups are being challenged openly in a way that was unthinkable before 9/11 and the U.S. invasion of Iraq.[6]

As we will now see, the ferment among Shi'is seeking democratic change has been even stronger in neighboring Bahrain, with beginnings as far back as the 1930s.

The Constitutional Movement in Bahrain

In contrast to Saudi Shi'is, whose protest essentially reflected the frustrations of a small and persecuted minority, their Bahraini core-ligionists have sought power in the state in proportion to their demographic preponderance in the population. Since the late 1930s, Bahraini Shi'is have played a growing role in the movement advocating a constitution and an elected parliament, seeking to use these institutions to curb the Al Khalifa's absolute power. The movements of 1938 and 1954–56 demonstrated increased political contacts between Shi'is and Sunnis in Bahrain in support of a legislative body. Yet on both occasions, the emir (who in 1954–56 was backed by the British and the Saudi king) sidelined the movement by splitting its Shi'i and Sunni members and sidetracking the demand for a parliament.[7]

The breakthrough came in 1973, two years after Bahrain gained independence. Unlike the 1954–56 popular movement, the driving force behind the introduction of a constitution and a parliament in 1973 was the ruler himself, Sheikh 'Isa ibn Salman. The emir's act was a gesture toward Bahrainis on the occasion of independence, inspired by Kuwait's constitutional experience beginning in 1962. As such, it was intended to provide a legitimate basis for the Al Khalifa's autocratic and tribal system of government, not to create institutions that would check the executive powers of the emir. In December 1972, a constitutional assembly of 22 elected and 20 appointed members was established. The very high voter turnout, in some areas as high as 90 percent, meant that 14 of the 22 elected members were Shi'is, mostly young and educated. All the elected Shi'is were Arabs, 3 of them defeating competing candidates of Iranian origin. Of the 20 government-appointed members (including 12 ministers), only 7 were Shi'is, which created a sectarian balance among the 42 members of the assembly. This body approved a constitution for Bahrain in June 1973 and called for a parliament, thus completing its task. The constitution defined Bahrain as a democracy and promised freedom of speech. It stipulated the separation of the judicial, legislative, and executive authorities, and entrusted the right of legislation to the emir together with the parliament.[8]

The parliament was established in December 1973. It was made up of 30 elected male members and 14 appointed male government ministers, including the prime minister. Like the assembly members, the Shi'i and Sunni parliament members were with few exceptions elected by their own communal constituencies. Three political groupings emerged among the elected members: the People's Bloc, the Religious Bloc, and independents. The 16 independent members included merchants, contractors, government employees, a pharmacist, and a real estate dealer. The 8 members of the People's Bloc were a mix of Sunnis and Shi'is elected in the cities of Manama and Muharraq; they included 4 Arab nationalists, a Ba'thist, 2 communists, and a socialist. Members of this bloc supported the establishment of labor unions, and most of them were active in the strikes of 1965. The Religious Bloc had 6 Shi'is, who were elected in rural areas; they included 3 clerics and a journalist (all graduates of the Shi'i seminaries in Najaf), as well as 2 schoolteachers. One of the clerics was 'Abd al-Amir al-Jamri, who would emerge as a national leader in the 1994–99 uprising. Unlike the members of the People's Bloc, those of the Religious Bloc were not politically organized prior to 1973, and they won the elections through the influence of higher religious figures in their localities. The Religious Bloc adopted a platform opposed to the sale of alcohol in Bahrain, the mixing of men and women in public, and the licensing of youth clubs not conforming to Islamic values. Its emergence reflected the rise of Islam as a political force among Shi'is in the Middle East since the 1960s.[9]

The events that followed the parliament's establishment demonstrated the ability of Bahrainis to unite in an attempt to influence the legislative process and check the power of the emir. During a large part of 1974 the parliament functioned as the emir had expected. Its members mainly commented on petitions submitted to the government, or debated projects already implemented; they did not participate in drafting laws. Yet this working relationship ended in December when the ruler issued a state security law without consulting the parliament. This law permitted the government to imprison for three years without trial any person considered a threat to national security. The demand by parliament members that the law be submitted for approval before being implemented was ignored by the government for fear that the bill might be defeated. Several months of negotiations between the government and parliament ended in a stalemate. Then, in an unexpected development, the Religious and the People's Blocs forged an alliance in opposition to the law. This alliance between Islamists and secularists altered the balance of power between the government and the parliament to the latter's advantage. To avoid defeat, the government ministers did not show up for the voting session on 15 June 1975, forcing parliament to adjourn for its summer vacation. In August, the emir dissolved the parliament. He subsequently ignored the clause in the constitution calling for either the election of a new parliament within two months or the reconvening of the dissolved parliament until a new one was elected. "The state," in the words of the Shi'i parliament member 'Abdallah al-Madani, "revolted against the parliament and against the constraints put upon it by the constitution."[10]

Several factors account for the emir's decision to dissolve the parliament. His move was intended to deny the three blocs a national platform that would enable them to act as a unified opposition force and gain greater clout vis-à-vis the government. The decision was a victory, too, for those within the ruling family led by the prime minister, who from the start had opposed the concept of a democratic system based on power sharing, checks and balances, and political transparency. It also reflected pressures from Saudi Arabia to abort the constitutional experiment for fear that it would encourage Saudis to push for similar reforms in the kingdom. Moreover, in granting a constitution and a parliament, the emir had created institutions that posed a threat to the welfare and survival of the ruling family. This manifested itself in parliamentary debates over three issues other than the state security law: first, the bill passed in 1974 limiting the emir's share of the state budget to six million dinars annually; second, an attempt by the People's Bloc to present a bill transferring control of land and the right to dispose of it from the emir to the state; and third, an attempt by the People's Bloc to present a bill ending the U.S. military presence in Bahrain.[11] The rise of a parliament that challenged the Al Khalifa's monopoly on power thus led to its dissolution by the emir. Accordingly, for twenty-seven years Bahrain had no constitution, and the country was in effect governed under the state security law of 1975.

It was only after the uprising of 1994–99 that the Al Khalifa reintroduced a constitution and a parliamentary system. This development was part of a strategy intended to trade reforms for popular consent to turning Bahrain from an emirate into a monarchy, and thereby further increasing the powers of the head of state—the king. In 1999 the government adopted a national charter: it envisaged the creation of a bicameral parliament composed of a house of elected members with legislative powers and a chamber of appointed members (including a Christian and a Jew) playing an advisory role. All men and women over the age of twenty were allowed to vote. Women were also permitted to run for office (although none succeeded in getting elected), and six were appointed to the advisory chamber. These measures put Bahrain ahead of other monarchies in the Persian Gulf, including Kuwait where only first-class male citizens could vote or put their names on the ballot.[12]

Hailed as a new social contract between the Al Khalifa and the people, the charter won overwhelming support (98.4 percent) in a national referendum held on the 14th and 15th of February 2001. The large turnout among Shi'is underscored the isolation of the Islamic Front for the Liberation of Bahrain, which conspicuously failed to persuade people to boycott the referendum. Yet the political process soon suffered a major blow. A few days after the referendum, the Bahraini government, in a surprising move, introduced an amended version of the 1973 constitution. The new version gave equal legislative powers to the appointed chamber and the elected house (each with forty members), and vested executive authority in the king and the government.[13] This amendment drained power from the house, making it impossible for this body to initiate legislation and parliamentary debate, or to oversee government policies. The initial euphoria of the opposition members gave way to disillusionment, prompting four Shiʻi-dominated groups to declare a boycott of the October 2002 elections to the house. Their action came only four months after a coalition led by Shiʻi clerics and professionals (the Wifaq National Islamic Association) won most of the votes in their constituencies during the municipal elections held in May. This boycott helps explain both the low voter turnout (52 percent by government account, below 40 percent according to the opposition) compared to the 90 percent rate in the 1973 parliamentary elections, as well as the ascendancy of Sunni Islamists, who won fourteen of the twenty-one seats in the elected house. Shiʻi opposition members, led by ʻAbd al-Amir al-Jamri and ʻAli Salman, charged that the amended version of the 1973 constitution effectively curtailed the power of the elected members and enabled the king to veto all measures passed by the parliament. They described the amendment as a government coup worse than the dissolution of parliament in 1975, and as an abrogation of the contract between the Al Khalifa and the people, while pledging to continue their struggle by peaceful means. As with the 1973–75 reforms, those of 1999–2002 amounted to royal decrees—acts of generosity on the part of the king, who could withdraw them at his will.[14]

The experience of constitutionalism in Bahrain demonstrates the resistance of governments in the Middle East to institutions that would formalize the legislative process, provide a national platform to organized opposition, and curb the power of the ruling elite. The 1999–2002 reforms in Bahrain, like those that had been introduced a few years earlier in Jordan and Morocco, were not intended to transfer real power and sovereignty from the ruling family to the people. Instead, they aimed to cope with a legitimacy crisis by creating some sense of national consensus and political stability, while allowing the ruling family to retain the upper hand in state affairs.[15] Moreover, the reforms in Bahrain fell afoul of the U.S.-declared war on terrorism in the wake of the 9/11 attacks. This led to an increase in the presence of U.S. forces on the islands and agitated Bahrainis. It also caused the Al Khalifa to impose new restrictions on freedom of expression and the right to criticize the royal family, and led them to depict Shi'is who continued to advocate a parliament with legislative and monitoring powers, and the restoration of the 1973 constitution, as dissenters seeking to foment civil strife. These developments largely account for the rise in political tension in Bahrain since 2001.[16]

Bahrain's constitutional experience has resulted in a government that commands little legitimacy among the Shi'i majority because it is neither accountable to the voters nor appointed by an elected body. This explains why Bahraini Shi'is have been holding their breath in anticipation of the political outcome in Iraq, hoping for the emergence of a strong parliamentary system that would redefine relations between people and government in the Arab world.

As in the case of Bahrain, the experience of Shi'is in Lebanon since the 1990s carries important lessons for Iraq today.

The Victory of Pragmatism in Lebanon

By the end of the civil war in 1990, Shi'is had emerged as the largest sect in Lebanon, determined to renegotiate their pact with the state. Both Amal, and to a much larger extent Hizballah, have used the idea of resistance to Israel to increase their clout within Lebanon and to gain legitimacy in the Arab and Islamic worlds. Amal has consistently presented such resistance as a national obligation of all Lebanese. In a 1988 speech on the occasion of the tenth anniversary of Musa Sadr's disappearance, for example, Nabih Berri declared that the second Lebanese republic should be the republic of resistance, arguing that only those who were part of the resistance deserved a say in state affairs.[17]

Hizballah has gone to greater lengths than Amal in exalting "the culture of resistance." During the 1980s Hizballah distinguished itself from Amal by portraying itself as the spearhead of an Islamic movement seeking to liberate not only southern Lebanon but Palestine as well. From the mid-1990s, however, after Hizballah had declared its openness toward Lebanese society, and sought to mend fences even with Christians, the organization shifted focus and began emphasizing Arab nationalist and Lebanese themes. Its members presented the resistance as the Arab front line in the fight against Israel and attempted to use the myth of resistance to gain acceptance in the country. The Israeli withdrawal from southern Lebanon in May 2000 was thus a victory for Hizballah. Yet support for the resistance within Lebanon dropped after 2000, even with regard to the disputed territory of Shab'a Farms. Subsequently, Hizballah shifted its public emphasis from liberating Shab'a to protecting Lebanon, and the idea of resistance gave way to the notion of deterrence. This change manifested itself in Hizballah's dealings with the second Palestinian uprising, which broke out in 2000. Although it provided weapons and training to Palestinian fighters, Hizballah has been careful not to compromise its political achievements at home, and its members have therefore not joined the fighting inside Israel or in the West Bank and Gaza. At the same time, Hasan Nasrallah, Hizballah's secretary-general, has acknowledged that a two-state solution between Israel and Palestine is a "Palestinian matter." The U.S. invasion of Iraq in 2003 generated widespread upheaval, reinforced by the assassination of former prime minister Rafiq Hariri, which, in turn, triggered mass demonstrations in Lebanon in March 2005, demanding the withdrawal of Syrian troops from the country. These events have further influenced Hizballah's priorities. Its major dilemma today is not how to preserve its image as the spearhead of Lebanese resistance to Israel, but how to respond to the shifting geopolitics of the Middle East following the rise of the Shi'is to power in post-Ba'th Iraq, and the subsequent Syrian withdrawal from Lebanon in April 2005, without compromising Hizballah's socio-

economic achievements and political clout in the country. This dilemma helps explain the decision of Hizballah's leaders to join the
Lebanese government in July 2005, for the first time in the organization's history.[18]

The changing priorities of Hizballah have also manifested themselves in the movement's acknowledgment that the conditions for
an Islamic state do not exist in Lebanon. Unlike Amal leaders, who
by and large have pursued a secular platform, during the 1980s
Hizballah's ideology was heavily influenced by Iran, and its officials advocated the establishment of an Islamic republic in Lebanon. Yet the idea of an Islamic state in Lebanon has remained an
abstraction. Already in the mid-1980s, the cleric Muhammad Hussein Fadlallah ruled out the practicality of an Islamic state, citing
the existence of a substantial Christian minority in Lebanon and
the fact that Sunnis and Shi'is had disagreements over the meaning
of an Islamic state.[19] Hizballah's pragmatism in dealing with the
question of Islamic government has become clear since the 1990s,
when Hasan Nasrallah admitted that Shi'i political Islam has no
place in Lebanon. An Islamic state, he explained in interviews in
1995 and 1998, requires overwhelming popular support that simply does not exist in Lebanon. In the absence of a sweeping majority, he said, the alternative was to participate in Lebanese politics
while remaining philosophically committed to the idea of an Islamic state. The extent to which Hizballah has been moving away
from the idea of Islamic government is evident from the attacks on
the Shi'i organization by Sunni Islamists, who have accused it of
capitulating to the idea of nation-state in Lebanon.[20]

How, then, did Lebanese Shi'is envisage the new Lebanon? Shi'is
have viewed postwar Lebanon as a "final" and unified state with
a special relationship with Syria—a view that is likely to endure
even after the Syrian withdrawal from the country. Hani Fahs, a
reform-minded cleric, urged Lebanese Shi'is to give priority to their
national identity, reach out to members of other sects, and extend
their unconditional support to the state despite its imperfections.
Fahs considered unity among Shi'is to be a precondition for the

achievement of national unity in Lebanon, calling on all groups, including Hizballah, to set limits to the idea of resistance. After the Israeli withdrawal in 2000, he urged Shi'is to turn their full energies to developing a national and cultural program that went beyond the resistance and aimed at bringing stability and prosperity to Lebanon. Fahs counseled Shi'is to be patient in their quest for social and political justice. He compared the process to a train ride: the time of the train's arrival at the station was not as important as ensuring that the train and the tracks were in good shape and that the direction of the journey was clear.[21]

Although initially Shi'is attempted to abolish the Lebanese confessional system, which would have allowed them to exploit their plurality among the population, by the mid-1990s they had accepted the political system of power sharing and checks and balances, as modified by the Ta'if accord. This important development is exemplified in the changing views of Mahdi Shams al-Din, head of the Higher Islamic Shi'i Council between 1994 and 2001. In the mid- and late 1980s Shams al-Din advocated rebuilding Lebanon as a parliamentary republic based on pluralism and the separation of the legislative, executive, and judicial branches. He objected to dividing Lebanon into several electoral regions along sectarian lines, and suggested treating the entire state as a single electoral domain. Shams al-Din rejected the historical justification the Maronites had given for their ascendancy—their fear of the Muslim majority—and instead was willing to offer Christians guarantees of political participation, but without allowing them to dominate politics as in the prewar period. Moreover, he advocated that the president of the republic be elected in a national referendum, which would have enabled a Muslim to become head of state and would thus have broken the Maronite monopoly on that position. By 1993, however, bowing to Syrian pressures, and realizing that a Shi'i push for political dominance could lead other sects to advocate a decentralized Lebanon, Shams al-Din adopted a more pragmatic line. He acknowledged that Christians, like the Copts in Egypt, have occupied a prominent position within Lebanese society and therefore could not be treated as second-class citizens. Shams al-Din began viewing Lebanon as a state governed neither by religion nor by ideology. Such a state, he said, would provide a political and national framework for its citizens and enable members of the different sects, irrespective of their ideological inclinations, to view themselves as Lebanese first. Shams al-Din called on Shi'is to reduce the intensity of the rituals commemorating the martyrdom of imam Hussein, arguing that excessive displays of religion undermined the national identity of Lebanese Shi'is and their integration within Lebanon. In his will, Shams al-din urged Lebanese Shi'is— as well as Shi'is in the larger Arab world—to espouse modernity, develop their national consciousness as Lebanese, Iraqis, or Bahrainis, and blend into their respective countries.[22]

Like Shams al-Din, Lebanon's leading Shi'i cleric, Hussein Fadlallah, has modified his views over time and has come to acknowledge that Christians are rooted in the soil of Lebanon. Fadlallah considered national dialogue and political compromise essential for achieving unity in Lebanon. During the 1980s he argued that minority groups deserved access to all state offices except the presidency. In subsequent years, however, he acknowledged that it was impossible to impose a Muslim ruler on a state as diverse as Lebanon. Fadlallah has accepted the spirit of the Ta'if accord, which transferred power from the Maronite president to the Sunni prime minister and the Shi'i speaker of parliament. While in his view Muslims and Christians could not fully embrace one another, he considered it important to reduce political tensions between the various sects and urged the Lebanese not to reject one another. Fadlallah has endorsed parliament as a national platform for all Lebanese and encouraged competition in mixed areas between Muslim and Christian candidates for municipal councils and the parliament. Both Catholic Christians and Shi'is, he said, were Lebanese, even though in religious matters the former looked to the pope in the Vatican and the latter to a cleric based in Lebanon, Iraq, or Iran. The Lebanese, he concluded, shared an Eastern heritage with a common culture, and therefore their national identity could not be compromised by religion or ideological preference.[23]

The Shi'i experience in Lebanon in the period following the civil war underscores the victory of pragmatism over Shi'i radicalism— an outcome that has implications for the political reconstruction of Iraq where Shi'is, together with other Iraqis, will need to agree on power sharing and a new government system to replace the former Ba'th regime.

The Price of Liberation in Iraq

Defying the expectations of the U.S. administration, Iraqi Shi'is did not rise up against Saddam Hussein during the invasion of 2003 and instead adopted a wait-and-see approach. This attitude reflected the strong national identity of Iraqi Shi'is and their sense that they had been betrayed by America in 1991, when President George H. W. Bush encouraged Iraqis to revolt against Saddam and then abandoned them, enabling the Iraqi leader to crush the uprising. While they yearned for the collapse of the Ba'th, Iraqi Shi'is were also concerned about their image in the Arab world, which is predominantly Sunni, and sought to avoid accusations similar to those leveled against them in 1991, namely, that they were an Iranian fifth column within Iraq and collaborators with Western powers. The U.S. invasion put Shi'is in the awkward position of having to choose between a Sunni Muslim oppressor and a foreign Christian invader. During March–April 2003 the Iraqi Shi'is opted for inaction. Their ambivalence was evident in the rarity of images of jubilant Iraqis celebrating their liberation in the Shi'i slum of Baghdad, Saddam City, now renamed Sadr City. Shi'is felt offended by the sight of American soldiers on Iraqi soil, considering it an affront to Iraq's honor, and they were ashamed that Western powers, not Iraqis, had toppled the regime. Fadil al-Shati, a young Shi'i of Hilla in southern Iraq, articulated the view of many of his coreligionists about the outcome of the war: "We sold our country," he told a *New York Times* reporter, "in order to get rid of Saddam Hussein."[24]

Iraqi Shi'is have also been leery of America's long-term goals in Iraq. But the U.S. occupation has forced them to redefine their self-image and their relations with this foreign power. Eighty-two years of Sunni domination led the Shi'i majority to adopt the mentality of a minority group, as is evident in their pleas for international protection during the Ba'th's suppression of the 1991 uprising.[25] By contrast, the collapse of the Ba'th regime has reenergized the Shi'is, who have sought to translate their demographic majority into political power. This change explains their tacit support of the early stages of the U.S. occupation. In contrast to the lethal Sunni rebellion in central Iraq, which had its origin in the summer of 2003, Sadr City at the time was said to be the safest place in Baghdad for U.S. soldiers. While Sunni clerics called for rebellion, the senior Shi'i mujtahids did not declare a jihad against the occupiers. Indeed, Shi'i leaders on the whole showed goodwill toward the Americans and even ignored accusations from fellow Iraqis that they were not part of the resistance.[26] Whereas 'Abd al-Majid Nuri, a Sunni cleric of Falluja, asserted that "the infidel had no right to relieve the oppression of believers," 'Abd al-Rahman al-Shuwayli, the outreach coordinator of the Shi'i Hikma mosque in Sadr City, said that he "would work with the Coalition Provisional Authority to serve the Iraqi people." Ibrahim al-Mutayri, secretary-general of Islamic Action in Karbala, echoed Shuwayli's words and emphasized that his group objected to jihad against the Americans. Khudayr Ja'far of the Islamic Da'wa Party went further: "We don't want the Americans to withdraw," he told the Arabic *Hayat* newspaper. "We want the Americans to help us so that we can build our Iraqi institutions."[27]

Shi'is disagreed, however, on how to engage the Americans and on the strategy to pursue in order to attain political power. Thus the young firebrand cleric Muqtada al-Sadr viewed the interim Governing Council appointed in July 2003 as an illegitimate and nonrepresentative body, tainted by its association with foreign powers, and instead advocated elections for a "popular Islamic government." Yet his calls for demonstrations in favor of his proposed government attracted only a few thousand supporters, forcing Sadr to concede that Iraqis were not ready for the idea. By contrast, the senior mujtahids led by 'Ali Sistani gave the council their tacit approval, paving the way for Shi'is to join this Iraqi political institution. In joining the council (as well as the interim government appointed in June 2004), Shi'i leaders broke with the path taken in the 1920s by their coreligionists who followed the rulings of the mujtahids and rejected employment under the British. This move demonstrated the determination of Shi'is not to repeat the mistakes of the past, and their willingness to adopt pragmatism as a precondition for leading the new Iraq.[28]

Nevertheless, a big gap in expectations, reinforced by several U.S. strategic blunders in handling Iraq, drove Shi'is and Americans further apart. Shi'is expected the Americans to provide security, give them food, electricity, and jobs, withdraw their troops from cities, and not block their bid for power. But the Bush administration did not commit the resources necessary to establish order and improve economic life, and had plans of its own for Iraq. The mayhem that followed the invasion and the ill-fated decision to dismantle the Iraqi army undercut the reconstruction effort and damaged American credibility in the country. While the sweeping "de-Baathification" measures of 2003 reassured Shi'is, their reversal in 2004 led them to believe that the United States intended to bring the Ba'thists back to power; the U.S. military decision in April to sign over the city of Falluja to former Ba'th Republican Guard officers reaffirmed this Shi'i fear. At the same time, the bombings in the shrine cities of Najaf, Karbala, and Kazimain—as well as scores of political assassinations of Shi'i leaders during 2003–4, including Muhammad Baqir al-Hakim, 'Aqila al-Hashimi, and 'Izz al-Din Salim—put Shi'is on edge and convinced them that America could not protect them against their militant Sunni adversaries. Moreover, Shi'is were enraged by the American-sponsored interim constitution (the Transitional Administrative

Law hailed as a bill of rights), which declared Iraq a federal state without defining the meaning of federalism, and gave veto powers to minorities. Sadr called the signing of the document in March 2004 by the Governing Council a betrayal of Iraq. Ayatollah Muhammad Taqi Modarressi of Karbala referred to it as a time bomb that could spark civil war. And Grand Ayatollah 'Ali Sistani warned the UN Security Council of dangerous consequences if it endorsed the document.[29]

The interim constitution bore the hallmark of L. Paul Bremer III, the top U.S. administrator in Iraq, who tightly controlled politics until his departure in June 2004, allowing hardly any input from Iraqis and alienating many Shi'is. A good example of Bremer's style was his attempt to force the Governing Council to select 'Adnan Pachahchi as Iraq's interim president, instead of Ghazi al-Yawar. As Raja al-Khuza'i, a female member of the council, related: "Bremer entered the room as we prepared to vote for Yawar. He told us: 'You do not represent the Iraqi people.' I was shocked by this. Two members of this council have been murdered. All of us have received death threats. And Mr. Bremer told us we don't represent Iraqis. He used us, and now that he is finished with us, he will throw us away. I used to say that I would cry when Mr. Bremer left Iraq. But not now. I will not miss him."[30] Iraqi Shi'is are likely to remember Bremer as a symbol of U.S. repression, much as Bahraini Shi'is have viewed Charles Belgrave—the once all-powerful British adviser to the emir.

Yet it was above all the U.S. attempt to sideline Shi'i Islamists, both religious figures and politicians, that radicalized Iraqi Shi'is and led to the two rebellions of Muqtada al-Sadr during April–August 2004. Polls sponsored by the Coalition Provincial Authority during 2003–4 consistently showed overwhelming Iraqi Shi'i support for Grand Ayatollah 'Ali Sistani, followed by Muqtada al-Sadr, and then by Ibrahim al-Ja'fari and 'Adil 'Abd al-Mahdi of the Islamic Da'wa Party and the Supreme Council for the Islamic Revolution in Iraq (SCIRI), respectively. Nevertheless, Washington was slow in coming to terms with Sistani's hidden power and put obstacles in the face of his demands for the direct election of a national assembly to appoint the government and write the constitution—demands that were democratic and reflected the aspirations of Sistani's constituency in Iraq. Washington also failed to acknowledge Sadr's growing popularity and did not permit his followers, mostly the urban Shi'i poor, to join the political process early on so as to mitigate the radicalism of his movement. The Sadr movement was denied a seat on the Governing Council appointed by Bremer in July 2003 (an action supported by SCIRI, Sadr's main Shi'i rival), leading Sadr to denounce the council as nonrepresentative, and thus putting Sadr and the Americans on a collision course. Making matters worse, the appointment of Iyad 'Allawi (a Shi'i and former Ba'thist with close ties to the CIA) as interim prime minister in June 2004 was intended in part to marginalize the Da'wa and SCIRI, two of Iraq's largest Shi'i parties, and led Iraqi Shi'i Islamists to conclude that the United States was targeting their political will. Those around Sadr began identifying America with Saddam Hussein and denounced it as anti-Shi'a.[31]

In announcing his rebellions, Sadr gave expression not only to the specific grievances of his movement, but also to the mood of larger segments of Iraqi Shi'i society that had begun to lose faith in America. As early as November 2003, a CIA report leaked to the press concluded that Iraqi Shi'is could soon join members of the Sunni minority in carrying out armed attacks against U.S. forces. In the months leading to the first rebellion of April–May 2004, Sadr had established himself as the leader of a grassroots movement with its own militia, the Mahdi Army, declaring it to be the military wing of the religious leadership, the *marja'iyya*. Like his father, Muhammad Sadiq al-Sadr, discussed in chapter 3, Muqtada claimed to represent the outspoken trend within the seminaries of Najaf (*al-hawza al-natiqa* or *al-fa'ila*) and protested the silence of the senior clerics. Muqtada al-Sadr's followers embarked on a drive to control Shi'i mosques and the income that comes with them, bullying their rivals and setting up religious and morality courts to prosecute their opponents. In an insult to Sistani, they highlighted Sadr's Arab background, as opposed to Sistani's Iranian origin, arguing that only an Iraqi could lead Iraq's Shi'a. At the same time, they referred to Sadr as the "Hasan Nasrallah of Iraq," after the secretary-general of Hizballah in Lebanon, and showed growing readiness to confront the U.S. military. "The people are burning," one of Sadr's supporters told a *Washington Post* reporter. "We have overcome our fear. We've come to the point where others are scared of us."[32]

Sadr's activism constituted a direct challenge to the nonconfrontational approach favored by the senior religious leaders led by Sistani, forcing the elder cleric to become more involved for fear of losing support among Iraqi Shi'is and in order to tame Sadr. Sistani had a keen sense of Iraq's history, and he knew that Iraqi Shi'is resented the Shi'i religious leaders for forbidding them to participate in elections and accept government office following the 1920 revolt against the British. In a meeting with tribal leaders in Najaf in January 2004, Sistani called them descendants of that revolt. Elections, he said, were the only way to ensure that their voices would be heard. Although Sistani disapproved of Sadr's tactics, he was nevertheless aware of his popularity and sympathized with the socioeconomic grievances of his followers. Moreover, Sistani realized the importance of retaining Sadr's Mahdi Army in the face of other militias in the country that refused to disarm, and as a counterweight to the Sunni insurgents and foreign jihadists determined to block the rise of Shi'is to power. He therefore did not sanction disarming the Mahdi Army; instead he shielded the young cleric during the rebellions, both from the U.S. military and from the Iraqi interim premier, who sought to destroy Sadr's militia and thus undermine his popularity and weaken him politically.[33]

The two rebellions signaled a tipping point in Shi'i-U.S. relations, both inside and outside Iraq, and threatened to cause internal strife within the Iraqi Shi'i community. As Sadr's sermons grew increasingly critical of America and of the Governing Council and later the interim government, U.S. commanders and Iraqi politicians sought a showdown with the cleric. The Coalition Provisional Authority provoked the first rebellion of April–May 2004 by closing down Sadr's newspaper, *al-Hawza*. Then, in June, shortly before his departure from Iraq, Bremer signed an order banning illegal militia members from holding political office for three years after ending their membership in the organization, thereby seeking to block the Sadr movement from contesting the January 2005 elections for a transitional national assembly. The timing and location of the August showdown around 'Ali's shrine in Najaf—a location of the highest Shi'i religious sensitivities—were reportedly a result of lapses in the American military command structure in Iraq.[34] That confrontation, which damaged the shrine and the cemetery adjacent to it, and dealt a blow to Najaf's economy based on the pilgrimage, drew condemnations from Shi'is around the world, including Hizballah and the Lebanese cleric Muhammad Hussein Fadlallah. Hizballah had apparently established a small presence in postwar Iraq, but according to U.S. intelligence estimates its members did not join forces with Iraqi Shi'is during the first rebellion. By contrast, because of U.S. attacks on the shrine during the outbreak of the second rebellion, Hizballah declared its support for the Iraqi Shi'i rebels. Likewise, in April 2004 Fadlallah urged Iraqi Shi'is to restrain themselves, but in August he called for ending "Shi'i neutralism" and for all Muslims to "expel the occupiers from Iraq through any means possible."[35]

Within the Iraqi Shi'i community, the rebellions represented a struggle to map the political direction of the new Iraq. The three-week battle in Najaf in August developed into a game of brinkmanship between 'Allawi and Sadr. The interim premier, backed by the Americans, needed a victory to build his authority in Iraq. He wanted to humiliate Sadr, crush his militia, and then go after the hubs of resistance in the Sunni areas. But Sadr rejected the notion that his movement could be pushed aside in favor of former exiles like 'Allawi, who lacked a broad social base in Iraq, and he dismissed the very idea that Iraq's political future could be determined under an American military umbrella. He therefore raised the stakes, letting his followers blow up oil pipelines near Basra and even threaten the secession of the Shi'i south from Iraq. In the event, the August showdown undermined 'Allawi's chances of gaining legitimacy in the eyes of Shi'is, turned Sadr into an Iraqi nationalist hero, and nearly tore the Shi'i community apart. It took the wisdom and political acumen of Sistani to avert a complete breakdown of relations between the Shi'is and the United States, and to focus Iraqi Shi'is on the approaching elections.[36]

The August showdown with Sadr obscured the real differences between the Shi'i rebellion centered in Najaf and the Sunni insurgency in Falluja. Washington's decision in April 2004 to hand Falluja over to former officers of the Ba'th Republican Guard had failed to pacify the city, turning it instead into a safe haven for former Ba'thists and Sunni Islamic extremists, primarily Iraqis but including some foreign jihadists. By August, the Islamic militants overshadowed the secular Ba'thi elements, establishing a city council of "holy warriors" and working in alliance with the militant Unity and Jihad organization of Abu Mus'ab al-Zarqawi, a Jordanian with links to al-Qaeda. Falluja had become a hub for Iraqi Sunni resistance fighters and for terrorists determined to undermine the U.S. reconstruction effort, expel Westerners from Iraq, kill Iraqis who cooperated with the United States, and block the rise of Shi'is to power. By November the strength of the hard-core Sunni rebels had swelled to more than twenty thousand, and the revolt spread from Falluja to a string of cities in central, western, and northern Iraq, including Ramadi and Mosul. The insurgency was financed in part by wealthy Ba'th loyalists who had fled Iraq before the U.S. invasion and now funneled money from Syria and Jordan to rebels on the ground. A U.S. military assault on Falluja reduced much of the city to rubble but failed to end the insurgency, which continued unabated through the January 2005 elections and gave expression to a Sunni community whose members felt disenfranchised in the politics of post-Ba'th Iraq.[37]

Although there were signs of solidarity between the Shi'i and Sunni rebels, it did not reach the level of tactical cooperation because of the conflicting political aspirations of Shi'is and Sunnis under U.S. occupation. In Najaf, the presence of Sadr's fighters irritated the senior religious leaders and the merchants, and eventually led Sistani to impose his will on the young rebel in order to avoid risking Shi'i political opportunities. In Falluja, by contrast, the insurgents had the support of the majority of the clerical and civilian population, who were seeking to reassert Sunni dominance in Iraq. Whereas the Sunni insurgents renounced the political process and the elections, inaugurated a campaign of civil disobedience against the government, and were even willing to push Iraq into a civil war to achieve their goals, Sadr desired a role in politics and did not want to cause civil strife in the country. He therefore condemned the presence of al-Qaeda in Iraq, as well as the beheading of Westerners and the bombing of churches belonging to Iraq's Christian minority. Amid the fighting with U.S. forces in August, he secured the release of a kidnapped American journalist, distancing his movement from the spate of hostage taking in Iraq. Moreover, Sadr initially gave his support to 'Allawi's government on condition that it set a timetable for the departure of the occupation forces. He withdrew his support only when he realized that 'Allawi and the Americans were determined to crush his power. In his toughest hour during the battle in Najaf he said: "I wish to be killed by a U.S. bomb, not by an Iraqi bullet."[38]

The political divide between Arab Sunnis and Shi'is widened in the months between the August 2004 showdown in Najaf and the January 2005 elections. While the Sunni rebels grew ever more determined to create chaos in Iraq and sow discord among Iraqis, Shi'is closed ranks in preparation for the elections and showed restraint in the face of suicide bombings and targeted assassinations. Within the Shi'i community, unity was given the highest priority. Establishing unity meant allowing members of the Sadr movement to join the political process. The first steps were not easy, however, and underscored the conflicting aspirations of Iraqi and U.S. officials on the one hand, and those of the major Shi'i players on the other. Encouraged by SCIRI and other Shi'i groups rivaling Sadr, government officials insulted the Sadr movement by offering its members only one seat on the preparatory committee for the national congress that convened in August to elect a council to oversee the interim government. Sadr turned down the invitation, as

did Iraqi Sunnis like Wamidh Nazmi, a newspaper editor and former dean of Baghdad University—both citing their refusal to participate in a political institution heavily controlled by the United
States. Sadr apparently also feared that his movement would be
marginalized in the congress because of the relatively small number
of seats allocated to Shi'i Islamists among the eleven hundred delegates, in comparison to secular Arabs and Kurds.[39] Under these
conditions, Sadr had no incentive to enter Iraqi politics. Instead,
he announced during the standoff in Najaf his willingness to hand
over control of the city and its shrine to the senior Shi'i clerics
led by Sistani, demanded complete freedom for his movement to
participate in politics, agreed to abide by the legitimate constitution of a freely elected Iraqi government, and pledged to work for
an independent and unified Iraq free of foreign control.[40] The deal
brokered by Sistani in late August reiterated the importance of
holding free elections to the interim assembly so as to make possible the participation of the Sadr movement. Yet a few days after
he had accepted the deal, 'Allawi reneged, overruling his national
security adviser, Muwaffaq al-Rubay'i, who favored coaxing the
Sadr movement into the political mainstream.[41] Both this move,
and the fighting that followed in Sadr City, signaled an attempt on
'Allawi's part to snatch victory from Sistani and further weaken
Sadr. Nevertheless, his actions failed to undermine Sistani's stature
or block the participation of members of the Sadr movement in the
elections. As it turned out, 'Allawi and the Americans, very much
like Sadr, had a stake in pushing the political process forward and
hence concluded a deal in October that granted the Sadr movement
a place at the negotiating table.

The moving figure behind the elections of 30 January 2005 was
'Ali Sistani, who demonstrated remarkable leadership in resisting
attempts inside and outside Iraq to postpone the elections, and in
mobilizing Shi'is and other Iraqis to participate in the political process. In the months leading to the elections, Sistani straddled the
role of a promoter of Shi'i political interests and that of an Iraqi
national leader. He worked to bridge gaps between former exile
groups, like SCIRI and the Da'wa, and other Shi'i opponents of

Saddam Hussein who had stayed in Iraq, as in the case of the Sadr movement and the Fadila Party of Muhammad al-Ya'qubi. At the same time, Sistani met with Kurdish and Christian leaders, and emphasized that Sunni representation in the government was vital to the working of a new Iraqi polity. In his rulings Sistani advocated free and transparent elections, considering voting the duty of all Iraqis. He affirmed that a married woman did not have to vote for the list preferred by her husband but should cast a ballot in accordance with her conscience and beliefs. While he tacitly supported the predominantly Shi'i United Iraqi Alliance, Sistani gave his blessing to all competing Iraqi parties and did not instruct his followers to vote for any particular list. The various Shi'i parties launched a massive get-out-the-vote campaign in defiance of the ferocious Sunni insurgency and the targeted killing of election workers. They also withstood propaganda by Sunni officials in the Iraqi interim government, and even by Jordan's king 'Abdallah, who warned of an Iranian attempt to control Iraq through the elections and create a crescent of Shi'i governments and movements stretching from Iran into Iraq, the Persian Gulf States, Syria, and Lebanon, thereby altering the balance of power between Shi'is and Sunnis in the Middle East. Both the senior clerics in Najaf and leaders of the major Shi'i parties denied plans to establish a Shi'i theocracy in Iraq. Instead, they stressed the importance of keeping Iraq unified, forming a representative national assembly, writing a constitution that guarded the Islamic character of Iraq and respected the rights of Iraqis of all religions and sects, and setting a timetable for the withdrawal of foreign troops from Iraq. The emphasis on unity among Iraqis was a theme also shared by Muqtada al-Sadr, who told his followers a few days before the elections: "Beware of letting sectarianism play a role in the elections. I want to elect only a noble Iraqi, neither a Shi'i nor a Sunni, but an Iraqi who will guard my religion and honor and my independence and unity."[42]

The elections were a historic moment that symbolized a shift of political hegemony in Iraq—a key Arab country—from the Sunni minority to the Shi'i majority and to the Kurds. Iraqi Shi'is viewed the elections as a sacrifice for progress with many prepared to die as martyrs at the gates of the polling stations. George Packer, reporting from Basra for the *New Yorker*, captured the spirit surrounding the vote and the meaning of the elections for Shi'is: "Sunday morning was strange and beautiful. Families, including small children and grandparents, walked along wide avenues, everyone dressed in fine clothes. At the polling places the queues were orderly. People seemed to keep their voices low out of respect, and the election workers were thanked as if they were heroes." Shadha Muhammad 'Ali, a fifty-year-old housewife wearing a black scarf, told Packer after casting her vote: "I spent thirty-five years of my life going from war to war. Now my hopes are for my children. We lost our future. We're looking for the future of our children." Muhsin Rahim Hashim, an Arabic teacher, added: "I've lived over fifty years, and I've never had such a feeling. My skin had strange feeling like goosebumps. We've had a great culture for six thousand years, and now I think our humanity is proved. We hope this democratic experiment brings this result, that the people are the real owners of the decisions in this country." The elections were in large part the culmination of a sustained effort by 'Ali Sistani. Yet by day's end, the biggest supporter of the elections had not cast a ballot. In fact, the Grand Ayatollah had not left his home all day. Sistani was born in Iran, and no one in Najaf seemed to know whether he was even qualified to vote in Iraq.[43]

In reality, the elections were only an incremental step toward the development of a representative government in post-Ba'th Iraq. Iraqi Sunnis by and large boycotted the elections, repeating the mistake made by Shi'is during the 1920s, which undermined their political position in Iraq until the U.S. invasion. By contrast, Shi'is and Kurds voted in large numbers, which resulted in a national voter turnout of 58 percent that exceeded all expectations. The elections had three purposes: First, electing a transitional national assembly of 275 members. Second, electing provincial councils, one for each of Iraq's 18 provinces. Third, in the Kurdish region voters also elected a local assembly of 105 members, called the Iraqi Kurdistan Assembly. More than a hundred parties competed for seats in the national assembly. The main Shi'i and Kurdish parties banded together into consensus lists, notably the United Iraqi Alliance, which won 140 seats in the national assembly, or 51 percent, and the Kurdistan Alliance, which won 75 seats, or 27 percent. They were followed by the Iraqi List, led by the interim premier Iyad 'Allawi, which won only 40 seats, or less than 15 percent. Interestingly, candidates affiliated with the Sadr movement within the United Iraqi Alliance won 23 seats in the assembly, in addition to 3 more seats won by the Independent Elites and Cadres Party, which ran with Sadr's implicit backing. The rules governing the elections stipulated that every third candidate on every list had to be a women, assuring that around 30 percent of the seats in the national assembly went to women. Seats in the assembly were allocated through a system of proportional representation—a system reminiscent of the one followed in Lebanon, and which in 2005 barred the Shi'i majority from a sweeping victory and forced them to compromise and form a coalition government. Shi'is succeeded, however, in dominating 11 of the 18 provincial councils in Iraq, with SCIRI winning most seats in 8 of the 11 councils dominated by Shi'is, including Baghdad.[44]

The transitional national assembly was seated in March, and May 2005 saw the installation of a transitional government, dominated by Shi'is and including three ministers belonging to the Sadr movement. Hajim al-Hassani, a Sunni, was elected speaker of the assembly. Jalal Talabani was named president of Iraq, making him the first Kurd to hold such a post in an Arab-dominated country. Iraqis also appointed Ibrahim al-Ja'fari, the Shi'i leader of the Islamic Da'wa Party, as prime minister—a development the U.S. administration probably had not anticipated on the eve of the 2003 invasion of Iraq.[45] These appointments indicate that confessionalism has become a principle of Iraqi politics, much as in Lebanon. Moreover, the protracted negotiations leading to the formation of the government—coupled with escalating Sunni insurgent violence, a decision of Shi'i and Kurdish leaders to retain their militias, and the formation of Shi'i death squads to retaliate against Sunnis—underscored the daunting challenges facing Iraqis in the coming years. These challenges were borne out already in the disputes over the draft constitution that was submitted to the transitional national assembly in August 2005, and which designated Islam as a main source of legislation, envisaged a Kurdish autonomous region in the north, and contained language that could lead to the creation of a large autonomous region in the south, dominated by Shi'is. The fierce opposition to the draft constitution by both Sunnis as well as some Shi'i groups suggests that Iraq's future will be determined by political battles accompanied by violence. As they move to consolidate power, Iraq's new leaders will need to deal firmly with the insurgents while giving the Sunni minority a stake in the political process. Iraqis will need to agree on relations between religion and state as well as on the role of religion in governing matters relating to personal status and women's rights. They will also need to devise a formula for sharing the country's oil revenues along geographic and communal lines, and define the meaning of federalism in a way that gives Shi'is, Sunnis, and Kurds a degree of cultural and religious autonomy without compromising either Iraq's political unity or Baghdad's role as the locus of national politics. In addition, Iraqis will need to redefine their country's relations with Iran, Turkey, and the Arab world, and to negotiate with the U.S. government over the future of the American presence in the country.

In the wake of the 2005 elections, Shi'is have come into their own as the politically dominant community in Iraq. Yet they are still pondering the price of liberation. The arrival of the Americans freed Iraqi Shi'is from Saddam Hussein and the Ba'th regime, but not from their own suspicions and grievances. Liberation by a foreign power was, in a way, humiliating and seemed to have brought new calamities. Still, liberation has also signaled a new beginning, and has provided the opportunity for Shi'is to take the lead in creating a more tolerant and inclusive Iraqi state.

Conclusion

In the past few decades there has been a surge in religious expression throughout the Middle East, among both Muslims and non-Muslims. Within Islam, religious revivalism has taken peaceful as well as violent forms, and has manifested itself differently among Shi'is and Sunnis. The upheaval generated by the Iranian Islamic Revolution of 1978–79 emboldened Shi'is in the Arab world and reinforced a trend toward activism within Shi'ism that continues to this day. During the late 1970s and 1980s Shi'is were often associated in the West with Islamic radicalism and terrorism. Yet in the period since the Gulf War of 1991, Shi'is have been moving away from violence and toward a dialogue both with the West and with other members of their societies. This trend toward accommodation among Shi'is reflects their desire for political empowerment. The cases of Saudi Arabia, Bahrain, Lebanon, and Iraq discussed in this book demonstrate this pivotal development within Shi'ism—a development that has taken shape against a background of growing militancy among Sunni groups hostile to the West and to the United States in particular. The roots of this wave of Sunni militancy go back to the Gulf War, when a U.S.-led coalition launched an offensive from Saudi Arabia to eject Saddam Hussein's army from Kuwait. Its dimensions have increased following the 9/11 attacks and the wars in Afghanistan and in Iraq.

The modern political experience of Saudi, Bahraini, Lebanese, and Iraqi Shi'is reveals communities and ruling elites that have had difficulties in agreeing on a common historical past. It also underscores the distinct characteristics of each of the four communities as well as the mutual influences shaping their political development. All Shi'i communities have experienced a degree of socioeconomic and political discrimination in their encounters with the state. Yet in each case, there were other decisive factors that influenced relations between Shi'is and governing elites.

Saudi Arabia stands out as a country where the religious-ideological divide has predominated over other factors in shaping the inferior status of Shi'is in the kingdom. At the same time, this case illustrates the major survival strategy of a small Shi'i minority seeking basic religious and citizenship rights within the kingdom. The Al Sa'ud have been reluctant to consider the Shi'is a partner worthy of inclusion in their system of alliances. And with the 1938 discovery of oil in the eastern province, where Shi'is predominate, the ruling family came to regard them as a security problem; this view was further reinforced following the Iranian revolution of 1978–79. The Al Sa'ud's adoption of Wahhabism as the state ideology, and their attempt to isolate rather than include the Shi'i minority, has led Shi'is to attach themselves to ideological movements originating outside the confines of Arabia that held the promise of political change and a better life at home.

In Bahrain, the home port of the U.S. Fifth Fleet in the Persian Gulf, a different reality prevails. There, a Sunni minority has dominated the Shi'i majority ever since the Al Khalifa ruling family conquered the islands in 1783. The tension between the Shi'is and the ruling family has its historical roots in the class and cultural differences distinguishing the two groups, as well as in the Al Khalifa's time-honored practice of relying on foreign powers and foreign workers to preserve their minority rule. More recently, the Al Khalifa's efforts to block the development of an elected parliament that might enable Shi'is to influence state affairs have further intensified political tension in Bahrain, accounting in large measure for the strained relations between Shi'is and the ruling family. Both Saudi and Bahraini Shi'is therefore have a considerable stake in the political outcome in post-Ba'th Iraq. While the former view a Shi'i-led Iraq as a development that could encourage the Al Sa'ud to introduce reforms and grant minority rights to the Shi'is, the latter hope for a strong parliamentary system in Iraq that would help redefine relations between parliament and the government in Bahrain.

The case of Lebanon, where Shi'is are today the largest community, reveals a country of seventeen sects organized politically along communal lines, with Syria acting as the power broker at least until April 2005, when its leaders withdrew Syrian troops from Lebanon in the face of U.S. and French pressures, and following mass demonstrations by the Lebanese opposition. Confessionalism as a system of political representation in Lebanon has its roots in the Ottoman period, and its endurance is a testimony to the difficulty of creating and sustaining nation-states in regions with multiethnic and multireligious populations. Much of the tension between the Shi'is and the Maronite and Sunni establishment in the twentieth century stemmed from the desire of Shi'is to run their own communal affairs independent of the Sunnis, and to gain political representation in proportion to their numbers. While in the first half of the twentieth century Shi'is were on the margin of Lebanese politics, they have since emerged as a powerful political community that no other group can ignore. The Iranian Islamic Revolution radicalized Lebanese Shi'is and led to the rise of Hizballah in the early 1980s. Yet in the course of two decades, Hizballah evolved from a revolutionary movement into a political party that courted Shi'i as well as Christian and Sunni voters in mixed areas, and sought a share of the country's power; this trend may continue following the departure of Syrian troops, provided the Lebanese succeed in maintaining peace in the country, and in renegotiating the Ta'if accord with a view to increasing political openness and giving preference to professional qualifications over communal affiliation in electing their leaders.

Like that of Lebanon, the case of Iraq demonstrates the changing fortunes of Shi'is. In pre-2003 Iraq, a Sunni minority elite held sway over the Shi'i majority. For eighty-two years the two groups essentially fought over the right to rule and to define the meaning of nationalism in the country. Whereas the majority of Shi'is preferred an Iraqi nationalism that stressed the Arab tribal and Islamic values of Iraqi society, Iraq's Sunni rulers adopted a wider Arab nationalism as their main ideology and portrayed Iraqi Shi'is as separatists with an "Iranian connection" seeking to undermine the Arab cause. The struggle between the two groups has not only intensified following the U.S. invasion but has also assumed a strongly religious dimension, as is evident from the emergence of clerics as community leaders, among both Shi'is and Sunnis. The U.S. occupation has transformed power relations between the two groups and led to the rise of the Shi'is as the politically dominant community in post-Ba'th Iraq. This profound change explains the different attitudes of the two groups toward the occupying power. While during 2003–5 most Iraqi Shi'is gave their tacit support to the U.S. reconstruction effort, Sunnis rebelled in large numbers, with some willing to push Iraq into a civil war in order to block the rise of Shi'is to power. Moreover, unlike the Sunnis, who rejected the U.S. attempt to impose a new order in Iraq, and by and large boycotted the January 2005 elections for a transitional national assembly, the Shi'is, including members of the Sadr movement, saw benefits in it and therefore entered the political process—in much the same fashion as the Lebanese Hizballah did in the early 1990s.

The political outcome in Iraq will reverberate throughout the Middle East. Although the January 2005 elections were fraught with problems, and were held under U.S. occupation and against the background of a violent Sunni insurgency, they could kick off an Iraqi political process. The key institution that ought to emerge out of the elections, and evolve in the coming years, is the national assembly. This assembly should be allowed to develop into an institution capable of checking the executive and guaranteeing the rights of women and minorities. If ordinary Iraqis can feel that through the assembly they can put pressure on the government to address their concerns, the political process will gain legitimacy. For its part, the U.S. government would need to accept the development of a strong assembly in Iraq even if this means that its members might pass laws that are not always to the liking of the United States, just as the Turkish parliament in 2003 denied the U.S. military the right to use Turkey as a platform to launch a ground offensive against Iraq. What is at stake in post-Ba'th Iraq is the creation of a strong legislature and a representative government accountable to the voters—a contentious issue that stands at the heart of the political debate in Iran and the Arab world. A dynamic political process in Iraq, even if influenced by Shi'i Islamists, could reinvigorate the reform movement in Iran and inspire change in the Arab world. And it could counter those Sunni militants who have been fighting Muslims seeking to build bridges to the West and willing to cooperate with Americans to realize sociopolitical change.

At the turn of the twenty-first century, Shi'is across the Middle East are searching for sociopolitical justice and for leaders who can uphold the rule of law. In a globalized world, Shi'is in Saudi Arabia or Bahrain or Lebanon are growing increasingly aware of developments in Iraq and Iran. Shi'is as a whole are looking for ways to reconcile Islamic and Western concepts of government and reshape Islam in conformity with modern times. Their debates have centered on the question of whether Shi'ism should be a set of fixed religious values, or a flexible identity shaped by the particular circumstances and environments in which Shi'is live. In his statements and actions in the period leading up to the January 2005 elections, Grand Ayatollah 'Ali Sistani responded precisely to such concerns among his followers in Iraq and all over the Shi'i world. Although he in no way attempted to do America's bidding in Iraq, Sistani nevertheless encouraged the trend toward accommodation among Shi'is, engaged America in a debate over the meaning of democracy and constitutional politics, and emerged as a strong advocate of free and direct elections.

The rise of Shi'is to power in Iraq may signal a positive start, but it could also lead to an all-out civil war in the country and to greater violence elsewhere in the Middle East. In the wake of the elections, Iraq's Shi'i majority and the United States share responsibility for the outcome of the political reconstruction of Iraq. Although Iraqis bear ultimate responsibility for the future of their country, the occupying power also needs to share the burden. What is required of U.S. policymakers is new thinking that responds to the changing geopolitics of the Middle East following the wars in Afghanistan and Iraq. The shift of focus among Shi'is since the 1990s from violence to accommodation, and the assertion of Shi'i power in Iraq, have signaled the rise of the Shi'is as a force that could potentially spur reform in the region. The United States would need to accept the consequences of that development, recognize that not all Islamists are alike, and develop a broad strategy for the Middle East that actively engages the moderates as part of the solution.

Such a strategy would inevitably acknowledge the positive role that Iran could play in a reconfigured Middle East, and seek a modus vivendi, if not full diplomatic relations, between the United States and Iran. Yet during 2003–5 the U.S. administration maintained an unyielding position on Iran, focusing on its nuclear intentions, its aid to Shi'i groups in Iraq, and the election of Mahmud Ahmadinejad as Iran's president. Meanwhile, as crude oil prices hit a record of $67 a barrel in August 2005, the administration moved to thaw relations with Saudi Arabia after the strains of the 9/11 attacks in New York and Washington in which 15 of the 19 hijackers were Saudi nationals. In so doing, the administration diverted attention from the more important problem of Sunni radicalism, with its sources in Saudi Arabia and in Afghanistan and Pakistan, and the danger that it poses to long-term U.S. strategic interests in the Middle East. The U.S. occupation of Iraq brought American troops to Iran's door, and as such it was bound to raise tensions between America and Iran as they vie for dominance in the Persian Gulf. But Iran, with its sixty-five million Shi'is, ultimately shares the U.S. goal of a unified Iraq with a Shi'i-led government, and it could play a supportive role in Washington's effort to bring stability to Iraq.

The circumstances leading up to the war in Iraq have resulted in an unprecedented loss of U.S. credibility in the international arena. Yet the war has also provided America with an opportunity to establish a relationship of trust not only with the Shi'is, but also with other people in the Middle East who have been craving change. Iraq has become the nexus where many critical issues are converging, most notably relations between Muslim and Western societies. Having gone to war in Iraq, and then proceeded to dismantle the Iraqi army, the United States has committed itself to remaining until Iraq can stand on its own feet. Nevertheless, any attempt to turn Iraq into a more permanent U.S. protectorate, and any failure to accept the leading role that Shi'i and Sunni Islamists are likely to play in the new Iraq and in the larger Middle East, will spark a brand of religious nationalism with strongly anti-American overtones, badly inflame relations between Islam and the West, and seriously undermine America's interests in the region. Success would mean an independent and unified Iraq with a representative government and a strong legislature. Achieving that goal will help restore America's standing in the world and, at the end of the day, will at least enable U.S. troops to leave Iraq with a sense of political accomplishment.

How the U.S. government handles Iraq and its people in the coming years will therefore be crucial not only for the future of that country and the Middle East, but also for America's global stature.

Abbreviations

AJIL	*American Journal of International Law*
ASQ	*Arab Studies Quarterly*
BJMES	*British Journal of Middle Eastern Studies*
BSOAS	*Bulletin of the School of Oriental and African Studies*
CSM	*Christian Science Monitor*
DI	*Der Islam*
DS	*Daily Star* (Beirut)
FA	*Foreign Affairs*
FCO	Foreign and Colonial Office, The Public Record Office, London
FO	Foreign Office, The Public Record Office, London
FT	*Financial Times*
IHT	*International Herald Tribune*
IJMES	*International Journal of Middle East Studies*
IO	India Office, The British Library, London
JP	*Journal of Politics*
LAT	*Los Angeles Times*
MA	*Monde Arabe*
MEF	*Middle East Forum*
MEI	*Middle East Insight*
MEINT	*Middle East International*
MEJ	*Middle East Journal*
MERIP	*Middle East Research and Information Project*
MES	*Middle Eastern Studies*
MW	*Moslem (Muslim) World*

Abbreviations

NYRB	*New York Review of Books*
NYT	*New York Times*
PRISM	*Project for the Research of Islamist Movements* (Herzliya)
TWQ	*Third World Quarterly*
WP	*Washington Post*
WSJ	*Wall Street Journal*

Notes

◈

Prologue
A Shi'i-Led Reformation

1. A'yatullah al-'Uzma al-Sayyid al-Sistani, "Hawla mashru' kitabat al-dustur al-'iraqi," 25 Rabi' al-Thani 1424; "Hawla qanun idarat al-'iraq li al-fatra al-intiqaliyya," 16 Muharram 1425; "Istifta' hawla asalib quwwat al-ihtilal fi baghdad wa-'adad min al-muhafazat," 16 Safar 1425; "Hawla tashkil al-hukuma al-'iraqiyya al-jadida," 14 Rabi' al-Thani 1425; "Hawla qanun idarat al-dawla al-'iraqiyya li al-marhala al-intiqaliyya," 17 Rabi' al-Thani 1425; "Istifta' jam' min al-mu'minin hawl al-intikhabat, 26 Sha'ban 1425, http://sistani.org/bayanat.

2. Yitzhak Nakash, *The Shi'is of Iraq*, 2d ed. (Princeton, 2003), 50–51.

3. 'Izz al-Din Salim, *Abhath fi shu'un al-nahdah* (Beirut, 1990), 162–63; Anon., "al-Shi'a 'ala abwab al-qarn al-hadi wa al-'ishrin," *al-Mawsim* 32 (1997): 5–15; Muhammad Sa'id al-Turayhi, *Dawlat al-najaf* (Oud-beijerland, 2004), 29–41, 47–48, 59–65, 89–92; news interview with Muhammad Husayn 'Ali al-Saghir, "Asatin al-marja'iyya al-'ulya: Shi'at 'arab wa-Shi'at 'ajam," *al-Mushahid al-Siyasi* 432 (20–26 June 2004): 12; Azadeh Moaveni, "Fall of Hussein Could Lead to a Shift in Center, Focus of Shiite Muslims," *LAT*, 17 April 2003; Anthony Shadid, "In Revival of Najaf, Lessons for a New Iraq," *WP*, 10 December 2003; Hamza Hendawi, "Shiite Leadership Clash in Iran, Iraq," Associated Press, 15 July 2004.

4. Muhammad Baqir al-Sadr, *al-Islam yaqud al-hayat* (Qum, 2000), 21; Salim al-Hasani, *al-Ma'alim al-jadida li al-marja'iyya al-Shi'iyya: dirasa wa-hiwar ma'a a'yatullah al-sayyid muhammad husayn fadlallah*, 2d ed. (Beirut, 1993), esp. 37–54, 57–74, 77–157, 169–75; Muhammad Husayn Fadlallah et al., *Ara' fi al-*

marja'iyya al-Shi'iyya (Beirut, 1994), 113–14, 119–20, 125–30; news interview with Muhammad Husayn Fadlallah, "Ma zilna ummat al-ashkhas, la al-mu'assasat," *al-Shira'* 1075 (17 March 2003): 15.

Chapter 1
The Burden of the Past

1. Fa'iq Hamdi Tahbub, *Ta'rikh al-bahrayn al-siyasi, 1783–1870* (Kuwait, 1983), 33–48.

2. J. G. Lorimer, *Gazetteer of the Persian Gulf, 'Oman and Central Arabia*, 5 pts. in 2 vols. (Calcutta, 1908–15), 1A:836–41; J. B. Kelly, *Britain and the Persian Gulf, 1795–1880* (Oxford, 1968), 26–27; Tahbub, *Ta'rikh al-bahrayn*, 33–52, 67, 73.

3. *The Encyclopaedia of Islam*, new ed., s.vv. "al-Ḳaṭif" and "al-Ḥasa;" Werner Ende, "The *Nakhawila*: A Shiite Community in Medina, Past and Present," *DI* 37 (1997): 266.

4. 'Ali Aba Husayn, "Dirasa fi ta'rikh al-'utub," *al-Wathiqa* 1 (July 1982): 83; 'Abdallah ibn Khalid Al Khalifa and 'Ali Aba Husayn, "Min ta'rikh al-'utub fi al-qarn al-thamin 'ashar," *al-Wathiqa* 2 (January 1984): 20–25; Khalid Khalifa al-Khalifa, "Tijarat al-bahrayn mundhu fath al-'utub wa-hatta zuhur al-naft," *al-Wathiqa* 4 (July 1985): 32–39. Cf. "The Utoob in the Eighteenth Century," and "Bahraini Trade from the 'Utub Conquest until the Appearance of Oil," in *Bahrain through the Ages: The History*, ed. Shaikh Abdullah bin Khalid al-Khalifa and Michael Rice (London, 1993), 302–13, and 339–43. See also Muhammad 'Abd al-Qadir al-Jasim and Sawsan 'Ali al-Sha'ir, *al-Bahrayn: qissat al-sira' al-siyasi, 1904–1956* (n.p., 2000), 9, 12, 16–18, 21.

5. The interview was reproduced in Khayr al-Din al-Zirikli, *Shibh al-jazira fi 'ahd al-malik 'abd al-'aziz*, 4 vols. (Beirut, 1970), 1:209–10.

6. Qadri Qal'aji, *Maw'id ma'a al-shaja'a: qabas min hayat 'abd al-'aziz al su'ud* (Kuwait, 1971), 14, 146, 167–69, 172, 176–77, 249–58, 277; 'Umar Abu Zilam et al., *'Abd al-'aziz al su'ud: al-'abqariyya fi al-tahrir wa al-tawhid wa al-tahdir* (Kuwait, 1984), 25, 171, 189–91, 215, 401, 404; Ahmad 'Abd al-Ghafur 'Attar, *Saqr al-jazira*, 2 pts. (Cairo, 1946), 1:249–61; Hasan Sulayman Mahmud and Sayyid Muhammad Ibrahim, *Ta'rikh al-mamlaka al-'arabiyya al-su'udiyya*, 4th ed. (Cairo, 1958), 76–77; Muhammad Ibrahim, *Ta'rikh al-mamlaka al-'arabiyya al-su'udiyya* (Riyadh, 1973), 191; 'Abdallah Salih 'Uthayman, *Ta'rikh al-mamlaka al-'arabiyya al-su'udiyya*, 2 vols. (n.p., 1984–95), 2:137; Ibrahim Sulayman al-Jabhan, *Ma yajib an ya'rifuhu al-muslim min haqa'iq 'an al-nasraniyya wa al-tabshir* (n.p., n.d.), 38–39. See also Madawi al-Rasheed, "Political Legitimacy and the Production of History: The Case of Saudi Arabia," in *New Frontiers in Middle East Security*, ed. Lenore Martin (New York, 1999), 33–35; Anon., "The Legacy of King Abdul Aziz," *Saudi Arabia* 16 (Fall 1999): 3–4.

7. Rabitat 'Umum al-Shi'a fi al-Su'udiyya, "al-Shi'a fi al-mamlaka al-'arabiyya al-su'udiyya: al-jughrafiyya wa al-sukkan," 6 September 1989, 1–2, 5; and "Ta'

rikh al-Shiʻa: al-tahawwulat al-raʼisiyya," 6 September 1989, 1–3; Hamza al-Hasan, *al-Shiʻa fi al-mamlaka al-ʻarabiyya al-suʻudiyya*, 2 vols. (Beirut, 1993), 1:26–32; Muhammad Saʻid al-Muslim, *al-Qatif: waha ʻala difaf al-khalij* (Riyadh, 1991), 95–98. See also Lorimer, *Gazetteer*, 2A:644–45, 2B:1536; Political Agent in Bahrain to Political Resident in the Persian Gulf, 5 October 1953, FO 371/104263/10110/2; Muhammad Ghanim al-Rumayhi, *Qadaya al-taghyir al-siyasi wa al-ijtimaʻi fi al-bahrayn, 1920–1970* (Kuwait, 1976), 49; Clive Holes, "Community, Dialect, and Urbanization in the Arabic-Speaking Middle East," *BSOAS* 55 (1995): 272–73.

8. Yusuf al-Bahrani, *al-Kashkul*, 3 vols. (Beirut, 1985), 1:99; ʻAli ibn al-Shaykh Hasan al-Biladi al-Bahrani, *Anwar al-badrayn fi tarajim ʻulamaʼ al-qatif wa al-ahsaʼ wa al-bahrayn* (Qum, 1986), 19, 27, 39; Hisham Muhammad al-Shakhs, *Aʻlam hajar min al-madiyyin wa al-muʻasirin*, 2 vols. (Beirut, 1990–98), 1:21–22, 2:48–52, 127; Muhammad ʻIsa Al Makabis, *Mawsuʻat shuʻaraʼ al-bahrayn, 1208–1966*, 4 pts. in 2 vols. (Qum, 1998), 1,1:20; Mahdi Abdalla Al-Tajir, *Language and Linguistic Origins in Bahrain: The Baharnah Dialect of Arabic* (London, 1982), 2, 7–8, 33–34; Hasan, *al-Shiʻa*, 1:15–19; Muhammad Saʻid al-Muslim, *Sahil al-dhahab al-aswad: dirasa taʼrikhiyya insaniyya li-mintaqat al-khalij al-ʻarabi* (Beirut, 1970), 93–99; idem, *al-Qatif*, 202; Muhsin al-Amin, *Aʻyan al-Shiʻa*, 56 vols. (Beirut, 1960), 1:32, 225; Muhammad Husayn al-Muzaffar, *Taʼrikh al-Shiʻa* (Qum, 1970), 111, 261–63. Cf. ʻAli Habiba, "Min qadaya al-taʼrikh fi al-bahrayn," *al-Wathiqa* 3 (1984): 101–2.

9. *The Encyclopaedia of Islam*, new ed., s.v. "Ḳarmaṭi"; Saʻid al-Shihabi, *al-Bahrayn, 1920–1971: qiraʼa fi al-wathaʼiq al-baritaniyya* (Beirut, 1996), 7; Muhammad ibn ʻAbdallah al-Ahsaʼi, *Tuhfat al-mustafid bi-taʼrikh al-ahsaʼ fi al-qadim wa al-jadid*, 2 pts. (Riyadh, 1960), 1:viii, 250–54; Biladi, *Anwar al-badrayn*, 277; Juan Cole, *Sacred Space and Holy War: The Politics, Culture, and History of Shiʻite Islam* (London, 2002), 4, 32–33, 56.

10. Rabitat ʻUmum al-Shiʻa fi al-Suʻudiyya, *al-Shiʻa fi al-suʻudiyya: al-waqiʻ al-saʻb wa al-tatalluʻat al-mashruʻa* (London, 1991), 28; Hasan, *al-Shiʻa*, 1:27, 75.

11. Hasan, *al-Shiʻa*, 1:29, 80–81, 108, 2:16; Muslim, *Sahil al-dhahab*, 99–101; Charles Belgrave, *Personal Column* (London, 1960), 56, 191; R. B. Serjent, "Fisher-Folk and Fish-Traps in al-Bahrain," *BSOAS* 31 (1968): 489, 506–7; Fuad Khuri, *Tribe and State in Bahrain: The Transformation of Social and Political Authority in an Arab State* (Chicago, 1980), 105, 112–13.

12. Rabitat ʻUmum al-Shiʻa fi al-Suʻudiyya, "Taʼrikh al-Shiʻa: al-tahawwulat al-raʼisiyya," 1; *The Encyclopaedia of Islam*, new ed., s.v. "Ḳatif."

13. Fuʼad al-Ahmad, *al-Shaykh hasan ʻali al badr al-qatifi* (Beirut, 1991), 97–101.

14. Tajir, *Language*, 8.

15. Khuri, *Tribe and State*, 28–29.

16. Anon., "al-Bahrayn: al-masar al-iqlimi wa-mustaqbal al-haraka al-islamiyya," *al-Thawra al-Islamiyya* 102 (September 1988): 27; Bahrain Freedom Movement, 26 August 1996, 25 December 1996, 19 January 1997, 10 February

1997, 3 May 1997, 19 June 1997, and 20 July 1997, http://vob.org; Shihabi, *al-Bahrayn*, 9. See also Yusuf al-Bahrani, *Lu'lu'at al-bahrayn fi al-ijazat wa-tarajim rijal al-hadith* (Najaf, 1966), 442; Yusuf al-Falaki, *Qadiyyat al-bahrayn bayn al-madi wa al-hadir* (n.p., n.d.), 10–16; Muhammad Ghanim al-Rumayhi, *al-Bahrayn: mushkilat al-taghyir al-siyasi wa al-ijtima'i* (Beirut, 1995), 287.

17. Nasir-i Khusru, *Safarnama-yi abu mu'in hamid al-din nasir-i bin khusru*, ed. Muhammad Dabir Siyaki (Tehran, 1956), 109–10; *The Encyclopaedia of Islam*, new ed., s.v. "Ḳarmaṭi"; William Palgrave, *A Personal Narrative of a Year's Journey through Central and Eastern Arabia, 1862–1863* (London, 1869), 368; S. M. Zwemer, *Arabia: The Cradle of Islam* (New York, 1900), 115–16; John Philby, *The Heart of Arabia: A Record of Travel and Exploration*, 2 vols. (London, 1922), 1:7; Habiba, "Min qadaya al-ta'rikh," esp. 107–10.

18. Hasan, *al-Shi'a*, 1:106–11, 124–30, 153–54. Cf. 'Uthman ibn Bishr, *'Unwan al-majd fi ta'rikh najd*, 2 pts. (Beirut, 1967), 1:99–100, 2:277–79; Husayn ibn Ghannam, *Ta'rikh najd* (Cairo, 1961), 179, 182–87, 192–95.

19. Muslim, *Waha*, 260–63; Hasan, *al-Shi'a*, 1:351–52, 2:9–16, 27; Rabitat 'Umum al-Shi'a fi al-Su'udiyya, *al-Shi'a fi al-su'udiyya*, 39; Hasan al-Saffar, *al-Shaykh 'ali al-biladi al-qudayhi* (Beirut, 1990), 48–51; Anon., "Madha fa'ala al su'ud fi al-ahsa' wa al-qatif," *al-Thawra al-Islamiyya* 102 (September 1988): 18–22. See also Guido Steinberg, "The Shiites in the Eastern Province of Saudi Arabia (al-Ahsa'), 1913–1953," in *The Twelver Shia in Modern Times: Religious Culture and Political History*, ed. Rainer Brunner and Werner Ende (Leiden, 2001), 243–45; Fahd al-Qahtani, *al-Islam wa al-wathniyya al-su'udiyya* (London, 1985), 31–35; Fouad Ajami, *The Dream Palace of the Arabs: A Generation's Odyssey* (New York, 1998), 153–54.

20. Yitzhak Nakash, *The Shi'is of Iraq*, 2d ed. (Princeton, 2003), 14–15, 25–48; Report on Arabia by Nakib Zade Talib Bey, 3 August 1904, Enclosure in No. 27, FO 416/20; Gökhan Çetinsaya, "The Ottoman Administration of Iraq, 1890–1908" (Ph.D. diss., University of Manchester, 1994), 222–44, 275–80, 327; Thomas Eich, "Abu al-Huda, the Rifa'iya, and Shiism in Hamidian Iraq," *DI* 80 (2003): 143, 148, 151.

21. Elie Kedourie, *England and the Middle East: The Destruction of the Ottoman Empire, 1914–1921* (London, 1956), 159–61, 203; idem, *The Chatham House Version and Other Middle Eastern Studies* (London, 1970), 239, 241–42, 255, 276; Paul Johnson, *Journey into Chaos* (London, 1958), 20–21; Muhammad Mahdi al-Basir, *Ta'rikh al-qadiyya al-'iraqiyya*, 2d ed., 2 pts. (London, 1990), 1:44–45; Salah al-Din al-Sabbagh, *Fursan al-'uruba fi al-'iraq: mudhakkirat al-shahid al-'aqid al-rukn salah al-din al-sabbagh* (n.p., 1956), 15; Lutfi Ja'far Faraj, *'Abd al-muhsin al-sa'dun wa-dawruhu fi ta'rikh al-'iraq al-siyasi al-mu'asir* (Baghdad, 1978), 15, 29–31, 45–47; 'Abd al-Razzaq Ahmad al-Nasiri, *Nuri al-sa'id wa-dawruhu fi al-siyasa al-'iraqiyya hatta 'am 1932* (Baghdad, 1987), 15–17, 21, 28, 31; 'Aqil al-Nasiri, *al-Jaysh wa al-sulta fi al-'iraq al-maliki, 1921–1958* (Damascus, 2000), 43, 55. A list of the ex-Ottoman officers may be found

in Ahmad al-Zaydi, *al-Bina' al-ma'nawi li al-quwwat al-musallaha al-'iraqiyya* (Beirut, 1990), 433–43.

22. Kamal Salibi, *A House of Many Mansions: The History of Lebanon Reconsidered* (Berkeley, 1988), 87, 90–91, 119, 137; idem, *The Modern History of Lebanon* (London, 1965), xvi–xvii; Elizabeth Picard, *Lebanon, a Shattered Country: Myths and Realities of the Wars in Lebanon*, trans. Franklin Philip (New York, 1996), 13–15.

23. Muhammad ibn al-Hasan al-Hurr al-'Amili, *Amal al-a'mal*, 2 vols. (Baghdad, 1964), 1:13; Muhsin al-Amin, *Khitat jabal 'amil* (Beirut, 1961), 35–37, 46, 65–67; idem, *A'yan al-Shi'a*, 1:30; Ahmad Rida, "al-Matawila aw al-Shi'a fi jabal 'amil," *al-'Irfan* 2 (1910): 239–40; Muhammad Kurd 'Ali, *Kitab khitat al-sha'm*, 6 pts. in 3 vols. (Damascus, 1925–28), 3:6, 252; Muhammad Taqi al-Faqih, *Jabal 'amil fi al-ta'rikh* (Beirut, 1986), 33–43; 'Ali Muruwwa, *al-Tashayyu' bayna jabal 'amil wa-iran* (London, 1987), 12–13; Muhammad Kazim Makki, *Muntalaq al-haya al-thaqafiyya fi jabal 'amil* (Beirut, 1991), 61; 'Ali Ibrahim Darwish, *Jabal 'amil, 1516–1697: al-haya al-siyasiyya wa al-thaqafiyya* (Beirut, 1993), 25; Hashim 'Uthman, *Ta'rikh al-Shi'a fi sahil bilad al-sha'm al-shimali* (Beirut, 1994), 25; Nawal Fayyad, *Safahat min ta'rikh jabal 'amil fi al-'ahdayn al-'uthmani wa al-faransi* (Beirut, 1998), 18.

24. Amin, *Khitat jabal 'amil*, 67–71; Muzaffar, *Ta'rikh al-Shi'a*, 163–68; Muruwwa, *al-Tashayyu'*, 14, 16; 'Uthman, *Ta'rikh al-Shi'a*, 47; Salibi, *A House of Many Mansions*, 118.

25. 'Uthman, *Ta'rikh al-Shi'a*, 108–13; Salih Ibn Yahya, *Ta'rikh bayrut*, ed. Fransis Hurs and Kamal Salibi (Beirut, 1969), 27–28, 195; Tanus al-Shidyaq, *Kitab akhbar al-a'yan fi jabal lubnan*, 2 vols. (Beirut, 1970), 2:208, 301; Muhammad 'Ali Makki, *Lubnan, 635–1516: min al-fath al-'arabi ila al-fath al-'uthmani* (Beirut, 1977), 213–32, 263–66; Muhammad Kurani, *al-Judhur al-ta'rikhiyya li al-muqawama al-islamiyya fi jabal 'amil* (Beirut, 1993), 55–60, 63; Muhammad Zu'aytar, *al-Maruniyya fi lubnan: qadiman wa-hadithan* (Beirut, 1994), 55–57; Abdul-Rahim Abu Husayn, "The Shiites in Lebanon and the Ottomans in the Sixteenth and Seventeenth Centuries," in *Convegno sul tema la Shi'a nell'impero ottomano*, Accademia Nazionale Dei Lincei (Rome, 1993), 109–11; Salibi, *A House of Many Mansions*, 14, 103–4.

26. Istifanus al-Duwayhi, *Ta'rikh al-azmina, 1095–1699* (Beirut, 1951), 308, 329; Philip al-Khazin, *Kisrawan 'ibr al-ta'rikh* (Harisa, 1970), 18–19, 31–37, 42–46; Bulus Qara'li, *Fakhr al-din al-ma'ni al-thani amir lubnan: idaratuhu wa-siyasatuhu, 1590–1635* (Bayt Shabab, 1937), 36–41; Yusuf Abi Sa'ab, *Ta'rikh al-kufur: kisrawan wa-usaruha* (Beirut, 1985), 73, 76–81, 88; Bulus Nujaym, *al-Qadiyya al-lubnaniyya* (Beirut, 1995), 84, 96; Anis Sayigh, *Lubnan al-ta'ifi* (Beirut, 1955), 86–87, 91; Sulayman Zahir, *Jabal 'amil fi al-harb al-kawniyya* (Beirut, 1986), 22–23; Zu'aytar, *al-Maruniyya*, 57–58, 95, 138–39; Amin, *Khitat jabal 'amil*, 72; Makki, *Muntalaq al-haya al-thaqafiyya*, 99–100; Darwish, *Jabal 'amil*, 128; Salibi, *A House of Many Mansions*, 105–6, 126; Richard Van Leeuwen,

Notables and Clergy in Mount Lebanon: The Khazins Sheikhs and the Maronite Church, 1736–1840 (Leiden, 1994), 82–83, 85, 106, 149–50, 178–79; Leila Fawaz, *An Occasion for War: Civil Conflict in Lebanon and Damascus in 1860* (London, 1994), 13, 15.

27. Rida, "al-Matawila," 237, 241–42; Amin, *Khitat jabal 'amil*, 52; idem, *A'yan al-Shi'a*, 1:16; Faqih, *Jabal 'amil*, 31–32; 'Ali al-Zayn, *Li al-bahth 'an ta' rikhina fi lubnan* (Sidon, 1973), 480–81; Darwish, *Jabal 'amil*, 27; al-Majlis al-Thaqafi li-Lubnan al-Janubi, *Safahat min ta'rikh jabal 'amil* (Beirut, 1979), 96–97; Makki, *Muntalaq al-haya al-thaqafiyya*, 65; Mundhir Jabir, "al-Shi'a fi jabal 'amil bayn al-mabda'iyya wa al-hifaz 'ala al-dhat," *al-Muntalaq* 105 (1993): 64, 66; Majed Halawi, *A Lebanon Defied: Musa al-Sadr and the Shi'a Community* (Boulder, Colo., 1992), 33. See also Ahmad ibn Muhammad al-Khalidi al-Safadi, *Lubnan fi 'ahd al-amir fakhr al-din al-ma'ni al-thani*, ed. Asad Rustum and Fuad al-Bustani (Beirut, 1969), 16, 66, 69–70, 76, 92, 131, 137, 150.

28. Zayn, *Li al-bahth 'an ta'rikhina*, 485–603; Muhammad Jabir Al Safa', *Ta'rikh jabal 'amil*, 2d ed. (Beirut, n.d.), 104, 117–38; Haydar Rida al-Rukayni, *Jabal 'amil fi qarn, 1163–1247* (Beirut, 1998), 11, 52–53, 99–100; Fouad Ajami, *The Vanished Imam: Musa al-Sadr and the Shia of Lebanon* (Ithaca, 1986), 52–54; Halawi, *A Lebanon Defied*, 20–21, 34–35.

29. Abdul-Rahim Abu Husayn, *Provincial Leaderships in Syria, 1575–1650* (Beirut, 1985), esp. 2, 130, 134, 144, 148–52; idem, *The View from Istanbul: Lebanon and the Druze Emirate in the Ottoman Chancery Documents, 1546–1711* (London, 2004), 127; idem, "The Shiites in Lebanon," 114–15; Salibi, *A House of Many Mansions*, 144–45, 149; *The Encyclopaedia of Islam*, new ed., s.v. "Harfush"; Ajami, *The Vanished Imam*, 127–28; Halawi, *A Lebanon Defied*, 35–36, 90, 150–51; Hani Fahs, *al-Shi'a wa al-dawla fi lubnan: malamih fi al-ru'ya wa al-dhakira* (Beirut, 1996), 92–93; Darwish, *Jabal 'amil*, 107–16, 140, 150–51, 229, 231.

30. Relations with Ibn Sa'ud, 12 January 1917, FO 371/3044/35392; Shakespear to Sir Percy Cox, Enclosure 2 in No. 458, 15 May 1913, FO 424/238; Jacob Goldberg, "The 1913 Saudi Occupation of Hasa Reconsidered," *MES* 18 (1982): 22–25.

31. Shakespear to Political Resident in the Persian Gulf, 4 January 1915, No. S-13, FO 371/2473/30472; Great Britain, Office of the Civil Commissioner, *The Arab of Mesopotamia* (Basra, 1917), 45–47; Political Resident in the Persian Gulf to Ibn Sa'ud, 14 June 1923, No. 173 of 1923, IO R/15/2/74; Jacob Goldberg, *The Foreign Policy of Saudi Arabia: The Formative Years, 1902–1918* (Cambridge, Mass., 1986), 124, 131, 145–47, 196–98; J. B. Kelly, *Eastern Arabian Frontiers* (New York, 1964), 112–13; John Philby, *Saudi Arabia* (London, 1955), 269–74.

32. Qal'aji, *Maw'id ma'a al-shaja'a*, 145–63, 169–71; Abu Zilam, *'Abd al-'aziz al su'ud*, 25, 51, 169, 419–20, 428, 437–39; Madiha Ahmad Darwish, *Ta'rikh al-dawla al-su'udiyya hatta al-rub' al-awwal min al-qarn al-'ishrin*, 2d ed. (Jidda, 1983), 84.

33. Hasan, *al-Shi'a*, 2:80–82, 101–4, 115–16; Anon., "al-Siyasa al-kharijiyya al-su'udiyya: bidayat al-nihaya," *al-Thawra al-Islamiyya* 45 (January 1984): 11. See also Muhammad Jalal Kishk, *al-Su'udiyyun wa al-hall al-islami: masdar al-shar'iyya li al-nizam al-su'udi*, 4th ed. (Cairo, 1984), 459–60; Translation of Treaty between Ibn Sa'ud and the Turks, 15 May 1914, FO 371/2769/236112.

34. Anon., "al-Za'im ahmad bin al-shaykh mahdi nasrallah," *al-Thawra al-Islamiyya* 104 (November 1988): 43–44; Rabitat 'Umum al-Shi'a fi al-Su'udiyya, *al-Shi'a fi al-su'udiyya*, 51–54; Hasan 'Ali Al Badr al-Qatifi, *Da'wat al-muwahhidin ila himayat al-din* (Najaf, 1911), 2–24; Ahmad, *al-Shaykh hasan 'ali al badr al-qatifi*, 112–14, 117; Hasan, *al-Shi'a*, 1:330, 333, 345, 2:106–9. See also Steinberg, "The Shiites in the Eastern Province," 245.

35. 'Ali al-Wardi, *Lamahat ijtima'iyya min ta'rikh al-'iraq al-hadith*, 6 vols. (Baghdad, 1969–78), 4:72–77; Hasan al-'Alawi, *Dawlat al-isti'ara al-qawmiyya: min faysal al-awwal ila saddam husayn* (London, 1993), 33–34; 'Ala' al-Lami, *Nusus mudadda: difa'an 'an al-'iraq, al-sha'b, al-watan wa al-huwiyya* (n.p., n.d.), 77; Nasiri, *al-Jaysh wa al-sulta*, 45–47, 50. See also Ibrahim al-Rawi, *Min al-thawra al-'arabiyya al-kubra ila al-'iraq al-hadith: dhikrayat* (Beirut, 1969), 19–22; Muhammad Ra'uf al-Shaykhli, *Marahil al-hayat fi al-fatra al-muzlima wa-ma ba'daha*, 2 vols. (Basra, 1972), 2:386–87, 409; Nasiri, *Nuri sa'id*, 38–56, 83–85; Kamal Mazhar Ahmad, *Safahat min ta'rikh al-'iraq al-mu'asir: dirasat tahliliyya* (Baghdad, 1987), 49–50, 75–77; Sabbagh, *Fursan al-'uruba*, 15; Kedourie, *The Chatham House Version*, 255.

36. A. J. Barker, *The Neglected War: Mesopotamia, 1914–1918* (London, 1967), 67–77; Russell Braddon, *The Siege* (London, 1969), 25–26; Arnold Wilson, *Loyalties: Mesopotamia, 1914–1917* (London, 1930), 22–23, 33–35.

37. Muhammad Rida al-Shabibi, "Yawm al-shu'ayba," *al-'Irfan* 6 (1921): 308–9; 'Abd al-Shahid al-Yasiri, *al-Butula fi thawrat al-'ishrin* (Najaf, 1966), 68–78; Hasan al-Asadi, *Thawrat al-najaf 'ala al-ingliz aw al-sharara al-ula li-thawrat al-'ishrin* (Baghdad, 1975), 91–92; Hasan Shubbar, "Dawr 'ulama' al-din fi al-jihad," *al-Jihad* 365 (7 November 1988): 7; Katib al-Turayhi, "Waqi'at al-shu'ayba didd al-ihtilal al-inglizi," *al-Mawsim* 19 (1994): 341–44; Anon., *al-Haraka al-islamiyya fi al-'iraq* (Beirut, 1985), 38–40; Salim al-Hasani, *Dawr 'ulama' al-Shi'a fi muwajahat al-isti'mar, 1900–1920* (Beirut, 1995), 79, 84, 101; 'Ali al-Ahmad, "al-Najaf wa-muqawamat al-istibdad al-dakhili wa al-istikbar al-khariji," *al-Muntalaq* 77 (1991): 103, 105; Khalid Hamud al-Sa'dun, *al-Awda' al-qabaliyya fi al-basra, 1908–1918* (Kuwait, 1988), 277–78; Pierre-Jean Luizard, "Shaykh Muhammad al-Khalisi (1890–1963) and His Political Role in Iraq and Iran in the 1910s and 1920s," in Brunner and Ende, *The Twelver Shia*, 226–27.

38. Fariq al-Muzhir Al Fir'awn, *al-Haqa'iq al-nasi'a fi al-thawra al-'iraqiyya sanat 1920 wa-nata'ijuha* (Baghdad, 1952), 36–37; 'Ali al-Sharqi, *al-Ahlam* (Baghdad, 1963), 97–99; 'Ali al-Khaqani, *Shu'ara' al-ghari aw al-najafiyyat*, 2d ed., 12 vols. (Qum, 1988), 9:149–50; Wardi, *Lamahat*, 4:129–30, 134, 146; Ra'uf al-Wa'iz, *al-Ittijahat al-wataniyya fi al-Shi'r al-'iraqi al-hadith, 1914–1941*

(Baghdad, 1974), 28–32; Hasan al-'Alawi, *al-Shi'a wa al-dawla al-qawmiyya fi al-'iraq* (Paris, 1989), 64; Anon., "Muhammad Sa'id al-Habubi," *al-Tayar al-Jadid* 24–25 (17 December 1984): 25; Ahmed al-Habbubi, "Itinéraire d'un nationaliste arabe," *MA* 163 (January–March 1999): 112, 116; Sa'id al-Samarra'i, *al-Ta'ifiyya fi al-'iraq: al-waqi' wa al-hall* (London, 1993), 111. See also 'Ali al-Bazirgan, *al-Waqa'i' al-haqiqiyya fi al-thawra al-'iraqiyya*, 2d ed. (Baghdad, 1991), 62–63, 73–74.

39. George Antonius, *The Arab Awakening: The Story of the Arab National Movement* (New York, 1946), 95, 106; Muhammad Jamil Bayhum, *Qawafil al-'uruba wa-mawakibuha khilal al-'usur*, 2 pts. (Beirut, 1948), 2:21; idem, *al-'Arab wa al-turk fi al-sira' bayn al-sharq wa al-gharb* (Beirut, 1957), esp. 153–58; Zeine N. Zeine, *Arab-Turkish Relations and the Emergence of Arab Nationalism* (Beirut, 1958), 75, 80, 124; Tawfiq Biru, *al-'Arab wa al-turk fi al-'ahd al-dusturi al-'uthmani, 1908–1914* (Damascus, 1991), esp. 479–84, 499–500. See also Adeed Dawisha, *Arab Nationalism in the Twentieth Century: From Triumph to Despair* (Princeton, 2003), 29–30, 33; C. Ernest Dawn, "The Origins of Arab National-ism," in *The Origins of Arab Nationalism*, ed. Rashid Khalidi et al. (New York, 1991), 16, 19, 23; Philip Khoury, *Urban Notables and Arab Nationalism: The Politics of Damascus, 1860–1920* (Cambridge, 1983), 53–74; Şükrü Hanioğlu, *The Young Turks in Opposition* (Oxford, 1995), 211, 216; Hasan Kayali, *Arabs and Young Turks: Ottomanism, Arabism, and Islamism in the Ottoman Empire, 1908–1918* (Berkeley, 1997), 12–13, 84, 114–15, 208–10, 212.

40. Muhammad Jabir Al Safa', "al-Haraka al-'arabiyya fi jabal 'amil (I)," and "Safahat min ta'rikh jabal 'amil (II)," *al-'Irfan* 28 (1939): 777–78, 900–901.

41. Jabir, *Ta'rikh jabal 'amil*, esp. 206–16. See also 'Adil al-Sulh, *Sutur min al-risala: ta'rikh haraka istiqlaliyya qamat fi al-mashriq al-'arabi sanat 1877* (Beirut, 1966), 71, 94–100, 143–48; Sabrina Mervin, *Un réformisme chiite: Ulémas et lettrés du Gabal 'Amil de la fin de l'empire ottoman à l'indépendance du Liban* (Paris, 2000), 331–34.

42. Amin, *A'yan al-Shi'a*, 43:300; 'Ali Muruwwa, *Ta'rikh juba': madiha wa-hadiruha* (Beirut, 1967), 364–70; Kurani, *al-Judhur al-ta'rikhiyya*, 117–18; 'Ali 'Abd al-Mun'im Shu'ayb, *Matalib jabal 'amil: al-wahda wa al-musawa fi lubnan al-kabir, 1900–1936* (Beirut, 1987), 49; Waddah Sharara, *al-Umma al-qaliqa: al-'amiliyyun wa al-'asabiyya al-'amiliyya 'ala 'atabat al-dawla al-lubnaniyya* (Beirut, 1996), 117–18.

43. Zeine, *Arab-Turkish Relations*, esp. 73; Hasan Muhammad Sa'd, *Jabal 'amil bayn al-atrak wa al-faransiyyin, 1914–1920* (Beirut, 1980), 27–28; Ghassan Ahmad 'Isa, "al-Haraka al-'arabiyya fi jabal 'amil, 1865–1920," *Amal* 543 (17 June 1988): 52, and 544 (24 June 1988): 60.

44. 'Ali al-Zayn, "Athar al-'an'anat fi ta'rikhina," *al-'Irfan* 58 (1970): 31–41; idem, *Li al-bahth 'an ta'rikhina*, 23–35; Mustafa Muhammad Bazi, *Jabal 'amil fi muhitihi al-'arabi, 1864–1948* (Beirut, 1993), 31–34; Fahs, *al-Shi'a wa al-dawla fi lubnan*, 27–28.

Chapter 2
Containment Politics in the Persian Gulf

1. Anon., "al-Kuwayt taghli..wa-lakin didd al sabah," *al-Jazira al-'Arabiyya* 3 (March 1991): 13; Anon., "al-Ikhtilasat min sanduq al-ajyal tumazziq ramziyyat al-usra al-hakima fi al-kuwayt," *al-Jazira al-'Arabiyya* 31 (August 1993): 36; Fallah al-Mudayris, "al-Shi'a fi al-mujtama' al-kuwayti," *al-Siyasa al-Dawliyya* 123 (1996): 34, 46; Rabitat 'Umum al-Shi'a fi al-Su'udiyya, *al-Shi'a fi al-su'udiyya: al-waqi' al-sa'b wa al-tatallu'at al-mashru'a* (London, 1991), 96; 'Abdallah Muhammad al-Gharib, *Wa-ja'a' dawr al-majus: al-ab'ad al-ta'rikhiyya wa al-'aqa'idiyya wa al-siyasiyya li al-thawra al-iraniyya* (Cairo, 1983), 329–35; Gregory Gause, *Oil Monarchies* (New York, 1994), 69–70, 101; Fouad Ajami, *The Dream Palace of the Arabs: A Generation's Odyssey* (New York, 1998), 156, 186–87; Graham Fuller and Rend Rahim Francke, *The Arab Shi'a: The Forgotten Muslims* (New York, 1999), esp. 155, 169–71.

2. Extracts from an untitled poem, *al-Thawra al-Islamiyya* 88 (July 1987): 1.

3. 'Abdallah al-Hasan, "Sira' al-huwiyyat wa al-aqalim fi al-mamlaka: al-sira' al-najdi al-hijazi," and Anon., "Watan yasir ila hatfihi: taqsim al-mamlaka..al-hajis al-akbar," *al-Jazira al-'Arabiyya* 16 (May 1992): 12–18, 25; Muhammad al-Husayn, "al-'Asabiyyat al-mahaliyya tatanama wa al-huwiyya al-wataniyya lam tulad ba'd: al-mamlaka muhaddada, al-musharaka al-siyasiyya aw al-taqsim," *al-Jazira al-'Arabiyya* 18 (July 1992): 24–29; 'Abd al-Amir Musa, "Wahdat al-mamlaka..wa-haqq lana an nakhaf 'alayha," *al-Jazira al-'Arabiyya* 11 (December 1991): 17–18; Khalid al-Rashid, "Hal hunak huwiyya wataniyya su'udiyya?" *Qadaya al-Khalij*, March 2003, http://gulfissues.net. See also Summary of Jedda Dispatch No. 30, 30 June 1963, FO 371/168869/1015/25; Madawi al-Rasheed, "The Shi'a of Saudi Arabia: A Minority in Search of Cultural Authenticity," *BJMES* 25 (1998): 125–29; idem, *A History of Saudi Arabia* (Cambridge, 2002), 113; Fuller and Rahim Francke, *The Arab Shi'a*, 181–82.

4. Ibrahim Sulayman al-Jabhan, *Tabdid al-zalam wa-tanbih al-niyam*, 2d ed. (Riyad, 1979), 29–33, 67, 71, 79, 139, 140, 153, 159–62, 165, 175, 188, 384, 490, 496; Muhibb al-Din al-Khatib, *al-Khutut al-'arida li al-usus allati qama 'alayha din al-Shi'a al-imamiyya al-ithna 'ashariyya*, 10th ed. (Cairo, 1981), 28, 42; Ihsan Ilhi Zahir, *al-Shi'a wa al-sunna*, 2d ed. (Cairo, 1986), 8, 10, 13, 15, 47–49, 56, 59; idem, *al-Shi'a wa al-tashayyu': firaq wa-ta'rikh* (Lahor, 1984), 40–41; idem, *al-Shi'a wa-ahl al-bayt*, 5th ed. (Lahor, 1983), 20, 28–29, 34; Muhammad Mal Allah, *Mawqif al-Shi'a min ahl al-sunna* (n.p., n.d.), 81; Safar al-Hawali, *Wa'd kisinjr wa al-ahdaf al-amirikiyya fi al-khalij* (Dallas, 1991), 92; idem, "Mudhakkirat al-nasiha," reproduced in *al-Jazira al-'Arabiyya* 7 (August 1991): 18; Anon., "'Ala khatt ibn jibrin: al-'abikan yuhaddid bi-madhbaha li al-muwatinin al-Shi'a," *al-Jazira al-'Arabiyya* 14 (March 1992): 47; Hamza al-Hasan, *al-Shi'a fi al-mamlaka al-'arabiyya al-su'udiyya*, 2 vols. (Beirut, 1993), 2:354–69, 397–98.

5. J. B. Philby, *The Heart of Arabia: A Record of Travel and Exploration* (London, 1922), 294–95.

6. *The Encyclopaedia of Islam*, new ed., s.vv. "'Abd Allah b. Saba' " and "Shi'a."

7. Muhammad Rashid Rida, *al-Sunna wa al-Shi'a aw al-wahhabiyya wa al-rafida*, 2d ed., 2 pts. (Cairo, 1947), 1:4–12, 2:249–52; Ahmad Amin, *Fajr al-islam*, 5th ed. (Cairo, 1945), 269.

8. Jabhan, *Tabdid al-zalam*, 159, 418, 483, 497; Zahir, *al-Shi'a wa al-sunna*, 16–27; idem, *al-Shi'a wa al-tashayyu'*, 45–77, 146; idem, *al-Shi'a wa-ahl al-bayt*, 117, 124, 126; Gharib, *wa-Ja'a' dawr al-majus*, 56–58; http://d-sunnah.net/rafedha-origin.htm; http://fnoor.com/fn0497.htm. For Shi'i responses, see Murtada al-'Askari, *'Abdallah ibn saba' wa-asatir ukhra*, 2d ed. (Baghdad, 1968), esp. 13–16, 29–31, 37–38, 41–45, 57; Muhammad Husayn Kashif al-Ghita', *Asl al-Shi'a wa-usuluha*, 9th ed. (Beirut, 1960), esp. 18, 66, 77–78; Badr al-Din al-Kazimi ila Ibrahim al-Jabhan, "Munaqasha 'aqa'idiyya fi maqalatihi wa-nashratihi" (Kuwait, 1977), 35–36; Muhammad Husayn al-Muzaffar, *Ta'rikh al-Shi'a*, 2d ed. (Beirut, 1979), 19; Ibrahim Ishkanani, *al-Tashayyu': nash'atan wa-tatawwuran* (n.p., 1979), 146–47; Muhammad Jawad al-Shirri, *al-Shi'a fi qafas al-ittiham* (Detroit, 1985), 39–78; Isma'il al-Baghdadi, *Mata wujidat al-Shi'a?* (n.p., 1986), esp. 29–30, 67–75, 186–91; Anon., "Al su'ud wa al-nasab al-yahudi," *al-Thawra al-Islamiyya* 70 (January 1986): 74–76; Pan-Shia Association in Saudi Arabia, *Ahl al-Bayt* 2 (1989): 5. See also Werner Ende, *Arabische Nation und Islamische Geschichte* (Beirut, 1977), 199–210, 300.

9. Yusuf al-Hajiri, *al-Baqi': qissat tadmir al su'ud li al-'athar al-islamiyya fi al-hijaz* (Beirut, 1990), 15–18; Hasan, *al-Shi'a*, 2:226–29; Yann Richard, *Shi'ite Islam*, trans. Antonia Nevill (Cambridge, Mass., 1995), 120. On Kuwait, see Mudayris, "al-Shi'a," 32, 35–36, 41, 45; Jill Crystal, *Oil and Politics in the Gulf: Rulers and Merchants in Kuwait and Qatar* (Cambridge, 1990), 83, 101; idem, *Kuwait: The Transformation of an Oil State* (Boulder, Colo., 1992), 77; Fuller and Rahim Francke, *The Arab Shi'a*, 157, 161.

10. John Philby, *Saudi Arabia* (London, 1955), 268; B. D. Hakken, "Sunni-Shia Discord in Eastern Arabia," *MW* 23 (1933): 304; Madawi al-Rasheed and Louloua al-Rasheed, "The Politics of Encapsulation: Saudi Policy towards Tribal and Religious Opposition," *MES* 32 (1996): 110; Hasan, *al-Shi'a*, 2:144, 307; Fahd al-Qahtani, *Sira' al-ajniha fi al-'a'ila al-su'udiyya: dirasa fi al-nizam al-siyasi wa-ta'assus al-dawla* (London, 1988), 252.

11. Hasan, *al-Shi'a*, 2:236, 241–52; Hasan al-Saffar, *al-Shaykh 'ali al-biladi al-qudayhi* (Beirut, 1990), 52–53; F. S. Vidal, *The Oasis of al-Hasa* (n.p., 1955), 97; Christine Helms, *The Cohesion of Saudi Arabia: Evolution of Political Identity* (Baltimore, 1981), 154–55, 167–68, 170.

12. Anwar 'Abdallah, "Nushu' al-mu'assasa al-salafiyya (II)," *al-Jazira al-'Arabiyya* 27 (April 1993): 36–38; Hamza al-Hasan, "Marakiz al-quwwa al-siyasiyya wa al-ijtima'iyya fi al-mamlaka al-'arabiyya al-su'udiyya," *al-Jazira al-'Arabiyya* 9 (October 1991): 29; idem, *al-Shi'a*, 2:146–54, 163–64, 262–64; Rabitat

'Umum al-Shi'a fi al-Su'udiyya, *al-Shi'a*, 28–29; Hasan al-Saffar, "al-Nizam al-su'udi wa-qatl al-kafa'at," *al-Thawra al-Islamiyya* 57 (January 1985): 41; Tawfiq al-Shaykh, "al-Nasaq al-ta'rikhi li al-'alaqa bayn al-mujtama' wa al-sulta wa-ta'thiruhu 'ala al-muthaqqafin (II)," *al-Jazira al-'Arabiyya* 19 (August 1993): 15; Abu al-Hasan al-Khunayzi, *al-Munazarat* (Cairo, 1977), 22. See also Hafiz Wahba, *Arabian Days* (London, 1964), 131–37; Ayman al-Yassini, *Religion and State in the Kingdom of Saudi Arabia* (Boulder, Colo., 1985), 49–50, 55–56; Joseph Kostiner, "On Instruments and Their Designers: The Ikhwan of Najd and the Emergence of the Saudi State," *MES* 21 (1985): 315–17; Guido Steinberg, "The Shiites in the Eastern Province of Saudi Arabia (al-Ahsa'), 1913–1953," in *The Twelver Shia in Modern Times: Religious Culture and Political History*, ed. Rainer Brunner and Werner Ende (Leiden, 2001), 238, 248–51.

13. Annual Review of Internal Conditions and External Relations of Saudi Arabia during 1953, FO 371/110095/1011/1; From Bahrain to Foreign Office, 19 June 1956, FO 371/120754/1015/13; Norman Walpole et al., *Area Handbook for Saudi Arabia* (Washington, D.C., 1966), 265; Anon., "Madha fi al-mamlaka al-'arabiyya al-su'udiyya," *al-'Irfan* 44 (1956): 198; Hasan, *al-Shi'a*, 2:287, 290, 295–300, 324–25, 377; Rasheed, *A History of Saudi Arabia*, 97, 100; Robert Vitalis, "Aramco World: Business and Culture on the Arabian Oil Frontier," in *The Modern Worlds of Business and Industry: Cultures, Technology, Labor*, ed. Karen Merrill (Brepols, 1999), 10.

14. Anon., "al-Yamani li al-amirikaniyyin: shukran lakum 'ala 'isti'marina," *al-Thawra al-Islamiyya* 38 (June 1983): 15–20; Anon., "al-Naft: min al-mustafid?" *al-Thawra al-Islamiyya* 40 (August 1983): 7–9; Anon., "As'ar al-bitrul: wahm al-irtifa' wa-bu's al-tajmid," *al-Thawra al-Islamiyya* 56 (December 1984): 24–30; Anon., "Lusus al-naft," *al-Thawra al-Islamiyya* 71 (February 1986): 11–19; Anon., "al-Wilayat al-muttahida al-amirikiyya wa-aramco: haqiqa isti'mariyya," *al-Thawra al-Islamiyya* 72 (March 1986): 50–58; Anon., "al-Siyasa al-'umaliyya li-sharikat aramco," *al-Thawra al-Islamiyya* 74 (May 1986): 63–70; Anon., "al-Haraka al-'umaliyya fi al-jazira al-'arabiyya: qiyamuha wa-tataw-wuruha," *al-Thawra al-Islamiyya* 92 (November 1987): 54–56; Hasan, *al-Shi'a*, 2:287–89, 323–29; J. B. Kelly, *Arabia, the Gulf, and the West* (New York, 1980), 252–62; Rasheed, *A History of Saudi Arabia*, 96; Robert Vitalis, "The Closing of the Arabian Oil Frontier and the Future of Saudi-American Relations," *MERIP* 204 (1997): 17. On Kuwait, see Mudayris, "al-Shi'a," 30, 41.

15. Anon., "al-Hukm al-su'udi: istratijiyyat al-takfir wa-sulukiyyat al-irhab," *al-Thawra al-Islamiyya* 65 (September 1985): 7–9; Anon., "Hal al-zira'a fi taqaddum?" *al-Thawra al-Islamiyya* 48 (April 1984): 30–33; M. al-Dughaythir, "Mulahazat hawla al-zira'a wa al-intaj al-zira'i," *al-Thawra al-Islamiyya* 50 (June 1984): 24–27; Anon., "al-Zira'a," *al-Thawra al-Islamiyya* 59 (March 1985): 66; Hasan, *al-Shi'a*, 1:317–18, 322, 2:91, 306–14, 329–37; Muhammad Sa'id al-Muslim, *Waha 'ala difaf al-khalij: al-qatif*, 2d ed. (Riyadh, 1991), 29, 269–71, 319–22. See also King to Stewart, Internal Security in Saudi Arabia, 14 August 1969, FCO 8/1165/1; 'Abdallah Nasir al-Subay'i, *Iktishaf al-naft wa-atharuhu*

'ala al-haya al-iqtisadiyya fi al-mintaqa al-sharqiyya, 1933–1960, 2d ed. (Khobar, 1989), 258–63; Nasir al-Sa'id, *'Alam al-muluk* (Beirut, n.d.), 4; Sharif Elmusa, "Faust without the Devil? The Interplay of Technology and Culture in Saudi Arabia," *MEJ* 51 (1997): 356.

16. Rabitat 'Umum al-Shi'a fi al-Su'udiyya, *al-Shi'a*, 40–41, 112–15; Hasan, *al-Shi'a*, 2:319, 392–93, 396–98; Anon., "Ila mata yastamir al-nizam al-su'udi fi idtihad al-Shi'a?" *Risalat al-Haramayn* 36 (January 1993): 16; Anon., "al-Wajh al-haqiqi li-nizam al-fasl al-madhhabi," *Risalat al-Haramayn* 42 (July 1993): 25; Hasan al-Saffar, "Nurahhib bi al-ta'awun ma'a atraf al-mu'arada fi al-bilad," *al-Jazira al-'Arabiyya* 2 (March 1991): 45.

17. Rasheed, *A History of Saudi Arabia*, 144–48; Jacob Goldberg, "The Shi'i Minority in Saudi Arabia," in *Shi'ism and Social Protest*, ed. Juan Cole and Nikki Keddie (New Haven, 1986), 238–45; Amnesty International, "Saudi Arabia: Detention without Trial of Suspected Political Prisoners" (January 1990), 7.

18. 'Abd al-Rahman al-Shaykh et al., *Intifadat al-mintaqa al-sharqiyya, 1400h/1979* (n.p., 1981), 22–25, 34, 105–6, 108–9, 113–15, 119, 125, 128, 136, 153, 160–63, 227–28, 280, 288; Munazamat al-Thawra al-Islamiyya bi al-Jazira al-'Arabiyya al-Su'udiyya, *Intifadat al-muharram fi al-mintaqa al-sharqiyya* (n.p., n.d.), 22; Anon., "The Regimes of Hypocrisy," *Mekka Calling* 11 (November 1984): 6–7; Anon., "Makasib al-intifada," *al-Thawra al-Islamiyya* 90–91 (September–October 1987): 3; Anon., "Fi al-dhikra al-sanawiyya al-tasi'a li-intifadat muharram 'am 1400," *al-Thawra al-Islamiyya* 103 (October 1988): 8, 10; Anon., "Intifadat al-muharram wa al-asala al-islamiyya," *Risalat al-Haramayn* 22 (August 1991): 19; Hasan, *al-Shi'a*, 2:384.

19. Shaykh, *Intifadat al-mintaqa al-sharqiyya*, 16, 98–99, 101, 106–7, 111–12, 129–30, 137, 172–75; Munazamat al-Thawra al-Islamiyya bi al-Jazira al-'Arabiyya al-Su'udiyya, *Intifadat al-muharram*, 24; Anon., "al-Intifada tasugh al-sha'b min jadid," *al-Thawra al-Islamiyya* 78 (September 1986): 33; Hasan, *al-Shi'a*, 2:385–86.

20. Shaykh, *Intifadat al-mintaqa al-sharqiyya*, 19, 61–85, 94–98, 117, 120, 135, 199–210; Munazamat al-Thawra al-Islamiyya bi al-Jazira al-'Arabiyya al-Su'udiyya, *Intifadat al-muharram*, 14, 39; Anon., "al-Thawra al-islamiyya bi-khayr wa-fi kull makan," *al-Thawra al-Islamiyya* 59 (March 1985): 14–15; Anon., "al-Intifada wa al-khiyar al-jamahiri," *al-Thawra al-Islamiyya* 78 (September 1986): 1–6; Anon., "Intifadat al-muharram," 19–21; Hasan al-Saffar, *al-Husayn wa-masu'liyyat al-thawra* (Beirut, n.d.), esp. 7–8, 55–65.

21. Hasan, *al-Shi'a*, 2:389–91; Anon., "al-Shi'a wa al-'alam: hiwar ma'a al-shaykh hasan al-saffar," *al-Mawsim* 11 (1991): 1045–48.

22. Hawali, *Wa'd kisinjr*, 91–92; idem, "Mudhakkirat al-nasiha," 18; Nasir ibn Sulayman al-'Umar, "Waqi' al-rafida fi bilad al-tawhid" (May 1993), esp. 23–25. See also Hamza al-Hasan, "Mawqif al-tayar al-salafi min al-muwatinin al-Shi'a fi al-mamlaka," *al-Jazira al-'Arabiyya* 6 (July 1991): 25–26; Anon., "Harb ta'ifiyya..harb taqsim," *al-Jazira al-'Arabiyya* 30 (July 1993): 31.

23. Said Aburish, *The Rise, Corruption, and Coming Fall of the House of Saud* (London, 1994), 110–11; Hamid Algar, *Wahhabism: A Critical Essay* (New York, 2002), 62.

24. Anon., "Ta'jij al-ta'ifiyya lan yuharrif al-ra'y 'an al-mutalaba bi al-huquq al-masluba," *Risalat al-Haramayn* 26 (December 1991): 4–5; Anon., "al-Su-'udiyya wa-siyasat al-tamyiz al-madhhabi didd al-Shi'a," *Risalat al-Haramayn* 35 (December 1992): 22–23; Anon., "Mu'aradat al-sulta am mu'aradat al-Shi'a: min wara' intishar ashritat al-jabhan?" *Risalat al-Haramayn* 29 (June 1992): 33; Anon., "I'tiqal wa-ta'dhib wa-tamyiz bi-haqq abna' al-ta'ifa al-Shi'iyya," *Risalat al-Haramayn* 48 (June 1994): 19, 21; Hamza al-Hasan, "Ta'ifiyyat al-tayar al-salafi tahudd min tawassu' sha'biyatihi fi al-wasat al-ijtima'i," *al-Jazira al-'Ara-biyya* 6 (July 1991): 27–28; idem, *al-Shi'a*, 2:400–409; Mirza al-Khuwaylidi, "al-Hukuma al-su'udiyya wara' 'arida sawda' tutalib bi-sahq al-muwatinin al-Shi'a wa-hadm masajidihim," *al-Jazira al-'Arabiyya* 21 (October 1992): 15–18.

25. Hasan ibn Farhan al-Maliki, "Mata kana sayf ibn 'umar mu'tamad al-'ulama'?" *al-Riyadh*, 17 March 1996; Sa'd al-Hamazani, "Bahith su'udi yanfi 'an ibn saba' dawruhu fi ish'al al-fitna al-kubra," *al-Hayat*, 13 January 1999.

26. British Embassy, Tehran, 2 September and 26 November 1966, FO 371/185331/BB103134/1 and FO 371/185331/BB103134/5; Good Offices Mission, Bahrain, The 1970 Referendum, 24 April 1970, FCO 8/1370; The Settlement of the Iranian Claim to Bahrain, 6 July 1970, FCO 8/1372; J. B. Kelly, *Britain and the Persian Gulf, 1795–1880* (Oxford, 1968), 319, 515–16; idem, *Arabia*, 54–55, 58–59, 179, 315; Fereydoun Adamiyat, *Bahrein Islands: A Legal and Diplomatic Study of the British-Iranian Controversy* (New York, 1955), esp. 124–252, 255–58; Majid Khadduri, "Iran's Claim to the Sovereignty of Bahrain," *AJIL* 45 (1951): 631–47; idem, ed., *Major Middle Eastern Problems in International Law* (Washington, D.C., 1972), 95–105.

27. L. Haworth to the Foreign Secretary to the Government of India, Enclosure 1 in No. 33, 1 September 1927, FO 406/60; Political Resident in the Persian Gulf to the Foreign Secretary to the Government of India, 22 July 1922, FO 371/7721/8918; From Viceroy, Foreign and Political Department, to Secretary of State for India, 11 May 1923, FO 371/8941/4838; From Political Resident in the Persian Gulf to Emir Faisal, 8 February 1862, IO 15/2/29; J. B. Kelly, *Eastern Arabian Frontiers* (New York, 1964), 62, 74, 78–79, 303–4; idem, *Britain*, 103–4, 126, 229–30; Mahdi Abdalla al-Tajir, *Bahrain, 1920–1945: Britain, the Shaikh, and the Administration* (London, 1987), 39–40, 65–66, 84–88; Fa'iq Hamdi Tahbub, *Ta'rikh al-bahrayn al-siyasi, 1783–1870* (Kuwait, 1983), 70–84, 128–35, 226, 245–52; Jamal Zakariya Qasim, *al-Khalij al-'arabi: dirasa li-ta'rikh al-imarat al-'arabiyya fi 'asr al-tawassu' al-urubi al-awwal* (Cairo, 1985), 423–28; idem, *al-Khalij al-'arabi: dirasa li-ta'rikh al-imarat al-'arabiyya, 1914–1945* (Cairo, 1973), esp. 225–37.

28. Anon., "al-Su'udiyya wa al-da'm al-la mahdud li-himayat amn wa-istiqlal al-bahrayn," *al-Mawaqif* 404 (28 December 1981): 3; 'Abd al-Latif Jasim Kanu, "al-Malik 'abd al-'aziz al su'ud wa al-bahrayn," *al-Wathiqa* 4 (January 1986):

32–48; 'Ali 'Abd al-Rahman Aba Husayn, "al-Silla al-ta'rikhiyya bayn al-bahrayn wa al-mamlaka fi 'ahd al-malik 'abd al-'aziz," *al-Wathiqa* 5 (July 1986): 64–95; Nadav Safran, *Saudi Arabia: The Ceaseless Quest for Security* (Cambridge, Mass., 1985), 134–37; Emile Nakhleh, *Bahrain: Political Development in a Modernizing Society* (Lexington, Mass., 1976), 96; Ghasan Qasim al-Mulla, *Riyah al-taghyir fi al-bahrayn* (n.p., n.d.), 231; Bahrain Briefing, March 2001, http://vob.org; Fuller and Rahim Francke, *The Arab Shi'a*, 152.

29. J. G. Lorimer, *Gazetteer of the Persian Gulf, 'Oman and Central Arabia*, 5 pts. in 2 vols. (Calcutta, 1908–15), 2A:48, 62–64, 68, 238–41, 249, 252, 1162, 1244, 1282–83, 1304–6, 1634, 1842–44, 1917–19, 1935, 1946; From Political Agent, Bahrain, to the Deputy Political Resident in the Persian Gulf, No. 284-G, 2 September 1920, IO 15/2/23; C. F. Daly to Political Resident, Bushire, 11 April 1922, FO 371/7721/5373; Talal Toufic Farah, *Protection and Politics in Bahrain, 1869–1915* (Beirut, 1985), 2–5, 10, 86–88; R. B. Serjent, "Fisher-Folk and Fish-Traps in al-Bahrain," *BSOAS* 31 (1968): 486–87; Charles Belgrave, *Personal Column* (London, 1960), 55; Tajir, *Bahrain*, 3, 15, 54; Fuad Khuri, *Tribe and State in Bahrain: The Transformation of Social and Political Authority in an Arab State* (Chicago, 1980), 48–49; Muhammad Ghanim al-Rumayhi, *al-Bahrayn: mushkilat al-taghyir al-siyasi wa al-ijtima'i*, 4th ed. (Beirut, 1995), 59, 313–14; Anon., "al-Bahrayn: al-Masar al-iqlimi wa-mustaqbal al-haraka al-islamiyya," *al-Thawra al-Islamiyya* 102 (September 1988): 27.

30. From Political Agent, Bahrain, to Political Resident in the Persian Gulf, No. 111/C, 13 July 1922, IO 15/1/336; Lorimer, *Gazetteer*, 2A:391–96; Belgrave, *Personal Column*, 20, 127; Tajir, *Bahrain*, 39–40, 56–58, 65–66, 84; Sa'id al-Shihabi, *al-Bahrayn, 1920–1971: qira'a fi al-watha'iq al-baritaniyya* (London, 1996), 34–38, 73, 86–88; Hasan, *al-Shi'a*, 2:176–79.

31. Telegram from Political Resident to the S.S.C.O., 31 January 1924, IO L/P&S 10/1039; Translation of a letter from A. P. Trevor to the Sultan of Najd, No. 49, 14 February 1924, IO L/P&S 10/1042; Translation of a letter from the Sultan of Najd to the Resident, No. 77, 22 February 1924, IO L/P&S 10/1042; Daly to Trevor, No. 88/C, 31 March 1924, IO 15/2/87; Haworth to F.S.G.I., No. 87-S, 27 March 1927, IO L/P&S 10/1042; Prideaux to F.S.G.I., No. 517-S, 4 December 1926, IO L/P&S 10/1042; Advisor to the Government of Bahrein to the Political Agent, No. 934, 20th Shawwal 1345, IO 15/2/87; Barrett to the Secretary to the Political Resident, No. C-53, 14 April 1927, IO L/P&S 10/1042; Haworth to F.S.G.I., No. 138-S, 1 May 1927, IO L/P&S 10/1042; Tajir, *Bahrain*, 84–88; Shihabi, *al-Bahrayn*, 38–43.

32. Translation of an Undated Petition from the Baharna to the Political Agent, IO 15/1/336; Daly to Trevor, Enclosures to Serials Nos. 2 and 3, November 1921 and 3 January 1922, IO 15/2/131; F. B. Prideaux to F.S.G.I., No. 521-S, 6 September 1924, IO 15/2/73; Belgrave to Political Agent, No. 105/SF, 5 Safar 1350, IO L/P&S 10/1044; Belgrave to Political Agent, No. 326/SF, 30 June 1935, IO 15/2/195; Belgrave to Loch, Nos. C/882 and C/129, 7 November 1934 and 28 January 1935, IO 15/2/176. See also Rupert Hay, *The Persian Gulf States* (Washington,

D.C., 1955), 91; Rumayhi, *al-Bahrayn*, 100–105; Ibrahim Khalaf al-'Ubaydi, *al-Haraka al-wataniyya fi al-bahrayn, 1914–1971* (Baghdad, 1976), 91–93; Yusuf al-Falaki, *Qadiyyat al-bahrayn bayn al-madi wa al-hadir* (n.p., n.d.), 17–20; Tajir, *Bahrain*, 2, 162–69; Bahrain Freedom Movement, 25 November 1997; Bahrain Briefing, March 2001, http://vob.org.

33. From Political Agent, Bahrain, to Political Resident in the Persian Gulf, Enclosure to Serial No. 29, 13 July 1922, IO 15/2/131; Belgrave to Prior, No. 1337/48, 9 February 1930, IO R/15/2/122; Belgrave, *Personal Column*, 41–42, 49–50, 126, 134; Tajir, *Bahrain*, 104–34; P.T.H. Unwin, *Bahrain*, World Bibliographical Series, vol. 49 (Denver, 1984), 24; Rumayhi, *al-Bahrayn*, 83–100; Shihabi, *al-Bahrayn*, 43–49, 77; Munira Fakhro, "The Uprising in Bahrain: An Assessment," in *The Persian Gulf at the Millennium: Essays in Politics, Economy, Security, and Religion*, ed. Gary Sick and Lawrence Potter (New York, 1997), 169.

34. Belgrave to Loch, 28 January 1935, IO R/15/2/176; Resident to F.S.G.I., No. C-43, 18 March 1935, FO 371/18920; Kelly, *Arabia*, 183; Khuri, *Tribe and State*, 217; Rumayhi, *al-Bahrayn*, 65–70, 144; Gause, *Oil Monarchies*, 150; Sick and Potter, *The Persian Gulf at the Millennium*, 18; Fuller and Rahim Francke, *The Arab Shi'a*, 137–38; Bahrain Freedom Movement, 29 September 1999 and 23 January 2004; Bahrain Briefing, March 2001, http://vob.org.

35. Belgrave, *Personal Column*, 81–85; Kelly, *Arabia*, 180–81; Jamal Zakariya Qasim, *al-Khalij al-'arabi: dirasa li-ta'rikhihi al-mu'asir, 1945–1971* (Cairo, 1974), 121.

36. Tajir, *Bahrain*, 173–78; Shihabi, *al-Bahrayn*, 120–26; Rumayhi, *al-Bahrayn*, 146–53; Belgrave, *Personal Column*, 86.

37. Qasim, *al-Khalij al-'arabi*, 122; Rumayhi, *al-Bahrain*, 154–60, 176–78; Khuri, *Tribe and State*, 224; Anthony Cordesman, *The Gulf and the Search for Strategic Stability* (Boulder, Colo., 1984), 407; Rodney Wilson, "The Evolution of the Saudi Banking System and Its Relationship with Bahrain," in *State, Society, and Economy in Saudi Arabia*, ed. Tim Niblock (London, 1982), 293–94, 297.

38. Belgrave, *Personal Column*, 10.

39. The information on Belgrave is derived largely from his *Personal Column*. See also Robert Belgrave, "Charles belgrave: mustashar qadim fi al-bahrayn," *al-Wathiqa* 3 (January 1985): 39–53; Khuri, *Tribe and State*, 115.

40. Falaki, *Qadiyyat al-bahrayn*, 58, 68–69; Anon., "Safahat min masar al-haraka al-islamiyya fi al-bahrayn," *al-Thawra al-Islamiyya* 92 (November 1982): 61; Shihabi, *al-Bahrayn*, 196–97, 204, 206–23, 241; 'Abd al-Rahman al-Bakir, *Min al-bahrayn ila al-manfa* (Beirut, 1965), 42–43; Qasim, *al-Khalij al-'arabi*, 120; Rumayhi, *al-Bahrayn*, 203–4, 379, 408–9; Anti-Belgrave Feelings in Bahrain between 10 July 1946 and 28 February 1948, FO 371/68331/2901.

41. Cordesman, *The Gulf*, 583–84, 586; 'Abd al-Hadi Khalaf, *Bina' al-dawla fi al-bahrayn: al-muhimma ghayr al-munjaza* (Beirut, 2000), 80–81, 91; Michelle Wallin, "U.S.-Bahrain Accord Stirs Persian Gulf Trade Partners," *NYT*, 24 December 2004.

42. Anon., "al-Bahrayn ila ayna?" *al-Bilad* 215 (7 January 1995): 32; Khalaf, *Bina' al-dawla fi al-bahrayn*, 86–89; Muhammad Mahdi, *al-Bahrayn: intihakat huquq al-insan, 1979–1990* (n.p., n.d.), 18–21; Mansur al-Jamri, "Prospects of a Moderate Islamist Discourse: The Case of Bahrain," 22 November 1997, http://vob.org; Fuller and Rahim Francke, *The Arab Shi'a*, 126.

43. Khalaf, *Bina' al-dawla fi al-bahrayn*, 92–99, 140, 142–47; idem, "Hal Yaqbal sha'b al-bahrayn majlis al-shura al-mu'ayyan?" *al-Jazira al-'Arabiyya* 26 (March 1993): 38–42; Anon., "al-Majlis al-istishari laysa badilan 'an al-majlis al-watani," *al-Jazira al-'Arabiyya* 23 (December 1992): 22–23; Anon., "Jadid al-bahrayn laysa jadidan," *al-Jazira al-'Arabiyya* 24 (January 1993): 28–30; Karim al-Mahrus, "Fi al-bahrayn: majlis al-shura al-mu'ayyan yufaqim azmat al-'a'ila al-hakima," *al-Jazira al-'Arabiyya* 27 (April 1993): 16; Fakhro, "The Uprising in Bahrain," 180–82; Bahrain Freedom Movement, 2 June 2000; Profile of Sheikh al-Jamri, http://vob.org.

44. From Political Resident in the Persian Gulf to the Foreign Secretary to the Government of India, 18 March 1935, FO 371/18920; Belgrave to Weightman, 13 November 1938, IO R/15/2/176.

45. Sheikh al-Jamri's Statements, http://vob.org; "Khutbat al-jum'a allati al-qaha al-shaykh 'abd al-amir al-jamri fi jami' al-imam al-sadiq bi al-daraz yawm al-jum'a," 5 January 1996, in *al-Haraka al-dusturiyya: nidal sha'b min ajl al-dimuqratiyya*, ed. Ahmad al-Shamlan et al. (n.p., 1997), 129; Khalaf, *Bina' al-dawla fi al-bahrayn*, 105; Qasim, *Riyah al-taghyir fi al-bahrayn*, 130, 249–50, 267–68, 281–86, 301–2.

46. "Bahrain Holds 44 It Says Are Tied to Pro-Iran Plot," *NYT*, 5 June 1996; "Bahrain Coup Suspects Say They Trained in Iran," *NYT*, 6 June 1996; Joe Stork, "Bahrain Regime Stages Confessions, Rejects Compromise," *MERIP* 200 (July–September 1996): 44; Bahrain Freedom Movement, 3, 6, 9, and 10 June 1996; 2 July 1996; 8 December 1996; 28 February 1997; 2, 9, and 17 March 1997; 30 April 1997, http://vob.org; Fakhro, "The Uprising in Bahrain," 182–83. See also Fuller and Rahim Francke, *The Arab Shi'a*, 135; Anon., "Ahdath al-bahrayn: taqrir khass," *al-Mawsim* 28 (1996): 294–304.

47. Mulla, *Riyah al-taghyir fi al-bahrayn*, 89–91, 114; Shihabi, *al-Bahrayn*, 277, 280–84, 300–301; Anon., "al-Bahrayn ila ayna?" 31; Bahrain Freedom Movement, 1, 7, 10, 14, and 16 July 1996, 14 September 1996, 1 and 28 October, and 24 December 1996; 7, 10, and 16 January, and 15 February 1997; 18 February, 5, 8 March, and 14 April 1998; 19 July, 18 August, 1, 13, 28, and 29 September, and 23 November 1999; 23 March 2000; Bahrain Briefing, March 2001, http://vob.org. See also Dispatch No. 7 from Political Agent in Bahrain to the Political Resident in the Persian Gulf, 5 October 1953, FO 371/104263/10110-2; K. V. Abraham, *British Justice in Bahrain* (Kerala, 1963), 58, 82; Khuri, *Tribe and State*, 122–23; Fuller and Rahim Francke, *The Arab Shi'a*, 144, 147.

48. Khalid Hamade, "Qadiyyat al-mahrumin min haqq al-jinsiyya fi al-bahrayn," *al-Jazira al-'Arabiyya* 11 (December 1991): 28–29; Bahrain Freedom Movement, 22 February and 1 June 1997, 29 September 1999, 12 October 2000,

http://vob.org. See also 'Abd al-Rahman al-Nu'aymi, "al-Ifraj 'an 'adad min al-mu'taqalin wa al-matlub hall siyasi," *al-Quds al-'Arabi*, 24 August 1995; Munira Fakhru, *al-Mujtama' al-madani wa al-tahawwul al-dimuqrati fi al-bahrayn* (Cairo, 1996), 77.

49. Fakhro, "The Uprising in Bahrain," 175–76; Bahrain Briefing, March 2001; Bahrain Freedom Movement, 25 November 1997 and 30 March 2001, http://vob.org; Ibrahim Bashmi, *Mashru' al-bahrayn al-islahi* (Manama, 2002), 87; Khalaf, *Bina' al-dawla fi al-bahrayn*, 45–48; "Bayan 'Ulama' al-Din fi al-Bahrayn," 18 December 1994, in Mulla, *Riyah al-taghyir fi al-bahrayn*, 24; Bakir, *Min al-bahrayn ila al-manfa*, 12–13.

50. See, for example, Muhammad 'Abd al-Qadir al-Jasim and Sawsan 'Ali al-Sha'ir, *al-Bahrayn: qissat al-sira' al-siyasi, 1904–1956* (n.p., 2000), esp. 345–49.

51. Bahrain Freedom Movement, 15 December 2000, and for the months of January and February 2001, http://vob.org; Khalaf, *Bina' al-dawla fi al-bahrayn*, 107–8.

Chapter 3
The Struggle for Power in Iraq

1. These affairs are discussed in Yitzhak Nakash, *The Shi'is of Iraq*, 2d ed. (Princeton, 2003), 61–72.

2. Fariq al-Muzhir Al Fir'awn, *al-Haqa'iq al-nasi'a fi al-thawra al-'iraqiyya sanat 1920 wa-nata'ijuha* (Baghdad, 1952), 55. See also Kamil Salman al-Juburi, *al-Kufa fi thawrat al-'ishrin* (Najaf, 1972), 6, 13–15, 21–23; Ja'far al-Mahbuba, *Madi al-najaf wa-hadiruha*, 3 vols. (Najaf, 1955–1958), esp. 1:374–75.

3. Salman Hadi Al Tu'ma, *Turath Karbala'* (Najaf, 1964), 282–93.

4. Furati, "al-Haqa'iq al-nasi'a fi al-thawra al-'iraqiyya al-kubra" (a response to Fir'awn), *al-Hatif* 1181 (23 June 1953): 2; 'Abud Shalash, "al-Najaf wa al-bayt al-hashimi," *al-'Irfan* 29 (1939): 839–40.

5. Nakash, *The Shi'is of Iraq*, 94–95.

6. Karim Wahid Salih, *Najm al-baqqal: qa'id thawrat al-najaf al-kubra didd al-ihtilal al-inglizi 'am 1918* (Najaf, 1980), esp. 5, 16–18, 24, 29–33, 43, 67–68, 71, 72, 92; Zuhayr Sadiq Rida, *Fi sabil al-watan: riwaya 'an thawrat al-'ishrin fi al-'iraq* (Beirut, 1979), esp. 7, 9, 12, 18, 20–23, 33, 67–68, 81, 89–94, 99–102, 120, 125–26. See also Yihya al-Safi al-Najafi, "Dhikra thawrat al-najaf," *al-'Irfan* 42 (1955): 427–28; Mahbuba, *Madi al-najaf*, 1:344–51; 'Abd al-Razzaq al-Hasani, *Thawrat al-najaf ba'da maqtal hakimuha al-kabtan marshal* (Sidon, 1978), 35–36; 'Abd al-Shahid al-Yasiri, *al-Butula fi thawrat al-'ishrin* (Najaf, 1966), 103, 107; 'Ali al-Wardi, *Lamahat ijtima'iyya min ta'rikh al-'iraq al-hadith*, 6 vols. (Baghdad, 1969–78), 5,2:216–21; Muhammad Mahdi al-Jawahiri, *Dhikrayati*, 2 vols. (Damascus, 1988–91), 1:97.

7. Rida, *Fi sabil al-watan*, esp. 49, 110–11, 115–16.

8. Salih, *Najm al-baqqal*, 15, 20–21; Hasan al-Asadi, *Thawrat al-najaf 'ala al-ingliz aw al-sharara al-ula li-thawrat al-'ishrin* (Baghdad, 1975), 371, 383–86;

Anon., "al-Thawrat wa-thawrata al-najaf," *al-'Irfan* 10 (1925): 629, 635; Anon., "al-Thawra fi al-najaf," *al-'Irfan* 24 (1934): 541; Hasani, *Thawrat al-najaf*, 69, 71, 133–34; idem, *al-'Iraq fi dawray al-ihtilal wa al-intidab* (Sidon, 1935), 38; Kazim al-Muzaffar, *Thawrat al-'iraq al-taharruriyya 'am 1920*, 3 pts. in 2 vols. (Najaf, 1972), 1:119; Muhammad 'Ali Kamal al-Din, *Thawrat al-'ishrin fi al-'iraq fi dhikriha al-khamsin* (Baghdad, 1970), 35, 66–67; Jawahiri, *Dhikrayati*, 1:98.

9. Kamal al-Din, *Thawrat al-'ishrin*, 71–74, 187, 214–18; 'Abdallah al-Fayyad, *al-Thawra al-'iraqiyya al-kubra sanat 1920* (Baghdad, 1963), 12, 81; Wardi, *Lamahat*, 5,1:19, 33, 36, 39, 65, 92, 124, 129, 172–76, 197, 200, 310, and 6:253; Ra'uf al-Wa'iz, *al-Ittijahat al-wataniyya fi al-Shi'r al-'iraqi al-hadith, 1914–1941* (Baghdad, 1974), 86–87, 95; Ibrahim al-Wa'ili, *Thawrat al-'ishrin fi al-Shi'r al-'iraqi* (Baghdad, 1968), 91, 93; Husayn al-Zalimi al-Rumaythi, "al-Dhikra al-rabi'a wa al-sab'in li al-thawra al-'iraqiyya al-kubra," *Nida' al-Rafidayn*, 8 July 1994.

10. Musa al-Karbasi, ed., *Mawsu'at al-shaykh 'ali al-sharqi al-nathriyya*, 2 vols. (Baghdad, 1988–89), 2:44–46; 'Ali al-Sharqi, *al-Ahlam* (Baghdad, 1963), 102–3; Muhammad Mahdi al-Basir, *Ta'rikh al-qadiyya al-'iraqiyya*, 2d ed., 2 pts. (London, 1990), 1:35, 46–47; Muhammad Mahdi Kubba, *Mudhakkirati fi samim al-ahdath, 1918–1958* (Beirut, 1965), 18–21; 'Adnan 'Ali, "Thawrat al-'ishrin fi dhikriha al-sittin," *al-Thaqafa al-Jadida* 123 (August 1980): 46.

11. See the correspondence of 'Abd al-Karim al-Jaza'iri, Sahib al-Jawahir, and Hibat al-Din al-Shahrastani in 'Abd al-Razzaq al-Hasani, *al-Thawra al-'iraqiyya al-kubra* (Sidon, 1952), 208–10; Muhammad Bahr al-'Ulum, "Dawr al-'ulama' al-qiyadi fi thawrat al-'ishrin" (London, n.d.), 2, 10, 13; 'Abd al-Sahib al-Musawi, *Harakat al-Shi'r fi al-najaf al-ashraf wa-atwaruhu khilal al-qarn al-rabi' 'ashar al-hijri* (Beirut, 1988), 91–92; Hasan Shubbar, *Ta'rikh al-'iraq al-siyasi al-mu'asir*, 2 vols. (Beirut, 1990), 2:219–24, 229–33; Salim al-Hasani, *Dawr 'ulama' al-Shi'a fi muwajahat al-isti'mar, 1900–1920* (Beirut, 1995), esp. 236–37, 244; 'Ali al-Tamimi, "al-'Ulama' qadat al-thawra wa al-masajid qawa'id li al-intilaq," *al-Jihad* 142 (25 June 1984): 7; Anon., "Qarar al-marja'iyya bi-i'lan al-thawra didd al-ingliz," *al-Jihad* 185 (6 May 1985): 7; a special issue on the occasion of the sixty-fifth anniversary of the 1920 revolt, *al-Jihad* 193 (1 July 1985): 5–15; Diya' al-Kufi, "Thawrat al-'ishrin: bidayat al-rafd al-mumtadda," *al-Jihad* 600 (28 July 1993): 6; Ayman al-Najafi, "Dawr al-marja'iyya al-diniyya fi thawrat al-'ishrin," *Liwa' al-Sadr* 556 (5 July 1992): 6.

12. Fayyad, *al-Thawra al-'iraqiyya*, 14, 78, 235–37, 243–47; Wardi, *Lamahat*, 5,1:15, 104, 341–45, 5,2:200, 205, 269, and 6:310. See also Hasan al-'Alawi, *Dawlat al-isti'ara al-qawmiyya: min faysal al-awwal ila saddam husayn* (London, 1993), 64.

13. Yasiri, *al-Butula*, 348–52; Wardi, *Lamahat*, 6:89, 106–10, 114; Sharqi, *al-Ahlam*, 126–27, 160–61; Ibrahim al-Wa'ili and Musa al-Karbasi, eds., *Diwan al-sharqi*, 2d ed. (Baghdad, 1986), 119–23. See also Pierre-Jean Luizard, "Shaykh Muhammad al-Khalisi (1890–1963) and His Political Role in Iraq and Iran in the 1910s and 1920s," in *The Twelver Shia in Modern Times: Religious Culture and*

Political History, ed. Rainer Brunner and Werner Ende (Leiden, 2001), 228–29; Elie Kedourie, *England and the Middle East: The Destruction of the Ottoman Empire, 1914–1921* (London, 1956), 208, 210, 212.

14. Sharqi, *al-Ahlam*, 132–37, 190; Karbasi, *Mawsuʻat al-shaykh ʻali al-sharqi*, 2:47–49; ʻArabi, "al-Shiʻa fi biladihim: ʻibar wa-ʻizza li-katib siyasi kabir min aqtab al-Shiʻa fi al-ʻiraq," *al-ʻIrfan* 20 (1930): 563–66; Muhammad Rida al-Shabibi's introduction in Fayyad, *al-Thawra al-ʻiraqiyya*, 3–4; Kamal al-Din, *Thawrat al-ʻishrin*, 382–83, 385; Ibrahim al-Waʼili, "Fi dhikra thawrat al-ʻishrin," *al-Rabita* 3 (1975): 9, 11; idem, *Thawrat al-ʻishrin*, 167, 171; idem, *Diwan al-waʼili*, 2 vols. (Baghdad, 1981–82), 2:345; ʻAbd al-Karim al-Dujayli, *al-Jawahiri: shaʻir al-ʻarabiyya* (Najaf, 1972), 273–74; Musawi, *Harakat al-Shiʻr*, 94–99; Muhammad Salih Bahr al-ʻUlum, *Diwan bahr al-ʻulum*, 2 vols. (Baghdad, 1968–69), 1:30, 33–34, 59, 73–75; Hasan al-ʻAlawi, *al-Shiʻa wa al-dawla al-qawmiyya fi al-ʻiraq* (Paris, 1989), 254–58, 264–65; idem, *Dawlat al-istiʻara al-qawmiyya*, 39; Saʻid al-Samarraʼi, *Saddam wa-Shiʻat al-ʻiraq* (London, 1991), 21–22. See also the poetry of Muhammad Mahdi al-Basir, Muhammad Baqir al-Shabibi, and Muhammad Salih Bahr al-ʻUlum in *al-Shiʻr al-ʻiraqi al-hadith wa-athar al-tayarat al-siyasiyya wa al-ijtimaʻiyya*, ed. Yusuf ʻIzz al-Din (Cairo, 1965), 160–61, 198–200, 204.

15. ʻAbd al-Hamid al-Radi, *Thawrat al-ʻiraq al-kubra: riwaya taʼrikhiyya shaʻbiyya* (Baghdad, 1938), esp. 23, 77–78, 93–94, 143–45; ʻAli al-Bazirgan, *al-Waqaʼiʻ al-haqiqiyya fi al-thawra al-ʻiraqiyya*, 2d ed. (Baghdad, 1991), 19, 41.

16. Salim Taha, "Sahafat thawrat al-ʻishrin," *al-Mawrid* 5 (1976): 7; Kamal Muzhir Ahmad, *Safahat min taʼrikh al-ʻiraq al-muʻasir: dirasat tahliliyya* (Baghdad, 1987), esp. 48, 53, 55, 65, 140.

17. See the introductions of ʻImad ʻAbd al-Salam Raʼuf and Hasan ʻAli al-Bazirgan in Bazirgan, *al-Waqaʼiʻ al-haqiqiyya*, 10, 12, 16.

18. Cited in Judith Yaphe, "The Challenge of Nation Building in Iraq," in *U.S. Policy in Post-Saddam Iraq: Lessons from the British Experience*, ed. Michael Eisenstadt and Eric Mathewson (Washington, D.C., 2003), 50.

19. Satiʻ al-Husri, *Abhath mukhtara fi al-qawmiyya al-ʻarabiyya, 1923–1963* (Cairo, 1964), 140; Mahmud al-Mallah, *al-Araʼ al-sariha li-binaʼ qawmiyya sahiha* (Baghdad, n.d.), 61–65, 84–85; idem, *al-Mujiz ʻala al-wajiz wa-mabahith ukhra* (Baghdad, 1956), 119; Malik Mufti, *Sovereign Creations: Pan-Arabism and Political Order in Syria and Iraq* (Ithaca, 1996), 21–22, 29–42; A. Shikara, "Faysal's Ambitions of Leadership in the Fertile Crescent: Aspirations and Constraints," in *The Integration of Modern Iraq*, ed. Abbas Kelidar (London, 1979), 32–45; Elie Kedourie, "The Iraqi Shiʻis and Their Fate," in *Shiʻism, Resistance, and Revolution*, ed. Martin Kramer (Boulder, Colo., 1987), 153–54; Michael Eppel, "The Elite, the *Effendiyya*, and the Growth of Nationalism and Pan-Arabism in Hashemite Iraq, 1921–1958," *IJMES* 30 (1998): 228, 232–35; Bassam Tibi, *Arab Nationalism: Between Islam and the Nation State*, 3d ed. (New York, 1997), esp. 116–22, 164–70; Adeed Dawisha, *Arab Nationalism in the Twentieth Century: From Triumph to Despair* (Princeton, 2003), 47–74.

20. Hani al-Fukayki, *Awkar al-hazima: tajrrubati fi hizb al-ba'th al-'iraqi* (London, 1993), 65–68, 79, 83–84, 96–106. See also Farhad Ibrahim, *al-Ta'ifiyya wa al-siyasa fi al-'alam al-'arabi: namudhaj al-Shi'a fi al-'iraq* (Cairo, 1996), 336–38.

21. Majid Ahmad al-Samarra'i, *al-Tayar al-qawmi fi al-Shi'r al-'iraqi al-hadith mundhu al-harb al-'alamiyya al-thaniyya 1939 hatta naksat huziran 1967* (Baghdad, 1983), esp. 5, 44; Tarad al-Kubaysi, *al-Tajruba al-khaliqa: qira'a jadida fi fikr al-ra'is saddam husayn* (Baghdad, 1984), 158–63, 166–67; Hasan Muhammad Tawaliba, *Muqtatafat min ahadith saddam husayn* (Beirut, 1979), 31–33; Fadil al-Barrak, *Hukumat al-difa' al-watani: al-badhra al-qawmiyya li al-thawra al-'arabiyya* (Baghdad, 1980), esp. 37–40; Sa'dun Hamadi, *Mulahazat hawla qadiyyat al-harb ma'a iran* (Baghdad, 1982), esp. 162–73; Ofra Bengio, *Saddam's Word: Political Discourse in Iraq* (Oxford, 1998), 45–48, 90–91, 168–70; Amatzia Baram, *Culture, History, and Ideology in the Formation of Ba'thist Iraq, 1968–1989* (New York, 1991), 121–22.

22. Many of Sharqi's articles were reproduced in Karbasi, *Mawsu'at al-shaykh 'ali al-sharqi*, esp. 1:55–58, 203–8, 2:52–54, 56, 61–68, 96–108, 163–66, 189–94. See also 'Ali al-Sharqi, "Lawhat al-qawmiyya al-'arabiyya fi al-'iraq," *al-'Irfan* 26 (1936): 773; idem, *al-Ahlam*, 194–95; Dujayli, *al-Jawahiri*, 404–6; Sami Zubaida, "The Fragments Imagine the Nation: The Case of Iraq," *IJMES* 34 (2002): 213.

23. 'Alawi, *Dawlat al-isti'ara al-qawmiyya*, 6, 8, 13, 15–19, 21–25, 27, 41, 42–44, 56–57, 63, 83–95; idem, *al-Shi'a wa al-dawla al-qawmiyya*, 254–58, 264–67, 299–302; Salim Matar, *al-Dhat al-jariha: ishkalat al-huwiyya fi al-'iraq wa al-'alam al-'arabi al-sharqani* (Beirut, 1997), 88, 126–31, 181–82, 185; Sa'id al-Samarra'i, *al-Ta'ifiyya fi al-'iraq: al-waqi' wa al-hall* (London, 1993), 108, 111–14; idem, *Saddam*, 22.

24. Sharqi, *al-Ahlam*, 143, 149–52; Mudhakkirat al-Shaykh Muhammad Rida al-Shabibi, 28 October 1965, reproduced in Anon., "Rijal min al-'iraq: al-shaykh muhammad rida al-shabibi," *al-Tayar al-Jadid* 21 (26 November 1984): 21. See also Hamid al-Bayati, *Shi'at al-'iraq: bayn al-ta'ifiyya wa al-shubuhat fi al-watha'iq al-sirriyya al-baritaniyya, 1963–1966* (London, 1997), 245–50; Ibrahim, *al-Ta'ifiyya*, 235–39; Sir Roger Allen to Mr. Stewart, Baghdad, 10 March 1965, FO 371/80807/1015/13.

25. Nakash, *The Shi'is of Iraq*, 82, 101–2; 'Abd al-Amir Hadi al-'Akkam, *al-Haraka al-wataniyya fi al-'iraq, 1921–1933* (Baghdad, 1975), 127–28; Majid Khadduri, *Republican Iraq: A Study of Iraqi Politics since the Revolution of 1958* (London, 1969), 226; Ibrahim, *al-Ta'ifiyya*, 297, 359; Ali Babakhan, *L'Irak, 1970–1990: Déportations des chiites* (Paris, n.d.), 46–47, 50, 54, 56, 61–63, 71–74, 102–6; 'Abd al-Husayn Sha'ban, *'Asifa 'ala bilad al-shams: dirasat fi qadaya al-harb wa al-fikr al-siyasi al-'iraqi* (Beirut, 1994), 223–26, 230–33; Ahmad 'Abd al-Hamid, "Mashakil al-jinsiyya fi al-'iraq," *al-Tayar al-Jadid* 13 (1 October 1984): 21–22; Abu Haydar, "al-Jinsiyya al-'iraqiyya wa-'amaliyyat al-tahjir," *al-Tayar al-Jadid* 22 (3 December 1984): 1, 11.

26. Jawahiri, *Dhikrayati*, 1:141, 146; Karbasi, *Mawsu'at al-shaykh 'ali al-sharqi*, 2:64; 'Arabi, "al-Shi'a fi biladihim," 564; Fukayki, *Awkar al-hazima*, 61; Hasan al-'Alawi, *al-Ta'thirat al-turkiyya fi al-mashru' al-qawmi al-'arabi fi al-'iraq* (London, 1988), 10, 71–75, 91–95, 102–5; idem, *al-Shi'a wa al-dawla al-qawmiyya*, 52; idem, *Dawlat al-isti'ara al-qawmiyya*, 34; Anon., "al-Jinsiyya al-'iraqiyya wa-'amaliyyat al-tahjir," *al-Tayar al-Jadid* 19 (12 November 1984): 12; 'Abd al-Karim al-Uzri, *Mushkilat al-hukm fi al-'iraq* (London, 1991), 253–54, 281–94; Samarra'i, *Saddam*, 27; idem, *al-Ta'ifiyya*, 56–57, 301–4, 309; Bayati, *Shi'at al-'iraq*, 35; 'Adnan 'Alian, "al-Shi'a wa-nash'at al-dawla al-'iraqiyya al-haditha wa al-badil al-matlub," and Sa'id Muhsin, "Hawla al-tamyiz al-ta'ifi fi al-'iraq," *al-Mawsim* 18 (1994): 36, 39, 81, 84; Hasan Isma'il, *Minhajiyyat al-ada' al-islami wa al-muwajaha ma'a al-nizam al-damawi fi al-'iraq* (n.p., 1984), 133–38. See also Lutfi Ja'far Faraj, *'Abd al-muhsin al-sa'dun wa-dawruhu fi ta' rikh al-'iraq al-siyasi al-mu'asir* (Baghdad, 1978), 346–47; Neil MacFarquhar, "Iraqis in Iran: Unwanted in Both Countries," *NYT*, 12 June 2003.

27. *The Encyclopaedia of Islam*, new ed., s.v. "al-Shu'ubiyya"; H. Norris, "Shu'ubiyyah in Arabic Literature," in *The Cambridge History of Arabic Literature, 'Abbasid Belles-Letters* (Cambridge, 1990), 31–38; Ignaz Goldziher, *Muslim Studies*, ed. S. M. Stern, 2 vols. (Chicago, 1966), esp. 1:137, 144, 146–48, 161; Sami Hanna and George Gardner, "Al-Shu'ubiyyah Updated: A Study of the Twentieth Century Revival of an Eighth Century Concept," *MEJ* 20 (1966): 336; Werner Ende, *Arabische Nation und Islamische Geschichte* (Beirut, 1977), 236, 292; Ibrahim, *al-Ta'ifiyya*, 271, 276.

28. Nakash, *The Shi'is of Iraq*, 82, 91.

29. Sati' al-Husri, *Mudhakkirati fi al-'iraq, 1921–1941*, 2 vols. (Beirut, 1967–68), 1:588–90; Jawahiri, *Dhikrayati*, esp. 1:147–50, 160, 163–64, 171–72; Hasan al-'Alawi, *al-Jawahiri: diwan al-'asr* (Damascus, 1986), 37, 39–40, 43. See also Samir al-Khalil, *Republic of Fear: The Inside Story of Saddam's Iraq*, 2d ed. (Berkeley, 1998), 153–55.

30. 'Abd al-Sahib al-Dujayli, *al-Shu'ubiyya wa-adwaruha al-ta'rikhiyya fi al-'alam al-'arabi*, 2d ed. (Najaf, 1960), 3–4, 22, 24–31; Michel 'Aflaq, *Fi sabil al-ba'th* (Beirut, 1959), 29–30, 71–72; Zaki al-Arsuzi, *al-Mu'allafat al-kamila*, 6 vols. (Damascus, 1972–76), 3:49–69; Sa'dun Hamadi, *Nahnu wa al-shuyu'iyya fi al-azma al-hadira* (Beirut, n.d.), 18–19; 'Abd al-'Aziz al-Duri, *Dirasat fi al-qawmiyya* (Beirut, 1960), esp. 14–15; idem, *al-judhur al-ta'rikhiyya li al-qawmiyya al-'arabiyya* (Beirut, 1960), 37–38; idem, *al-Judhur al-ta'rikhiyya li al-shu'ubiyya* (Beirut, 1962), 120–25; 'Abd al-Hadi al-Fukayki, *al-Shu'ubiyya wa al-qawmiyya al-'arabiyya* (Beirut, 1962), esp. 30–32, 41, 43–44, 97–100; Khayrallah Tulfah, *al-Shu'ubiyya: 'adu al-'arab al-awwal* (Baghdad, 1973), esp. 3–6, 169–72, 179–82, 188; Samir 'Abd al-Karim, *Adwa' 'ala al-haraka al-shuyu'iyya fi al-'iraq*, 5 vols. (Beirut, 1979), 3:83–85; Khalil, *Republic of Fear*, 216–20, 226, 264; Bengio, *Saddam's Word*, 104; Silvia Naef, "*Shi'i-Shuyu'i* or How to Become a Communist in a Holy City," in Brunner and Ende, *The Twelver Shia*, 255; Ibrahim, *al-Ta'ifiyya*, 273.

31. Muhammad Baqir Shirri, *al-'Iraq al-tha'ir* (Beirut, n.d.), 72, 107.

32. Hasan al-'Alawi, *'Abd al-karim qasim: ru'ya ba'd al-'ishrin* (London, 1983), 5–6, 69–71, 90–91, 102–5, 157, 164–65; idem, *Dawlat al-isti'ara al-qaw-miyya*, 28, 36, 81–82; Fukayki, *Awkar al-hazima*, 106, 116, 118, 219; Uzri, *Mushkilat al-hukm*, 269–71; Samarra'i, *al-Ta'ifiyya*, 47; Jawahiri, *Dhikrayati*, 2:176, 179; Ahmad al-Zaydi, *al-Bina' al-ma'nawi li al-quwwat al-musallaha al-'iraqiyya* (Beirut, 1990), 76–80; 'Adnan Fadil, "'Abd al-karim qasim wa al-ta' ifiyya," *al-Mu'tamar* 162 (2 August 1996): 15. See also Ibrahim, *al-Ta'ifiyya*, 236, 239, 257; 'Aflaq, *Fi sabil al-ba'th*, 246–51; Hamadi, *Nahnu wa al-shuyu'iyya*, 47, 49; Ahmad Fawzi, *Qissat 'abd al-karim qasim kamilatan* (Cairo, 1963), 109–113; Subhi 'Abd al-Hamid, *Asrar thawrat 14 tamuz 1958 fi al-'iraq*, 2d ed. (Beirut, 1994), 134, 136, 160–61; Uriel Dann, *Iraq under Qassem: A Political History, 1958–1963* (New York, 1969), 67; Eric Davis, *Memories of State: Politics, History, and Collective Identity in Modern Iraq* (Berkeley, 2005), 118–19; Lutfi al-Sayyid in *al-Musawwar*, 5 May 1950, as cited by Husri, *Abhath mukhtara fi al-qawmiyya al-'arabiyya*, 218.

33. Bengio, *Saddam's Word*, 100–102; Nakash, *The Shi'is of Iraq*, 113.

34. 'Abdallah Salum al-Samarra'i, *al-Shu'ubiyya: haraka mudadda li al-islam wa al-umma al-'arabiyya* (Baghdad, 1984), esp. 5, 11, 48–53, 126, 137, 145–52, 155–56; Mustafa 'Abd al-Qadir al-Najjar et al., *Ta'rikh al-khalij al-'arabi al-ha-dith wa al-mu'asir* (Basra, 1984), 6; Subhi Muhammad Jamil et al., *al-Shu'ubiyya wa-dawruha al-takhribi fi al-fikr al-'arabi al-islami* (Baghdad, 1988), 122–32; Ibrahim Khalil Ahmad, "Judhur al-sira' al-'arabi al-farisi wa al-'alaqat al-'iraqiyya al-iraniyya," and Tawfiq Sultan al-Yuzbiki, "al-Khumayniyya al-'unsu-riyya al-farisiyya wa-silatuha bi al-majusiyya," *al-Jami'a* 2 (1980): 8–12 and 108–111; Muhammad Jalub Farhan, "al-Shu'ubiyya: barnamaj tathqif mudadd wa-mashru' tamarrud," 2 pts., *al-Jami'a* 8 (1981): 8–13, 28–35. See also Adeed Dawisha, "Arabism and Islam in Iraq's War with Iran," *MEI* 2 (1984): 32; Bengio, *Saddam's Word*, 139–44; Ibrahim, *al-Ta'ifiyya*, 274.

35. Eric Davis and Nicolas Gavrielides, "Statecraft, Historical Memory, and Popular Culture in Iraq and Kuwait," in *Statecraft in the Middle East: Historical Memory and Popular Culture*, ed. Davis and Gavrielides, (Miami, Fla., 1991), 135–37; Samarra'i, *al-Shu'ubiyya*, 166, 181–82.

36. Anon., "Madha hasala fi awakhir 'am 1990 wa-hadhihi al-ashhur min 'am 1991 wa-limadha hasala alladhi hasala?" reproduced by the Center for Iraqi Studies as *Maqalat jaridat al-thawra al-'iraqiyya bi-sha'n al-harb wa-intifadat a'dhar 1991 fi al-'iraq* (London, 1993), esp. 7–24. See also Khalid 'Abd al-Rah-man, "Hadha ma fa'alahu al-'umala' ashab al-fitna fi babil," *Alif Ba'* 1174 (27 March 1991): 26–27; Hasan Hamid 'Ubayyid al-Gharbawi, *al-Shu'ubiyya wa-dawruha al-takhribi fi majal al-'aqida al-islamiyya* (Baghdad, 1993), esp. 34–39, 218–20.

37. Ahmad al-Wa'ili, *Huwiyyat al-tashayyu'* (Beirut, 1980), esp. 53, 63–64, 84–85, 226–42; Tawfiq al-Fukayki, *Difa' 'an shu'ara'* (Beirut, 1975), esp. 8–12; 'Alawi, *al-Ta'thirat al-turkiyya*, 142–56; idem, *Dawlat al-isti'ara al-qawmiyya*,

20; Uzri, *Mushkilat al-hukm*, 255–61; Anon., "al-Shu'ubiyya al-mu'asira," *al-Tayar al-Jadid* 64 (9 March 1987): 1, 6, 7; Samarra'i, *Saddam*, 28, 43–47; Bayati, *Shi'at al-'iraq*, 215–17; Zaydi, *al-Bina' al-ma'nawi*, 83–84, 87–93, 157–63, 212–13.

38. 'Alawi, *al-Shi'a*, 235–48, 276, 288–89; Fukayki, *Awkar al-hazima*, 22–27; Samarra'i, *al-Ta'ifiyya*, 35, 36, 43–48, 81, 98, 123–28, 141, 150–51, 162–63, 186–87, 264–66; idem, *Saddam*, 10–11, 90; Matar, *al-Dhat al-jariha*, 58, 394–99; Bayati, *Shi'at al-'iraq*, 14–19, 25–26, 29, 259; Muhammad Salih Bahr al-'Ulum, *Diwan*, 1:59, 93–94; Mudhakkirat al-Shaykh Muhammad Rida al-Shabibi, 21–22; Uzri, *Mushkilat al-hukm*, 273–80; Muhammad Baqir al-Nasiri, "'Alayna takhlis al-sha'b al-'iraqi min al-ta'ifiyya al-siyasiyya," *al-Jihad* 569 (9 November 1992): 5; Isma'il, *Minhajiyyat al-ada' al-islami*, 126; Musawi, *Harakat al-Shi'r*, 71–73; Kanan Makiya, *Cruelty and Silence: War, Tyranny, Uprising, and the Arab World* (New York, 1993), 223, 225; Sami al-'Askari, "Shi'at al-'iraq bayn al-mawqif al-watani wa al-tarh al-ta'ifi," *al-Hayat*, 19 December 2002. See also Davis, *Memories of State*, 261–62.

39. Nakash, *The Shi'is of Iraq*, 128–32.

40. D. K. Haskell to C. M. St. E. Burton, Baghdad, 14 May 1965, FO 371/80807/1015/22; S. L. Egerton to C. T. Brant, Baghdad, 26 November 1965, FO 371/180809/1015/98.

41. Salim al-Hasani, *al-Ma'alim al-jadida li al-marja'iyya al-Shi'iyya* (Beirut, 1993), 87–90, 159–75; Anon., "Wasiyyat al-imam al-sadr," and Jalal al-Hadi, "Umma fi rajul," *al-Rafidayn* 9 (7 April 1984): 1, 9–10; Zayn al-'Abidayn al-Bakri, "Shurut al-thawra 'ind al-sayyid al-shahid al-sadr," *Liwa' al-Sadr* 544 (12 April 1992): 4–5; Ghalib Hasan, "Shi'at al-'iraq ila ayn?" *al-Raya al-'Alawiyya* 1 (February 1997): 4–5; Talib Aziz, "The Political Theory of Muhammad Baqir al-Sadr," in *Ayatollahs, Sufis, and Ideologues: State, Religion, and Social Movements in Iraq*, ed. Faleh Abdul-Jabar (London, 2002), 238–39.

42. 'Adil Ra'uf, *Muhammad muhammad sadiq al-sadr, marja'iyyat al-maydan: mashru'uhu al-taghyiri wa-waqa'i' al-ightiyal* (Damascus, 1999), esp. 15, 27–32, 55–57, 69, 78, 86–97, 113–57, 171–86, 198–200, 208–18, 228, 233, 247; Mukhtar al-Asadi, *al-Sadr al-thani: al-shahid wa al-shahid* (n.p., 1999), esp. 12–13, 17–19, 62, 79, 102, 125, 133–35; Faleh Jabar, *The Shi'ite Movement in Iraq* (London, 2003), 183–84; Juan Cole, "The United States and Shi'ite Religious Factions in Post-Ba'thist Iraq," *MEJ* 57 (2003): 550–54; Pierre-Jean Luizard, *La question irakienne*, 2d ed. (Paris, 2004), 187, 400–401.

43. Fukayki, *Awkar al-hazima*, 274–75; 'Alawi, *Dawlat al-isti'ara al-qawmiyya*, 73; Ibrahim, *al-Ta'ifiyya*, 257; Dann, *Iraq under Qassem*, 246–47; Khadduri, *Republican Iraq*, 226; British Embassy, Baghdad, 29 January 1966 and 20 December 1969, FO 371/186743/EQ1015/3 and FCO 17/871.

44. Amir Iskandar, *Saddam husayn: munadilan wa-mufakkiran wa-insanan* (Paris, 1980), 17–18, 21; Yunis Ibrahim al-Samarra'i, *al-Qaba'il al-'iraqiyya*, 2d ed., 2 vols. (Baghdad, 1989), 2:655–58; Anon., "Bayn al-qa'id saddam husayn

wa al-najaf al-ashraf," *al-Turath al-Sha'bi* 3 (1990): 4–5; Anon., "Madha hasala fi awakhir 'am 1990 wa-hadhihi al-ashhur min 'am 1991," 12.

45. Talal Salim al-Hudaythi, "Min suwwar al-muqawama wa al-tahaddi fi al-amthal al-sha'biyya," *al-Turath al-Sha'bi*, nos. 11 and 12 (1980): 21–30; Muhammad Husayn al-Zubaydi, "al-Batal al-sha'bi fi al-ta'rikh," and Shakir al-Barmaki, "al-Ahazij wa al-aghani al-sha'biyya al-'iraqiyya fi al-harb," *al-Turath al-Sha'bi*, nos. 7 and 8 (1984): 17–44; Salih Mahdi al-'Azzawi, "Qira'at fi adab al-harb 'ind al-'arab," *al-Turath al-Sha'bi*, no. 2 (1985): 17–22; Suhayl Qasha, "al-Harb fi al'ab al-sibyan al-'iraqiyyin," *al-Turath al-Sha'bi*, no. 4 (1985): 17–31; Khalid ibn Muhammad al-Qasimi, "al-Dawr al-qawmi li al-aghniya al-'iraqiyya fi muwajahat al-atma' al-farisiyya," *al-Turath al-Sha'bi*, no. 3 (1988): 5–8. See also Ibrahim, *al-Ta'ifiyya*, 411–12.

46. See the many articles in a special issue entitled "Millaf al-basra," *al-Mawrid* 14 (1985): esp. 4, 7, 10–11, 17–18, 51–53, 65–66; Mundhir 'Abd al-Karim al-Bakir, "Dawlat maysan al-'arabiyya," Muhammad Baqir al-Husayni, "Nuqud mamlakat maysan al-'arabiyya wa-dawruha al-ta'rikhi wa al-hadari wa al-i'lami," and Faruq 'Umar Fawzi, "Dawr ahl maysan fi al-difa' 'an 'urubat al-'iraq," *al-Mawrid* 15 (1986): 19, 21, 35–42; Jabbar 'Abdallah al-Juwaybrawi, *Ta'rikh maysan wa-'asha'ir al-'amara: dirasa ijtima'iyya, iqtisadiyya, siyasiyya* (Baghdad, 1990), esp. 1–20, 69–73, 99–111, 165–71, 190–97, 282–91.

47. Amir Tahiri, "Saddam husayn yuhawil ihya' nizam al-'asha'ir ba'da inhiyar nizam al-saytara al-hizbiyya," *al-Sharq al-Awsat*, 15 May 1996, reproduced by the Center for Iraqi Studies (London, 1996), 23–24; Nakash, *The Shi'is of Iraq*, 88–89, 93–94, 278; Amatzia Baram, "Neo-Tribalism in Iraq: Saddam Hussein's Tribal Policies, 1991–1996," *IJMES* 29 (1997): 7, 12–13, 19–20; Faleh Jabar, "Shaykhs and Ideologues: Detribalization and Retribalization in Iraq, 1968–1998," *MERIP* 215 (2000): 31, 48; Keiko Sakai, "Tribalization as a Tool of State Control in Iraq: Observations on the Army, the Cabinets, and the National Assembly," in *Tribes and Power: Nationalism and Ethnicity in the Middle East*, ed. Faleh Abdul-Jabar and Hosham Dawod (London, 2003), 137–38, 149, 152, 156–59; Asadi, *al-Sadr al-thani*, 139–44; Ra'd Kamil, "Saddam assasa jaysh muhammad qabla suqutihi," *al-Sharq al-Awsat*, 17 November 2004.

Chapter 4
The Revival of Shi'ism in Lebanon

1. "al-Su'al wa al-jawab," *al-'Irfan* 17 (1929): 624.

2. Kamal Salibi, *A House of Many Mansions: The History of Lebanon Reconsidered* (Berkeley, 1988), 25–26, 32–33, 35, 183; Elizabeth Picard, *Lebanon, a Shattered Country: Myths and Realities of the Wars in Lebanon*, trans. Franklin Philip (New York, 1996), 66–67; Meir Zamir, *The Formation of Modern Lebanon* (London, 1985), 126–32; idem, *Lebanon's Quest: The Road to Statehood, 1926–1939*, 2d ed. (New York, 2000), esp. 108–12, 206; Najla 'Atiyya, *Lubnan: al-mushkila wa al-ma'sa* (Beirut, 1977), 30–38; Muhammad Jamil Bayhum, *Lubnan*

bayna mashriq wa-maghrib, 1920–1969 (Beirut, 1969), 34; Muhammad 'Ali Dannawi, *al-Muslimun fi lubnan: muwatinun la ra'aya* (Beirut, 1973), 46–47.

3. Salibi, *A House of Many Mansions*, 27, 31–33, 37, 41, 53, 180; Fouad Ajami, *The Arab Predicament: Arab Political Thought and Practice since 1967*, 2d ed. (Cambridge, 1992), 192; Samir Khalaf, *Lebanon's Predicament* (New York, 1987), 274; Michael Hudson, *The Precarious Republic: Political Modernization in Lebanon* (New York, 1968), 190–97; Malcolm Kerr, "Political Decision Making in a Confessional Democracy," in *Politics in Lebanon*, ed. Leonard Binder (New York, 1966), 209; Clovis Maksoud, "Lebanon and Arab Nationalism," in Binder, *Politics in Lebanon*, 239; John Entelis, *Pluralism and Party Transformation in Lebanon: Al-Kata'ib, 1936–1970* (Leiden, 1974), 29–32; Nazih Ayubi, *Over-Stating the Arab State: Politics and Society in the Middle East* (London, 1995), 115–16; 'Atiyya, *Lubnan*, 60.

4. Hani Fahs, *al-Shi'a wa al-dawla fi lubnan: malamih fi al-ru'ya wa al-dhakira* (Beirut, 1996), 67–68; Fouad Ajami, *The Vanished Imam: Musa al-Sadr and the Shia of Lebanon* (Ithaca, 1986), 205.

5. Muhammad Jabir Al Safa', *Ta'rikh jabal 'amil*, 2d ed. (Beirut, n.d.), 213–15, 223–24; Sulayman Zahir, *Jabal 'amil fi al-harb al-kawniyya* (Beirut, 1986), 72–73; Ahmad Rida, "Li al-ta'rikh: min mudhakkirat al-ustadh al-shaykh ahmad rida," *al-'Irfan* 33 (1946–47): 257, 989; 'Ali 'Abd al-Mun'im Shu'ayb, *Matalib jabal 'amil: al-wahda, al-musawa fi lubnan al-kabir, 1900–1936* (Beirut, 1986), 66–77, 80–85; idem, "Ittijahat qadat al-ra'y fi jabal 'amil, 1914–1936," *al-Muntalaq* 104 (1993): 89–96; Mustafa Muhammad Bazzi, *Jabal 'amil fi muhitihi al-'arabi, 1864–1948* (Beirut, 1993), 89–91, 161–83, 200–236, 244; Waddah Sharara, *al-Umma al-qaliqa: al-'amiliyyun wa al-'asabiyya al-'amiliyya 'ala 'atabat al-dawla al-lubnaniyya* (Beirut, 1996), 249–51, 267–71, 277, 298, 305–9; Fahs, *al-Shi'a*, 31, 87; Muhammad Murad, "Jabal 'amil wa-ishkaliyyat al-khiyarat fi marhalat ta'sis lubnan al-kabir, 1918–1926," *al-Muntalaq* 106 (1994): 158; Anon., "al-Shi'a wa al-waza'if" and "huquq al-Shi'a al-mahduma," *al-'Irfan* 6 (1921): 293–94, 405; Zamir, *Modern Lebanon*, 68, 82, 84–86, 135–36; idem, *Lebanon's Quest*, 111.

6. Murad, "Jabal 'amil," 163–64; Shu'ayb, *Matalib jabal 'amil*, 94–98; idem, "Ittijahat qadat al-ra'y," 96; Bazzi, *Jabal 'amil*, 253–62; Zamir, *Modern Lebanon*, 175, 182–83, 188–90, 210–11; idem, *Lebanon's Quest*, 111; Majed Halawi, *A Lebanon Defied: Musa al-Sadr and the Shi'a Community* (Boulder, Colo., 1992), 40–41.

7. Nawal Fayyad, *Safahat min ta'rikh jabal 'amil fi al-'ahdayn al-'uthmani wa al-faransi* (Beirut, 1998), 89; Shu'ayb, *Matalib jabal 'amil*, esp. 113–20, 151–63; idem, "Ittijahat qadat al-ra'y," 97–104; Bazzi, *Jabal 'amil*, 262, 346–57; Zamir, *Lebanon's Quest*, 59, 156–57, 196–97, 205–8.

8. Iskandar al-Riyashi, *Qabla wa-ba'd: 1918 ila 1941* (Beirut, n.d.), 215. See also Hani Faris, *al-Niza'at al-ta'ifiyya fi ta'rikh lubnan al-hadith* (Beirut, 1980), 121; Fahs, *al-Shi'a*, 65, 69–72, 87–95; Theodor Hanf, *Coexistence in Wartime*

Lebanon: Decline of a State and Rise of a Nation, trans. John Richardson (London, 1993), 406.

9. Muhsin al-Amin, *Khitat jabal 'amil* (Beirut, 1961), 47–52; Muhammad Kazim Makki, *Muntalaq al-hayah al-thaqafiyya fi jabal 'amil* (Beirut, 1991), 46; Muhammad Kurd 'Ali, *Khitat al-sha'm*, 6 pts. in 3 vols. (Damascus, 1925–28), 3,6:253; Shu'ayb, *Matalib jabal 'amil*, 43, 89–90; Salam al-Ra'si, *Li-'ala tadi'*, 2 vols. (Beirut, n.d.), 1:60–63; Mas'ud Zahir, *Ta'rikh lubnan al-ijtima'i, 1914–1926* (Beirut, 1974), 85–87; al-Majlis al-Thaqafi li-Lubnan al-Janubi, *Safahat min ta' rikh jabal 'amil* (Beirut, 1979), 84, 94–95; Muhammad Taqi al-Faqih, *Jabal 'amil fi al-ta'rikh* (Beirut, 1986), 15–16; Muhammad Zu'aytar, *al-Maruniyya fi lubnan: qadiman wa-hadithan* (Beirut, 1994), 84.

10. Muhammad Jawad Mughniyya, *al-Wad' al-hadir fi jabal 'amil fi matla' al-istiqlal: bidayat al-qahr wa al-hirman*, 2d ed. (Beirut, 1984), 29–35, 81–87; idem, "al-'Ulama' wa al-zu'ama' fi jabal 'amil," *al-'Irfan* 32 (1946): 364; Nabil Khalifa, *al-Shi'a fi lubnan: thawrat al-dimugrafiyya wa al-hirman* (Beirut, 1984), 54; Augustus Richard Norton, *Amal and the Shi'a: Struggle for the Soul of Lebanon* (Austin, 1987), 16–18; Halawi, *Lebanon Defied*, 42, 74–75; Ajami, *The Vanished Imam*, 60–61; Farid el-Khazen, *The Breakdown of the State in Lebanon, 1967–1976* (London, 2000), 42; Hanf, *Coexistence*, 79, 93–94, 110, 554.

11. Mughniyya, *al-Wad' al-hadir*, 41–63, 67–71, 75; Waddah Sharara, *Dawlat hizballah: lubnan mujtama'an islamiyan* (Beirut, 1996), 24–46, 58–59; al-Majlis al-Thaqafi li-Lubnan al-Janubi, *Wujuh thaqafiyya min al-janub*, 2 vols. (Beirut, 1981–1984), 1:7–24; Bazzi, *Jabal 'amil*, 279–85; Fahs, *al-Shi'a*, 52–53; 'Ali al-Sha'mi, "'Ulama' jabal 'amil wa-mushkilat al-intima' al-siyasi," *Amal* 406 (1985): 61; Ajami, *The Vanished Imam*, 72–73, 112; Halawi, *Lebanon Defied*, 90, 103–6.

12. Mughniyya, *al-Wad' al-hadir*, 13–25, 67–71, 75; idem, "'Ulama' al-din: ma lahum wa-ma 'alayhum," *al-'Irfan* 31 (1945): 326, 483–84; idem, "al-'Ulama' wa al-zu'ama'," 362–65; idem, *Tajarub muhammad jawad mughniyya* (Beirut, 1980), 452–57. See also Muhammad Kurani, *al-Judhur al-ta'rikhiyya li al-muqawama al-islamiyya fi jabal 'amil* (Beirut, 1993), 266–68; Murad, "Jabal 'amil," 164.

13. Yusuf Qazma Khuri, *al-Ta'ifiyya fi lubnan: min khilal munaqashat majlis al-nuwwab* (Beirut, 1989), esp. 20–24, 26, 29–30, 42–44, 50–56, 88, 186–96, 280, 289–92, 296–99, 346. See also *al-'Irfan* 49 (1962): 698–702, 1011–14; 50 (1962–63): 114–21, 333–35; and 51 (1963–64): 117–22, 776.

14. Fahs, *al-Shi'a*, 77–84.

15. Bishara Khalil al-Khuri, *Haqa'iq lubnaniyya*, 2 vols. (Harisa, 1960), 2:7–9, 17, 289–99; George Dib, "Selections from Riyad Solh's Speech in the Lebanese Assembly (October 1943) Embodying the Main Principles of the Lebanese National Pact," *MEF* 34 (January 1959): 6–7. See also Basim al-Jisr, *Mithaq 1943: li-madha kana wa-hal saqata?* (Beirut, 1978), 14, 133, 142–59; Riyad al-Samad, *al-Ta'ifiyya wa-lu'bat al-hukm fi lubnan* (Beirut, 1977), 94; Entelis, *Pluralism*, 25–26; Salibi, *A House of Many Mansions*, 179, 185–86.

16. Hasan al-'Alawi, *al-Shi'a wa al-dawla al-qawmiyya fi al-'iraq* (Paris, 1989), 235, 237–38; Sa'id al-Samarra'i, *al-Ta'ifiyya fi al-'iraq: al-waqi' wa al-hall* (London, 1993), 141; Farhad Ibrahim, *al-Ta'ifiyya wa al-siyasa fi al-'alam al-'arabi: namudhaj al-Shi'a fi al-'iraq* (Cairo, 1996), 355; Sami Ofeish, "Lebanon's Second Republic: Secular Talk, Sectarian Application," *ASQ* 21 (1999): 100.

17. Anis Sayigh, *Lubnan al-ta'ifi* (Beirut, 1955), 17, 19, 22–23, 145–47, 157–58, 162; Mishal Gharib, *al-Ta'ifiyya wa al-iqta'iyya fi lubnan* (Beirut, 1964), esp. 48–52; Nasif Nassar, *Nahwa mujtama' jadid: muqaddamat asasiyya fi naqd al-mujtama' al-ta'ifi* (Beirut, 1970), 64, 103–29; Iliya Hariq, *Man yahkum lubnan* (Beirut, 1972), esp. 61–62; Samad, *al-Ta'ifiyya*, 97–99, 101, 107; Dannawi, *al-Muslimun*, 55–57; Fu'ad Shahin, *al-Ta'ifiyya fi lubnan: hadiruha wa-judhuruha al-ta'rikhiyya wa al-ijtima'iyya* (Beirut, 1980), 5–6, 18–19, 169–75; Mahdi 'Amil, *Fi al-dawla al-ta'ifiyya* (Beirut, 1986), esp. 186–90; Burhan Ghalyun, *Nizam al-ta'ifiyya: min al-dawla ila al-qabila* (Beirut, 1990), 5–7, 25–26, 42–43, 109, 202; Sami Makarim, "al-Ta'ifiyya wa al-musawa: al-waqi' wa al-mustaqbal," *al-Ghadir*, nos. 23–24 (1993): 106–9. See also Hisham Sharabi, "The Problems of the Lebanese Intellectual Today," in Binder, *Politics in Lebanon*, 258; Ralph Crow, "Religious Sectarianism in the Lebanese Political System," *JP* 24 (1962): 489–520; Ussama Makdisi, *The Culture of Sectarianism: Community, History, and Violence in Nineteenth-Century Ottoman Lebanon* (Berkeley, 2000), esp. 6–7, 164–65.

18. Kamal Yusuf al-Hajj, *al-Ta'ifiyya al-bana'a aw falsafat al-mithaq al-watani* (Beirut, 1961), esp. 14, 140–43, 150, 155, 157–63, 194–96, 241, 251–55.

19. Henri Lammens, *La Syrie: Précis historiques*, 2 pts. (Beirut, 1921), esp. 2:8–22; Asad Rustum and Fu'ad Afram al-Bustani, *Ta'rikh lubnan al-mujaz li-talabat al-shahada al-ibtida'iyya* (Beirut, 1937), esp. 57–64; Antwan Najm, *al-Wahda al-lubnaniyya* (Beirut, 1960), 16–22, 104–6, 115–17; Jawad Bulus, *Lubnan wa al-buldan al-mujawira*, 2d ed. (Beirut, 1969), 414; Philip Hitti, *Lebanon in History* (New York, 1957), 246–47, 257; Salibi, *A House of Many Mansions*, 36, 130–36, 186, 198; Khazen, *Breakdown of the State*, 131; Anon., *Fi al-qadiyya al-lubnaniyya: maqalat jaridat al-'amal, 1974–1976* (Beirut, 1979), 29.

20. Ajami, *The Vanished Imam*, 61–62, 72–73, 112, 114–15, 157; Faris, *al-Niza'at al-ta'ifiyya*, 128–29; Salibi, *A House of Many Mansions*, 47–48, 50–53; idem, *Crossroads to Civil War: Lebanon, 1958–1976* (New York, 1976), 143; Hudson, *The Precarious Republic*, 199; Riyashi, *Qabla wa-ba'd*, 211.

21. Graham Fuller and Rend Rahim Francke, *The Arab Shi'a: The Forgotten Muslims* (New York, 1999), 203.

22. Meir Zamir, "Emile Eddé and the Territorial Integrity of Lebanon," *MES* 14 (1978): 232–35. See also Zu'aytar, *al-Maruniyya fi lubnan*, esp. 479–85.

23. Eliahu Sasson, *Baderekh El ha-Shalom: Igrot ve-Sihot* (Tel-Aviv, 1978), 224–25. See also Moshe Sharett, *Yoman Medini*, 4 vols. (Tel-Aviv, 1968–74), 2:141; Eliahu Elath, *Shivat Tzion ve-'Arav* (Tel-Aviv, 1974), 294–96, 308; Zamir, *Lebanon's Quest*, 221; Itamar Rabinovich, *The War for Lebanon, 1970–1985* (Ithaca, 1985), 21–22; Avner Yaniv, *Dilemmas of Security: Politics, Strategy, and*

the Israeli Experience in Lebanon (Oxford, 1987), esp. 29–30; Badr al-Hajj, *al-Judhur al-ta'rikhiyya li al-mashru' al-sahyuni fi lubnan* (Beirut, 1982), 102–4; Zu'aytar, *al-Maruniyya fi lubnan*, 486.

24. Ajami, *The Vanished Imam*, 91, 112, 116, 160.

25. Leila Fawaz, *Merchants and Migrants in Nineteenth-Century Beirut* (Cambridge, 1983), 50, 155; Halawi, *Lebanon Defied*, 52, 59–60, 68–70, 74–75; Norton, *Amal and the Shi'a*, 23, 27, 91; Hala Jaber, *Hezbollah: Born with a Vengeance* (New York, 1997), 1.

26. "Aham al-akhbar wa al-'ara'," *al-'Irfan* 54 (1966): 407; Musa al-Sadr, "al-Watan haqq wa-wajib wa la yumkin fasluhuma abadan," 2 pts., *Amal* 493 and 494 (3 and 10 July 1987): 1:41–43 and 2:47–49; idem, "Mafhum al-watan wa al-muwatin wa al-muwatiniyya," *Amal* 584 (31 March 1989): 4–5; Najib Jamal al-Din, *al-Shi'a 'ala al-muftaraq aw musa al-sadr* (n.p., n.d.), 71; 'Adil Rida, *Ma'a al-i'tidhar li al-imam al-sadr* (Cairo, 1981), 93–94. See also 'Ali al-Sha'mi, "Lubnan al-kabir wa-ma'ziq al-ijtima' al-'amili," *al-Muntalaq* 104 (1993): 73; "Mudhakkirat al-majlis al-islami al-Shi'i al-a'la al-sadira 'am 1977," reproduced in Fahs, *al-Shi'a*, 20, 185–87; Ajami, *The Vanished Imam*, 27, 62, 127.

27. "Aham al-akhbar wa al-'ara'," 406, 408–9; Muhammad Husayn Shams al-Din, "al-Majlis al-islami al-Shi'i al-a'la," *al-'Irfan* 47 (1960): 767–68; "Nida' min al-'allama muhammad jawad shirri ila 'ulama' al-muslimin fi lubnan hawla qadiyyat insha' al-majlis al-milli," *al-Nahar*, 17 December 1966; "Bayan al-ta'ifa al-islamiyya al-Shi'iyya fi lubnan," *Amal* 614 (27 October 1989): 42–43; Hasan S., "Hakadha wulida al-majlis al-Shi'i," *al-Shira'* 97 (23 January 1984): 12–13; Rida, *Ma'a al-i'tidhar*, 94–97; Faris, *al-Niza'at al-ta'ifiyya*, 129–30; Jamal al-Din, *al-Shi'a 'ala al-muftaraq*, 113–22; Fahs, *al-Shi'a*, 22; Ajami, *The Vanished Imam*, 113–19; Halawi, *Lebanon Defied*, 139–42, 157.

28. Mustafa Sadr al-Din, "Yaqzat jabal 'amil," *Amal* 209 (26 March 1982): 6–7; Fahs, *al-Shi'a*, 26; Hasan S., "al-Shi'a hum sabab al-harb fi lubnan," *al-Shira'* 94 (2 January 1984): 16; idem, "al-Infijar alladhi walada amal," *al-Shira'* 98 (30 January 1984): 18–19; Ajami, *The Vanished Imam*, 123–57; Norton, *Amal and the Shi'a*, 35, 40–41, 46–48; Halawi, *Lebanon Defied*, 129, 131–32, 150–51, 165, 183–84; Andreas Rieck, *Die Schiiten und der Kampf um den Libanon: Politische Chronik, 1958–1988* (Hamburg, 1989), 94–98.

29. Hudson, *The Precarious Republic*, 194; Shahin, *al-Ta'ifiyya fi lubnan*, 117–23, 153–63, 186–87; Fouad Ajami, "The End of Pan-Arabism," in *Pan-Arabism and Arab Nationalism: The Continuing Debate*, ed. Tawfic Farah (Boulder, Colo., 1987), 102–3; idem, *The Arab Predicament*, 193–94; Najm, *al-Wahda al-lubnaniyya*, esp. 9, 111; Entelis, *Pluralism*, 36–37, 77–79; Tewfik Khalaf, "The Phalange and the Maronite Community: From Lebanonism to Maronitism," in *Essays on the Crisis in Lebanon*, ed. Roger Owen (London, 1976), 44–45, 51, 55; Salibi, *Crossroads to Civil War*, 3–4, 7, 21–22, 126–27, 144; idem, *The Modern History of Lebanon* (London, 1965), 198–202; idem, *A House of Many Mansions*, 170–75; Anon., *Fi al-qadiyya al-lubnaniyya*, 210, 215, 219, 224–25, 427, 436, 468; 'Ali Muhammad Lagha, *al-Ittijahat al-siyasiyya fi lubnan, 1920–1982*

(Beirut, 1991), 389–401, 421–36; Khazen, *Breakdown of the State*, esp. 108, 379–81; Asher Kaufman, *Reviving Phoenicia: The Search for Identity in Lebanon* (London, 2004), 141–83.

30. Ajami, *The Vanished Imam*, 161–63, 173, 178–79, 205, 213, 218; idem, "Lebanon and Its Inheritors," *FA* 63 (1985): 779, 784–87; Augustus Richard Norton, "Shi'ism and Social Protest in Lebanon," in *Shi'ism and Social Protest*, ed. Juan Cole and Nikki Keddie (New Haven, 1986), 168–70; Khazen, *Breakdown of the State*, 367.

31. Ajami, *The Vanished Imam*, 169–70; Norton, *Amal and the Shi'a*, 88–106; Magnus Ranstorp, *Hizballah in Lebanon: The Politics of the Western Hostage Crisis* (New York, 1997), 25–34; Jaber, *Hezbollah*, 67; Martin Kramer, "Muhammad Husayn Fadlallah," *Orient* 26 (1985): 148; Hasan Fadlallah, *al-Khiyar al-akhar: hizballah, al-sira al-dhatiyya wa al-mawqif* (Beirut, 1994), 88; Sharif al-Husayni, "Hizballah: haraka 'askariyya am siyasiyya am diniyya?" *al-Shira'* 209 (17 March 1986): 14–21; Muhammad al-Safwani, "Ihtiwa' hizb al-da'wa bi-hizballah," *al-Shira'* 625 (25 April 1994): 38–39; Khalifa, *al-Shi'a fi lubnan*, 21–25; 'Akif Haydar, *al-Ashya' bi-asma'iha: min jabal lubnan afdal* (Beirut, 1995), 70; Shimon Shapira, *Hizballah: Bein Iran ve-Levanon* (Tel-Aviv, 2000), 96–114.

32. Sharara, *Dawlat hizballah*, 56, 60–61, 71, 85, 88–89, 97, 103, 116, 153, 178–80, 189, 195–24; Fahs, *al-Shi'a*, 132–34; 'Ali Kurani, *Tariqat hizballah fi al-'amal al-islami* (Beirut, 1986), 77–78; Hasan Fadlallah, *al-Khiyar al-akhar*, 85; Shapira, *Hizballah*, 116–44. For the citation, see Jaber, *Hezbollah*, 168.

33. Anon., "al-Khawarij yutliqun qadhifa 'ala al-nas wa-tasrihan didd al-majlis," *Amal* 540 (28 May 1988): 16–17; Anon., "al-khawarij yujhidun furas al-hall al-amni isti'dadan li-mughamara jadida" and "Rafa'u Shi'ar al-muqawama al-islamiyya li al-tastir 'ala jara'imihim," *Amal* 574 (20 January 1989): 28–29, 44. See also Jad al-Amin and Sina' 'Aytani, "Hal yasqut qarar ahl al-janub?" *al-Shira'* 406 (1 January 1990): 14–17.

34. Anon., "Hizballah yatruh afkaran li-tanzim al-'alaqa ma'a amal: al-matlub hafz al-muqawama wa-tafwit al-furas 'ala al-muta'amirin," *al-'Ahd* 208 (17 June 1988): 1 and 11; Anon., "al-Majlis al-Shi'i: waqi' murr wa-dawr mawhum," *al-'Ahd* 210 (1 July 1988): 5.

35. Sharara, *Dawlat hizballah*, 337, 339; Anon., "Berri yasta'id qarar al-janub," *al-Shira'* 285 (7 September 1987): 10; Muhammad Baqir Shirri, "'Uqdat al-awhadiyya fi za'amat al-janub," *al-Shira'* 288 (28 September 1987): 19–22; Zayn Hamud, "Hasan nasrallah: sayyi' al-tali'," *al-Shira'* 603 (22 November 1993): 17–22. See also Ranstorp, *Hizballah*, 34–39; Hanf, *Coexistence*, 317–18; Martin Kramer, *Arab Awakening and Islamic Revival: The Politics of Ideas in the Middle East* (New Brunswick, 1996), 242; Shapira, *Hizballah*, 170.

36. Picard, *Lebanon*, 145, 156–59; Hanf, *Coexistence*, esp. 583–90, 610, 617–18, 622; Augustus Richard Norton, "Lebanon after Ta'if: Is the Civil War Over?" *MEJ* 45 (1991): 460–64; Ofeish, "Lebanon's Second Republic," 104–13; Neil MacFarquhar, "President of Syria Defends His Nation's Role in Lebanon," *NYT*,

10 October 2004. For the text of the Ta'if accord, see Ahmad Sirhal, *Azmat al-hukm fi lubnan: 'awamil wa-hulul* (Beirut, 1990), 149–60.

37. News interview with Muhammad Mahdi Shams al-Din, *al-Bilad* 18 (8 October 1990): 13–14; Nasir Sharara, "Rabi' intikhabat al-majlis al-islami al-Shi'i: al-ma'raka fi muntasaf al-tariq," *al-Shira'* 563 (1 February 1993): 24; Zayn Hamud, "Amal-hizballah: sira' 'ala haffat al-huwiyya," *al-Shira'* 710 (18 December 1995): 19; idem, "al-Imam shams al-din: law 'ada stalin," *al-Shira'* 731 (27 May 1996): 15–20; Hasan Sabra, "Harb salat al-jum'a: safqa bayna fadlallah wa-nasrallah," *al-Shira'* 731 (27 May 1996): 3–7; Anon., "Lubnan: qissat khilafat al-Shi'a," *al-Majalla* 852 (15 June 1996): 36.

38. Anon., "Li-hadha qarara hizballah dukhul al-intikhabat al-niyabiyya," *al-Bilad* 87 (4 July 1992): 16; Muhammad Husayn Fadlallah, "Hizb al-umma aw ummat al-hizb," *al-Muntalaq* 29 (1985): 4–12; news interviews with Fadlallah, "li-Nanfatih ma'an 'ala al-masih wa-muhammad," *al-Bilad* 64 (11 January 1992): 46–50, and "Da'watuna li al-hiwar ba'ida 'an ayy istihlak mahhali," 2 pts., *al-Bilad* 103 and 104 (24 and 31 October 1992): 1:48–53, 2:46–49; Ahmad Khalid, "Hizballah: budhur inshiqaq yantazir al-daw' al-akhdar al-irani," *al-Shira'* 562 (25 January 1993): 22–23; Zayn Hamud, "Nasrallah: 'uqdat musadarat al-intisar," *al-Shira'* 729 (13 May 1996): 14–16; Hasan Sabra, "Hizballah yaltazim al-labnana rasmiyyan al-'an," *al-Shira'* 889 (5 July 1999): 3; Hasan Fadlallah, *al-Khiyar al-akhar*, 96, 104–17; Fahs, *al-Shi'a*, 126–30, 137, 149–56; Ahmad Nizar Hamzeh, "Lebanon's Hizbullah: From Islamic Revolution to Parliamentary Accommodation," *TWQ* 14 (1993): 321, 324, 334; Fuller and Rahim Francke, *The Arab Shi'a*, 218–19; Ranstorp, *Hizballah*, 51–52, 119–33; Jaber, *Hezbollah*, 66, 71–74, 210–11; Kramer, *Arab Awakening*, 227; Shapira, *Hizballah*, 184–92, 203–4.

39. News interview with Hasan Nasrallah, "Itma'inu: sa-abqa aminan 'amman," *al-Shira'* 826 (30 March 1998): 17; Amal Saad-Ghorayeb, *Hizbu'llah: Politics and Religion* (London, 2002), 32–33, 46, 53–54, 117; Sami Hajjar, "Hizballah: Terrorism, National Liberation, or Menace?" Strategic Studies Institute, U.S. Army War College (Washington, D.C.; August 2002), 16, http://au.af.mil/au/awc/awcgate/ssi/hizbala.pdf; Judith Palmer Harik, *Hezbollah: The Changing Face of Terrorism* (London, 2004), 50, 77, 96, 100–101, 149; Anon., "Hizballah: al-hiwar ma'a 'awn mustamir wa-nu'ayyid baqa' lahud," *al-Anwar*, 16 June 2005; Anon., "Washinton sara'at ila al-tarhib lakinnaha tarfid al-ta'amul ma'a wazir hizballah," *al-Nahar*, 20 July 2005.

40. Haydar, *al-Ashya' bi-asma'iha*, 71–72; Amin Sha'lan, "al-Janub ila ayn? hizballah yataqadam wa-harakat amal ma zalat tahlum," *al-Shira'* 622 (4 April 1994): 19–22; Amir Qansuh, "Siyasat al-sulta tajhil abna' al-biqa'," *al-'Ahd* 644 (25 June 1996): 8; Anon., "Berri-Nasrallah: i'tilaf am ikhtilaf?" *al-Shira'* 742 (12 August 1996): 13–15; Zayn Hamud, "Berri: isti'adat al-mubadara," *al-Shira'* 730 (20 May 1996): 17–22; Husayn 'Abdallah, "Hizballah-harakat amal: ta'awun 'ala thalath mahawir," *al-Bilad* 327 (15 March 1997): 12; Hasan Sabra, "Amal-hizballah: sira' ma ba'd 425," *al-Shira'* 832 (18 May 1998): 3–5; Wisam al-Amin,

"Amal tabhath 'an nasiha wa-hizballah yughliq al-abwab," *al-Shira'* 942 (24 July 2000): 25–27; Nasir Sharara, "Hizbuna hizballah wa-amal tanzimuna," *al-Shira'* 984 (28 May 2001): 20–22; Anon., "Hizballah yud'if amal wa la yaktasihha," *al-Hayat*, 25 May 2004; Augustus Richard Norton, "Hizballah of Lebanon: Extremist Ideals vs. Mundane Politics," Council on Foreign Relations (New York, 1999), 9, 20, http://cfr.org/pdf/Norton.pdf; Graham Usher, "Why Hizbullah's Wings Have Been Clipped," *MEINT* 535 (4 October 1996): 18–19; Farid el-Khazen, "Political Parties in Postwar Lebanon: Parties in Search of Partisans," *MEJ* 57 (2003): 615, 617, 619; Palmer Harik, *Hezbollah*, 51, 95, 107–9, 151; Ahmad Nizar Hamzeh, *In the Path of Hizbullah* (New York, 2004), 116–35.

Chapter 5
Between Aspirations and Reality

1. From Jedda to Foreign Office, 1 July 1964, FO 371/174672/1017/2; Possible Change of Regime in Saudi Arabia, 1963, FO 371/174671/1015/8/G; Hamza al-Hasan, "al-Shi'a wa-masar al-'amal al-watani fi al-mamlaka," *al-Jazira al-'Arabiyya* 8 (September 1991): 19; idem, "al-Mu'arada fi al-su'udiyya: al-ta'rjuh bayn al-hawa al-iqlimi wa al-wataniyya al-jami'a," *al-Jazira al-'Arabiyya* 18 (July 1992): 44–47; idem, *al-Shi'a fi al-mamlaka al-'arabiyya al-su'udiyya*, 2 vols. (Beirut, 1993), 2:379–83; Tawfiq al-Shaykh, "'Ala hamish ijtima' al-qimma li-duwwal majlis al-ta'awun fi al-kuwayt: da'wa li-tahwil al-majlis ila itar li al-wahda," *al-Jazira al-'Arabiyya* 11 (December 1991): 2–5; Rabitat 'Umum al-Shi'a fi al-Su'udiyya, *al-Shi'a fi al-su'udiyya: al-waqi' al-sa'b wa al-tatallu'at al-mashru'a* (London, 1991), 77–90.

2. Anon., "Mahzalat al-'alam: al-aktaf al-'ariyya tahmi al-shawarib," "al-Muthaqqafun wa al-shakhsiyyat al-wataniyya yutalibun al-usra al-malika bi al-taghyir," "al-ta'addudiyya: waqi' ma'ash tantazir al-i'tiraf al-rasmi," "al-A'ila al-malika wa al-'amaliyya al-dusturiyya," and "al-Adyan tajtami' fi jazirat al-'arab," *al-Jazira al-'Arabiyya* 1 (January 1991): 1–3, 20, 26–27, 49; Anon., "al-Infitah al-fikri bayn al-madhahib al-islamiyya," *al-Jazira al-'Arabiyya* 2 (February 1991): 35–37; Anon., "Risala ila al-malik tutalib bi al-islah al-siyasi" and "Watha'iq muta'addida tasubb fi majra al-taghyir," *al-Jazira al-'Arabiyya* 3 (March 1991): 24–25, 31; Anon., "I'adat al-tasalluh wa-durus al-azma," *al-Jazira al-'Arabiyya* 6 (July 1991): 5–6; Anon., "al-Amn al-watani bayn mafhumayn: al-sha'bi al-da'i li al-tatwir wa al-rasmi al-qa'im 'ala ta'ziz al-rad' al-khariji li-mushkilat al-dakhil," *al-Jazira al-'Arabiyya* 9 (October 1991): 8; Hasan al-Saffar, "al-Wahda al-wataniyya: man yaduqq naqus al-khatar?" *al-Jazira al-'Arabiyya* 12 (January 1992): 3–7; Hasan 'Abd al-Hadi, "Mafhum al-wahda wa-ishkaliyyat al-intima' al-khass," *al-Jazira al-'Arabiyya* 28 (May 1993): 34–35; Anon., "al-quwwat al-su'udiyya al-musallaha wa al-taghyir," *al-Jazira al-'Arabiyya* 31 (August 1993): 32–34.

3. Anon., "Da'wa ila al-hiwar wa al-musalaha al-wataniyya," *al-Jazira al-'Arabiyya* 31 (August 1993): 2–4; Anon., "Hal yasbah al-Shi'a muwatinun am fatrat

naqaha yastaghilluha al-nizam didd al-tayar al-salafi?" *Risalat al-Haramayn* 45 (November 1993): 2; Anon., "Fatawa al-takfir tulahiq al-Shi'a wa al-'a'idun fi mu'taqal kabir," *Risalat al-Haramayn* 49 (August 1994): 29; Riyad Najib al-Rayyis, "Safqat al-'asr al-siyasiyya: al-qissa al-kamila li al-ittifaq al-su'udi al-Shi'i," *al-Nahar*, 7 March 1994; Madawi al-Rasheed, "The Shi'a of Saudi Arabia: A Minority in Search of Cultural Authenticity," *BJMES* 25 (1998): 136; Mamoun Fandy, *Saudi Arabia and the Politics of Dissent* (New York, 1999), 200–201; Graham Fuller and Rend Rahim Francke, *The Arab Shi'a: The Forgotten Muslims* (New York, 1999), 189–91.

4. David Johnston, "14 Indicted by U.S. in 96 Saudi Blast; Iran Link Is Cited," *NYT*, 22 June 2001; Anon., "Saudi Militants Are Sentenced in 96 Bombing," *NYT*, 2 June 2002; Anon., "Al Qaeda Is Now Suspected in 1996 Bombing Barracks," *NYT*, 14 May 2003. See also Reuven Paz, "From Riyadh 1995 to Sinai 2004: The Return of al-Qaeda to the Arab World," *PRISM* 3 (October 2004): 4.

5. Hamza al-Hasan, "Nahwa mashru' watani jadid," *Qadaya al-Khalij*, December 2002, http://gulfissues.net; Nora Boustany, "Shiite Muslims in Saudi Arabia Emboldened by Hussein's Fall," *WP*, 23 April 2003; Abdulali, "Shia in Saudi Arabia Demand Basic Rights," 12 May 2003, http://jafariyanews.com; Michael Doran, "The Saudi Paradox," *FA* 83 (January/February 2004): 46–49.

6. Hasan bin Farhan al-Maliki, "Manahij al-ta'lim: qira'a naqdiyya li-muqararat al-tawhid li-marahil al-ta'lim al-'am" (n.p., n.d.), esp. 5–8; Neil MacFarquhar, "Under Pressure to Change, Saudis Debate Their Future," *NYT*, 23 November 2003; idem, "Saudis Uneasily Balance Desires for Change and Stability," *NYT*, 4 May 2004; idem, "Saudi Shiites, Long Kept Down, Look to Iraq and Assert Rights," *NYT*, 2 March 2005; David Ottaway, "U.S.-Saudi Relations Show Signs of Stress," *WP*, 21 April 2004; International Crisis Group, "Can Saudi Arabia Reform Itself?" (Cairo and Brussels, 14 July 2004); idem, "Saudi Arabia Backgrounder: Who Are the Islamists?" (Amman, Riyadh, and Brussels, 21 September 2004), http://crisisgroup.org.

7. Muhammad 'Abd al-Qadir al-Jasim and Sawsan 'Ali al-Sha'ir, *al-Bahrayn: qissat al-sira' al-siyasi, 1904–1956* (n.p., 2000), 175–200, 229–48, 269–71, 277–91, 306–7, 311–14, 333, 341–42, 353; Muhammad Ghanim al-Rumayhi, *al-Bahrayn: mushkilat al-taghyir al-siyasi wa al-ijtima'i* (Beirut, 1995), 345–53, 367–72, 379–83, 386–89, 392–95; Sa'id al-Shihabi, *al-Bahrayn, 1920–1971: qira'a fi al-watha'iq al-baritaniyya* (London, 1996), 97–119, 194, 199–200, 206–8, 230–39; 'Abd al-Rahman al-Bakir, *Min al-bahrayn ila al-manfa* (Beirut, 1965), 15–29, 75–141, 171–74; Charles Belgrave, *Personal Column* (London, 1960), 202–5, 210–13, 216, 218–23, 226–33; From Belgrave to Loch, 28 January 1935, IO R/15/2/176; From Political Resident, Bahrain, to Political Resident, Bushire, 18 February 1935, and From Political Resident in the Persian Gulf to the Foreign Secretary to the Government of India, 18 March 1935, FO 371/18920; From Belgrave to Weightman, 13 November 1938, IO R/15/2/176; British Residency, Bahrain, 26 December 1954, FO 371/114586/EA1016/1; Annual Administration Report on Bahrain, 1954, FO 371/114576/EA1011/5; Political Agency, Bahrain, 20

November 1955, FO 371/114587/EA1016/43; Update on the Situation, Bahrain, 17 March 1956, FO 371/120544/EA1016/30; British Residency, Bahrain, 31 July 1956, FO 371/120548/EA1016/135; Resume of the Proceedings against Five Members of the Committee of National Union, 22–23 December 1956, FO 371/126894/EA1016/17.

8. Emile Nakhleh, *Bahrain: Political Development in a Modernizing Society* (Lexington, Mass., 1976), 117, 124–25, 129, 135, 149, 154–61; Fuad Khuri, *Tribe and State in Bahrain* (Chicago, 1980), 214. For the text of the constitution, see Ghasan Qasim al-Mulla, *Riyah al-taghyir fi al-bahrayn* (n.p., n.d.), 330–56.

9. Khuri, *Tribe and State*, 191–93, 219–23, 225–30; Munira Fakhro, "The Uprising in Bahrain: An Assessment," in *The Persian Gulf at the Millennium: Essays in Politics, Economy, Security, and Religion*, ed. Gary Sick and Lawrence Potter (New York, 1997), 173–74.

10. 'Abdallah al-Madani, "Madha yahduth fi al-bahrayn?" *al-Mawaqif* 96 (1 September 1975): 3. See also idem, "Tawahhadat kalimat nuwwab al-sha'b," *al-Mawaqif* 84 (9 June 1975): 3, 6; idem, "Ma hall al-azma al-mutafajjira bayn al-hukuma wa al-majlis al-watani?" and 'Abd al-Amir al-Jamri, "Qanun amn al-dawla la yakhda' li-dawabit islamiyya," *al-Mawaqif* 85 (16 June 1975): 3–4, 5; 'Isa Ahmad Qasim, "al-Itaha bi-bina' al-dimuqratiyya," *al-Mawaqif* 87 (30 June 1975): 5; Anon., "li-Madha istaqallat al-wizara?" *al-Mawaqif* 95 (25 August 1975): 5; Khuri, *Tribe and State*, 230–34.

11. Nakhleh, *Bahrain*, 135, 144, 149; Khuri, *Tribe and State*, 11, 234, 242, 246; Fakhro, "The Uprising in Bahrain," 174–75; Anon., "Qadaya al-musharaka al-siyasiyya fi al-khalij wa al-jazira al-'arabiyya," *al-Thawra al-Islamiyya* 115 (December 1989): 39–40; al-Jabha al-Sha'biyya fi al-Bahrayn, *Fi al-wahda al-wataniyya al-bahrayniyya* (Beirut, 1979), 69–71, 104–5, 110–11; 'Abd al-Hadi Khalaf, *Bina' al-dawla fi al-bahrayn: al-muhimma ghayr al-munjaza* (Beirut, 2000), 67–68.

12. Bahrain Freedom Movement, 15 December 2000, and reports for the months of January and February 2001, http://vob.org; Khalaf, *Bina' al-dawla fi al-bahrayn*, 107–8; Ahmad Munaysi, *al-Bahrayn min al-imara ila al-mamlaka: dirasa fi al-tatawwur al-siyasi wa al-dimuqrati* (Cairo, 2003), 132, 134, 136, 183.

13. Kingdom of Bahrain, "Constitution of the Kingdom of Bahrain," 14 February 2002, http://bahrain.gov.bh/pdfs/constitution.pdf.

14. Sa'id al-Shihabi, "al-Bahrayn: 'awdat al-tawattur bayn al-hukuma wa al-mu'arada," 11 December 2002, and Mansur al-Jamri, "Khiyarat al-dimuqratiyya fi al-bahrayn," *Qadaya al-Khalij*, n.d., http://gulfissues.net; Abdulhadi Khalaf, "A Year of Political Reform Brings Few Real Changes to Bahrain" and "Local Polls in Bahrain: A Royal Triumph," *DS*, 11 February and 19 May 2002; Bahrain Freedom Movement, 21 September 2001; 13, 21, and 25 February, 2 March, 19 May, 22 and 29 June, 7, 10, 12, 18, and 21 July, 8 August, 3 and 4 September, 8, 15, 18, 19, 22, 24, 25, and 30 October, 8, 19, and 13 November, 3 and 18 December 2002; 5 March, 21 April, 3 June, 22 August, and 19 December 2003, 19 April and 28 May 2004; Voice of Bahrain Commentary, December 2001; Abduljalil

Alsingace, "Bahrain: A Gateway to Reforms in the Persian Gulf," December 2004, http://vob.org; Munaysi, *al-Bahrayn*, 137–45, 172, 176, 229–30.

15. On Jordan and Morocco, see Glenn Robinson, "Defensive Democratization in Jordan," *IJMES* 30 (1998): 387–410; Kathrine Rath, "The Process of Democratization in Jordan," *MES* 30 (1994): 540–43, 548–49; Abdeslam Maghraoui, "Political Authority in Crisis: Mohammed VI's Morocco," *MERIP* 218 (Spring 2001): 12–17.

16. Anon., *al-Haraka al-dusturiyya: nidal sha'b al-bahrayn min ajl al-dimuqratiyya* (Manama, 1997), 104; Bahrain Freedom Movement, 21 September 2001; 16 and 19 June, 7 and 10 July, 8 and 13 November, and 3 December 2002; 5 March, 21 April, 30 June, 24 July, 22 August, 5 September, and 29 October 2003, 13 February and 21 May 2004; Voice of Bahrain Commentary, December 2001; Anon., "Nahwa 'amal sha'bi mutawasil li-tahqiq al-mufasala bayn al-diktaturiyya al-khalifiyya," 24 March 2005; http://vob.org; Neil MacFarquhar, "Death in Bahrain Brings Demand That U.S. Leave," *NYT*, 8 April 2002; Mahdi Rabi', "Malik al-bahrayn yuhaddir min itharat al-fitna wa al-mass bi al-wahda warumuz al-hukm," *al-Hayat*, 26 September 2004; idem, "al-Hukuma al-bahrayniyya tu'akkid 'azmiha ittikhadh ijra'at 'iqabiyya didd masirat al-wifaq," *al-Hayat*, 28 March 2005.

17. "Kalima: al-jumhuriyya al-thaniyya jumhuriyyat al-muqawama," *Amal* 555 (9 September 1988): 9. See also al-Majlis al-Thaqafi li-Lubnan al-Janubi, *al-Muqawama al-wataniyya al-lubnaniyya: tariq al-tahrir wa al-wahda* (Beirut, 1984), 45, 50–56; Harakat Amal, 6 *Shubat 1984: al-maghza al-siyasi wa al-ab'ad al-mustaqbaliyya* (n.p., n.d.), 64; Anon., "Nadwa fikriyya fi al-nabatiyya hawla huwiyyat al-muqawama," *Amal* 582 (17 March 1989): 42–46; Zayn Hamud, "Amal tath'ar li-hizballah," *al-Shira'* 797 (8 September 1997): 23–24.

18. Anon., "Khususiyyat al-muqawama al-islamiyya wa a'faquhah al-mustaqbaliyya," 2 pts., *al-Ahd* 121 (19 October 1986): 2:8; news interview with Muhammad Hasan al-Amin, "al-Haymana al-thaqafiyya tastatbi' haymana siyasiyya wa-iqtisadiyya," *al-Bilad* 50 (28 September 1991): 48; Na'im Qasim, "al-'Alaqa bayn al-qawmiyya wa al-islam," *al-Bilad* 244 (12 August 1995): 46–47; news interview with Hasan Nasrallah, "Itma'inu: sa-abqa aminan 'amman," *al-Shira'* 826 (30 March 1998): 22–23; Husayn 'Abdallah, "al-Dars al-lubnani," *al-Bilad* 476 (26 February 2000): 1; Hasan Sabra, "Ba'da tahrir al-janub: mata yataghayyar hizballah?" *al-Shira'* 1034 (27 May 2002): 6–7; Hasan Fadlallah, *al-Khiyar al-akhar: hizballah, al-sira al-dhatiyya wa al-mawqif* (Beirut, 1994), 14, 55, 64–65; Amal Saad-Ghorayeb, *Hizbu'llah: Politics and Religion* (London, 2002), 78, 117, 187; International Crisis Group, "Old Games, New Rules: Conflict on the Israeli-Lebanon Border" (Amman and Brussels, 18 November 2002), 17–19; idem, "Hizbollah: Rebel without a Cause?" (Amman and Brussels, 30 July 2003), 7–10, 16–18, http://crisisgroup.org; Judith Palmer Harik, *Hezbollah: The Changing Face of Terrorism* (London, 2004), x, 122–23, 161–62, 186–87, 191; Ahmad Nizar Hamzeh, *In the Path of Hizbullah* (New York, 2004), 135–41; Adam Shatz, "In Search of Hezbollah," 2 pts., *NYRB*, 29 April and 13 May 2004; Anon., "Militant

Urges Restraint as Lebanese Chafe under Syria's Grip," *NYT*, 20 February 2005; Riyad 'Ilm al-Din, "Ma'ziq hizballah: bayn al-sistani wa-khamina'i," *al-Watan al-'Arabi*, 1461 (4 March 2005): 20–23; Anon., "Hizballah yubdi infitahihi 'ala bahth silah al-muqawama lubnaniyyan wa-yatlub min al-mu'taridin 'alayhi taqdim bada'il li-himayat al-watan," *al-Sharq al-Awsat*, 23 March 2005; Anon., "Nasrallah: al-muqawama laysat mihna wa-musta'idun li-hiwar hawla silahiha," *al-Anwar*, 15 April 2005.

19. News interviews with Muhammad Husayn Fadlallah, "al-Zuruf al-mawdu'iyya la tasmah bi-tahwil lubnan ila jumhuriyya islamiyya," *al-Shira'* 122 (16 July 1984): 13, 15–16; "al-'Allama Muhammad Husayn Fadlallah: al-jumhuriyya al-islamiyya fi iran laysat hukumat kull al-muslimin," *al-Shira'* 219 (26 May 1986): 19. See also Fadlallah's rulings in *al-Mawsim* 21–22 (1995): 659–60, 662–63; Salim al-Hasani, *Sira' al-iradat: dirasa fi al-fikr al-haraki li-samahat a'yatullah muhammad husayn fadlallah*, 2d ed. (Beirut, 1990), 81, 99–100.

20. News interviews with Hasan Nasrallah, "Lubnan sha'b wahid muta'ddid al-adyan," *al-'Ahd* 602 (29 September 1995): 6; "Itma'inu: sa-abqa aminan 'amman," 15, 18; 'Abd al-Mun'im Mustafa Halima Abu Basir al-Tartusi, "Hizballah al-lubnani wa-tasdir al-madhhab al-Shi'i al-rafidi," 2 February 2004, http://abubaseer.bizland.com/articles/read/a65.doc; Augustus Richard Norton, "Hizballah of Lebanon: Extremist Ideals vs. Mundane Politics," Council on Foreign Relations (New York, 1999), 11–12, 16, 20–21, http://cfr.org/pdf/Norton.pdf; Saad-Ghorayeb, *Hizbu'llah*, 36–37, 46, 49–50, 57; Shatz, "In Search of Hezbollah," 29 April 2004.

21. Hani Fahs, *al-Shi'a wa al-dawla fi lubnan: malamih fi al-ru'ya wa al-dhakira* (Beirut, 1996), 9–12, 17–18, 20, 39–40, 60, 119–20; idem, "al-Shi'a wa al-mujtama' fi lubnan: al-i'tiraf bi al-akhar," *al-Shira'* 741 (5 August 1996): 31; idem, "Hizballah wa al-intikhabat: bayn al-siyasa wa al-tahrir," *al-Shira'* 950 (18 September 2000): 16.

22. News interviews with Muhammad Mahdi Shams al-Din, "al-Dimuqratiyya al-'addudiyya al-qa'ima 'ala mabda' al-shura," *al-Shira'* 176 (29 July 1985): 8; "al-khutut al-'amma li-nizam al-dimuqratiyya al-'addudiyya 'ala mabda' al-shura," *al-Amal* 519 (1 January 1988): 18–20; "Na'am lubnan watan niha'i wa-dawla bi-la din: quburuna fi jizzin 'umruha alf sana," *al-Ghadir* 3 (1993): 23; "Hadha mashru'i li-muwajahat al-tatbi' wa-man ladayhi badil fa li-yataqadam," *al-Bilad* 157 (20 November 1993): 49; "Ad'u li-mujtama' ahli mutadayyin wa li-dawla bi-la din," *al-Bilad* 203 (15 October 1994): 45–46; "Lan askut 'ala fasl al-Shi'a min al-islam," *al-Shira'* 683 (12 June 1995): 5–6; "Wasaya shams al-din li al-Shi'a: al-mashari' al-khassa sharr mutlaq," *al-Shira'* 1055 (21 October 2002): 14–17.

23. News interviews with Muhammad Husayn Fadlallah, "Li-nanfatih ma'an 'ala al-masih wa-muhammad," *al-Bilad* 64 (11 January 1992): 49; "Da'watuna li al-hiwar ba'ida 'an ayy istihlak mahalli," *al-Bilad* 103 (24 October 1992): 50, 52–53; "al-Islam la yatanakar li al-khususiyyat al-qawmiyya," *al-Bilad* 148 (18 September 1993): 48; Martin Kramer, "The Oracle of Hizbullah: Sayyid Muham-

mad Husayn Fadlallah," in *Spokesmen for the Despised: Fundamentalist Leaders in the Middle East*, ed. R. Scott Appleby (Chicago, 1997), 125–28, 158; Saad-Ghorayeb, *Hizbu'llah*, 45.

24. Cited in Susan Sachs, "A Graveyard Window on Hussein's Iraq," *NYT*, 1 June 2003. See also Anthony Shadid, "In Shiite Slums, Focus Is on Survival, Not Revolt," *WP*, 30 March 2003; Yaroslav Trofimov et al., "History of Betrayal Makes Iraqi Shiites Wary of Liberators," *WSJ*, 1 April 2003; Peter Galbraith, "The Ghosts of 1991," *WP*, 12 April 2003; Hazim Saghiya, "Qissat al-ba'th fi al-'iraq: mihnat al-Shi'a bi-wasfihim taburan khamisan li al-iraniyyin," *al-Hayat*, 22 April 2003; Ibrahim al-Zubaydi, "al-Suqut al-akhar li-baghdad: man saraqa timthal 'abd al-muhsin al-sa'dun?" *al-Hayat*, 16 July 2003.

25. Mu'assasat al-Imam al-Khu'i al-Khayriyya, *Azmat shi'at al-'iraq* (London, n.d.), 23, 42–44.

26. Hazim al-Amin, "Balad al-shi'iyya tatanassal min muqawamat al-ihtilal wa al-dhulu'iyya al-sunniyya amamaha ayam sa'ba," *al-Hayat*, 15 June 2003; idem, "al-Hakim li al-hayat: nuqawim silman wa la-nuqirr al-'amaliyyat didd al-amirikiyyin," *al-Hayat*, 18 June 2003; idem, "Jumhuriyyat muqtada al-sadr wa-jadid al-'iraq II," *al-Hayat*, 12 July 2003; 'Isam al-'Ariyan, "al-Ma'ziq al-amiriki yatafaqam fi al-'iraq wa-bi'at al-muqawama tatashakkal," *al-Hayat*, 20 June 2003; Anon., "Muhammad Baqir al-Hakim yu'arid al-'inf didd quwwat al-ihti-lal," *al-Hayat*, 27 June 2003; 'Abdallah al-Ash'al, "al-Muqawama al-'iraqiyya wa ab'aduha al-qanuniyya wa al-siyasiyya," *al-Hayat*, 5 July 2003; Rajiv Chandrasekaran, "Sunnis in Iraq Protest U.S. Occupation," *WP*, 19 April 2003; Patrick Tyler, "In Iraq's Disorder, the Ayatollahs May Save the Day," *NYT*, 6 July 2003.

27. Neil MacFarquhar and Neela Banerjee, "Army Is Reluctant to Flaunt Photos of Hussein's Sons," *NYT*, 24 July 2003; Anthony Shadid, "A Struggle for Iraqi Clergy's Soul," *WP*, 30 June 2003; Anon., "Munazamat al-'amal al-islami: namudhaj al-inqisam al-manatiqi li al-marja'iyya" and "Hizb al-da'wa al-dakhil: al-amirikiyyun azhaqu al-batil wa-'alayhum ihqaq al-haqq," *al-Hayat*, 15 July 2003.

28. Yitzhak Nakash, *The Shi'is of Iraq*, 2d ed. (Princeton, 2003), esp. 108–11; Mu'assasat al-Khu'i, *Azmat shi'at al-'iraq*, 46–47; Anon., "Iraqi Shiite Leader Blasts Governing Council," Reuters, 18 July 2003; Ian Fisher, "Anti-U.S. Iraqi Cleric Declares Own Government," *NYT*, 12 October 2003; Anon., "Muqtada al-sadr yushakkil jaysh al-mahdi wa-'ulama' al-sunna yuhajimun majlis al-hukm," *al-Hayat*, 19 July 2003; 'Ali 'Abd al-Amir, "Muqtada al-sadr yad'u ila majlis sha'bi: quwwat badr ja'at min al-kharij wa la tumaththil al-sha'b," *al-Hayat*, 27 July 2003; Anon., "Muqtada al-Sadr," *al-Hayat*, 18 October 2003.

29. Larry Diamond, "What Went Wrong in Iraq," *FA* 83 (September/October 2004): 34–56; Neil MacFarquhar, "Iraqi Shiites Flex Muscle Even as They Mourn" and "After Cleric's Assassination, Fears for the Future," *NYT*, 1 and 2 September 2003; Ian Fisher, "Iraqi Shiite Anger Raises New Fears for U.S. Soldiers," *NYT*, 11 October 2003; idem, "For Hussein's Ouster, Many Thanks, but Iraqis Are Expecting More," *NYT*, 23 October 2003; Dexter Filkins and Eric

Schmitt, "Other Attacks Averted in Iraq, a General Says," *NYT*, 4 March 2004; "America Adrift in Iraq," editorial, *NYT* 15 May 2004.

30. Cited in Jeffrey Gettleman, "Iraqis Start to Exercise Power Even before Date for Turnover," *NYT*, 13 June 2004.

31. Noah Feldman, *What We Owe Iraq: War and the Ethics of Nation Building* (Princeton, 2004), 40–41; International Crisis Group, "Governing Iraq" (Washington and Brussels, 25 August 2003), http://crisisgroup.org; W. Andrew Terril, "The United States and Iraq's Shi'ite Clergy: Partners or Adversaries?" Strategic Studies Institute, U.S. Army War College (Washington, D.C., February 2004), 2, 33–34, http://carlisle.army.mil/ssi/pubs/2004/clergy.htm; Ibrahim Khayyat, "Hamlat shi'iyya 'ala al-dustur al-'iraqi wa-muqtada al-sadr yatabarra' min al-khiyana," *al-Hayat*, 10 March 2004; John Burns, "Shiites May Demand Lifting of Limits on Their Power," *NYT*, 10 March 2004; idem, "Shiite Ayatollah Is Warning U.N. against Endorsing Charter Sponsored by U.S.," *NYT*, 23 March 2004; Dexter Filkins, "Agreement by U.S. and Rebels to End Fighting in Najaf" and "Exile with Ties to CIA Is Named Premier of Iraq," *NYT*, 28 and 29 May 2004; James Drummond, "Shia Party Voices Dissent over Iraqi Interim Government," *FT*, 3 June 2004; Rajiv Chandrasekaran, "Mistakes Loom Large as Handover Nears," *WP*, 20 June 2004; Peter Galbraith, "Iraq: The Bungled Transition," *NYRB*, 23 September 2004.

32. Cited in Anthony Shadid, "Shiites Organize to Block U.S. Plan," *WP*, 29 March 2004. See also Douglas Jehl, "CIA Report Suggests Iraqis Are Losing Faith in U.S. Efforts," *NYT*, 13 November 2003; Hazim al-Amin, "Jumhuriyyat muqtada al-sadr wa-jadid al-'iraq I," *al-Hayat*, 18 June 2003; Jeffrey Gettleman and Douglas Jehl, "A Rebel Cleric's Militia Keeps Up Attacks," *NYT*, 7 April 2004.

33. Shadid, "A Struggle for Iraqi Clergy's Soul"; idem, "Call of History Draws Iraqi Cleric to the Political Fore," *WP*, 1 February 2004; Halim al-A'raji, "Shaykh mashayikh bani zurayyij fi al-rumaytha: al-sistani da'a ila muqata'at al-ihtilal," *al-Hayat*, 18 January 2004; Anon., "Ayatollah al-Sistani's Silence Causes Divisions among Shiites," http://asianews.it, 11 May 2004.

34. Jonathan Steele, "U.S. Bars Cleric from Iraq Elections," *Guardian*, 8 June 2004; "The Road to Confrontation in Najaf," editorial, *NYT*, 21 August 2004; Eric Schmitt and Thom Shanker, "Pentagon Sets Steps to Retake Iraq Rebel Sites," *NYT*, 8 October 2004.

35. James Risen, "Account of Broad Shiite Revolt Contradicts White House Stand," *NYT*, 8 April 2004; Neil MacFarquhar, "Arabs Worry over Extremism While Evoking Vindication," *NYT*, 9 April 2004; Nazila Fathi, "Shiite Muslims Condemn U.S. for Attacks on Holy City," *NYT*, 13 August 2004; Wahid Taja, "Liqa' ma'a samahat al-sayyid muhammad husayn fadlallah," *al-Tharwa*, 8 April 2004, http://tharwaproject.com; Anon., "al-Sadr musta'id li al-tafawud hawl al-insihab wa-'allawi yutalibuhu bi-i'lanihi rudukhhihi shakhsiyyan," *al-Hayat*, 8 August 2004; Anon., "al-Marinz yuhasirun al-sadr fi masjid al-imam 'ali wa-mi'a qatil fi gharat 'ala al-kut," *al-Hayat*, 13 August 2004; Scott Baldauf, "Standoff Bolstered Sadr's Support," *CSM*, 30 August 2004.

36. James Bennet, "The Parallels of Wars Past," *NYT*, 10 April 2004; Alex Berenson and John Burns, "Marines Pushing Deeper into City Held by Shiites," *NYT*, 8 August 2004; Karl Vick, "For Iraqis Preparing to Invade Shrine, First an Internal Battle," *WP*, 20 August 2004; John Burns, "Two Power Brokers Collide in Iraq," *NYT*, 22 August 2004; Anne Barnard, "Shiite Support Eludes New Iraqi Government," *IHT*, 6 September 2004; Anon., "Ma'arik tahina fi al-najaf wa-waqf dakh naft al-basra wa ansar al-sadr yulawwihun bi-infisal iqlim al-janub," *al-Hayat*, 10 August 2004; Roula Khalaf, "Southern Iraqi Provinces Push for Autonomy," *FT*, 29 September 2004.

37. Jeffrey Gettleman, "The Re-Baathification of Falluja," *NYT* (magazine), 20 June 2004; John Burns and Erik Eckholm, "In Western Iraq, Fundamentalists Hold U.S. at Bay," *NYT*, 29 August 2004; Eric Schmitt and Thom Shanker, "Estimates by U.S. See More Rebels with More Funds," *NYT*, 22 October 2004; Edward Wong, "Showing Their Resolve, Rebels Mount Attacks in Northern and Central Iraq," *NYT*, 18 November 2004; idem, "Rebels Keep Up Attacks in Sunni-Dominated Cities of Central and North Iraq," *NYT*, 21 November 2004; idem, "Iraqi Leaders Plan to Meet Insurgents in Jordan," *NYT*, 26 November 2004; Kamil al-Tawil, "al-Zarqawi: hukuma islamiyya fi al-'iraq wa al-intilaq minhu li-qalb anzimat duwwal al-jiwar," *al-Hayat*, 10 September 2004.

38. Cited in Jackie Spinner and Saad Sarhan, "U.S. Battles Mahdi Army for Fifth Day," *WP*, 9 August 2004. See also Abdul Razzaq al-Saeidy and Edward Wong, "Radical Cleric Is Unwanted by His Neighbors," *NYT*, 24 April 2004; Edward Wong, "In Shift, Rebel Iraqi Cleric Backs New Government He Had Once Mocked," *NYT*, 12 June 2004; Ian Fisher, "Iraqi Liquor Store Owners Fear Fundamentalists' Rise," *NYT*, 16 July 2004; idem, "Iraqi Insurgents Add an Egyptian Diplomat to Spate of Recent Kidnapping Victims," *NYT*, 24 July 2004; idem, "Leading Muslim Clerics in Iraq Condemn Bombing of Churches," *NYT*, 3 August 2004; Dexter Filkins and Alex Berenson, "Reporter Freed as Rebel Cleric Brokers a Deal," *NYT*, 23 August 2004; Dexter Filkins and Eric Schmitt, "U.S. Intensifying Bombing Attacks on Falluja Sites," *NYT*, 16 October 2004.

39. Robin Wright, "New Iraqi Government Facing Its First Big Test," *WP*, 25 July 2004; Ian Fisher, "Early Steps, Maybe, toward a Democracy in Iraq," *NYT*, 27 July 2004; Alex Berenson and Sabrina Tavernise, "Cleric Rebuffs Iraqi Mediators, Battle in Najaf Continues," *NYT*, 18 August 2004.

40. Anon., "Muqtada al-Sadr (al-musab) yuhaddid 10 shurut li-waqf itlaq al-nar wa al-insihab min al-najaf," *al-Sharq al-Awsat*, 14 August 2004; Anon., "al-Sadr yanju min shadhaya wa-yashtarit insihaban amirikiyan wa-idarat al-marja 'iyya al-najaf," *al-Hayat*, 14 August 2004.

41. Erik Eckholm, "Rebel Shiite Cleric's Aides Hint He May Enter Politics," *NYT*, 31 August 2004; Dexter Filkins and Erik Eckhom, "Talks to Disarm Shiites Collapse," *NYT*, 1 September 2004; Dexter Filkins, "Militia Leaders Charging Betrayal by Iraqi Premier," *NYT*, 3 September 2004; idem, "Battles in Baghdad Slum Leave 40 Iraqis and a G.I. Dead," *NYT*, 8 September 2004; idem, "Raising the Pressure in Iraq," *NYT*, 14 September 2004.

42. Cited in Nu'man al-Haymas, "Mumaththil al-sistani yuhadir min al-ta-la'ub fi nata'ij al-intikhabat wa al-sadr yushakkik fi sihhat ijra'iha," *al-Sharq al-Awsat*, 11 January 2005. See also Istifta' jam' min al-mu'minin hawl al-intikha-bat, 26 Sha'ban 1425; Istifta' jam' min al-mu'minin hawla musharakat al-zawja fi al-intikhabat, 6 Dhi al-Hijja 1425, http://sistani.org; Ja'far al-Ahmar, "al-Mar-ja'iyya al-Shi'iyya tad'u al-'iraqiyyin ila taghlib al-masalih al-'amma," *al-Hayat*, 17 November 2004; Su'dad al-Salihi, "al-Marja'iyya fi al-najaf tanfi al-sa'y ila iqamat dawla Shi'iyya fi al-'iraq," *al-Hayat*, 30 December 2004; Wafiq Qansuh, "Marja'iyyat al-najaf tu'ayyid tamthilan fa'ilan li al-sunna fi al-hukuma," *al-Hayat*, 9 January 2005; Anon., "Maktab al-marja' al-a'la: al-sistani la yulzim muqallidihi ikhtiyar ayy min al-qawa'im al-intikhabiyya," *al-Ra'y al-'Am*, 16 December 2004; Rory McCarthy, "Sistani Pulls Main Shia Parties Together to Dominate Iraq Poll," *Guardian*, 1 December 2004; Robin Wright and Peter Baker, "Iraq, Jordan See Threat to Election from Iran," *WP*, 8 December 2004; Robert Worth, "Shiites Signal Concern over Sunni Turnout amid Violence," *NYT*, 10 December 2004; John Burns and Robert Worth, "Iraqi Campaign Raises Question of Iran's Sway," *NYT*, 15 December 2004; Khaled Yacoub Oweis, "Sistani Pushes Shiites to Vote in Iraq Poll," Reuters, 6 January 2005.

43. George Packer, "Testing Ground: In the Shiite South, Islamists and Secularists Struggle over Iraq's Future," *New Yorker* (28 February 2005): 43. See also Anthony Shadid, "In Cafe Debate, a Victory for Elections," *WP*, 14 January 2005; Edward Wong, "Shiite Leader Inspires Many to Cast Ballots," *NYT*, 31 January 2005.

44. Jim Hoagland, "Mickey Mouse and the U.N.," *WP*, 20 June 2004; Dexter Filkins, "Top Shiite Cleric Is Said to Fear Voting in Iraq May Be Delayed," *NYT*, 23 September 2004; "Iraq's Disappearing Elections," editorial, *NYT*, 26 September 2004; Steven Weisman, "U.S. Officials Are Haunted by Initial Plan for Nationwide Candidate Lists for Iraqi Election," *NYT*, 9 January 2005; John Burns and James Glanz, "Iraqi Shiites Win, but Margin Is Less Than Projected," *NYT*, 14 February 2005; "Democracy Wins," *WSJ*, editorial, 15 February 2005; Basil Muhammad and Su'dad al-Salihi, "Tihran tudhakkir washinton bi al-ta'awun fi al-'iraq," *al-Hayat*, 18 February 2005.

45. Edward Wong, "Iraq Takes Step toward New Government," *NYT*, 4 April 2005; idem, "A Kurd Is Named Iraq's President as Tensions Boil," *NYT*, 7 April 2005; Robert Worth, "Shiite Leader Named Iraq Premier to End Two Months of Wrangling," *NYT*, 8 April 2005; idem, "Iraq's Assembly Accepts Cabinet despite Tension," *NYT*, 29 April 2005.

Further Reading

◈

Since the Iranian Islamic Revolution of 1978–79, a large volume of publications on Shi'i Islam have appeared, focusing mostly on Iran. I have listed some of the classical works, as well as recently published works in English that contain useful bibliographies. These publications have also helped me develop the themes discussed in the prologue. There are many excellent works in Western languages, as well as in Arabic and Persian, not to speak of archival sources, not mentioned here but cited in the notes to the chapters of this book.

General Works on Shi'ism

There are three primers: Yann Richard, *Shi'ite Islam: Polity, Ideology, and Creed*, trans. Antonia Nevill (Oxford: Blackwell Publishers, 1995); Moojan Momen, *An Introduction to Shi'i Islam: The History and Doctrines of Twelver Shi'ism* (New Haven: Yale University Press, 1985); and Heinz Halm, *Shi'a Islam: From Religion to Revolution*, trans. Allison Brown (Princeton: Markus Wiener Publishers, 1997). Juan Cole, *Sacred Space and Holy War: The Politics, Culture, and History of Shi'ite Islam* (London: I. B. Tauris, 2002), and Rainer Brunner and Werner Ende, eds., *The Twelver Shi'a in Modern Times: Religious Culture and Political History* (Leiden: E. J. Brill, 2001), contain chapters and articles covering a wide range of topics and territories. Recent trends within the Shi'i religious leadership are discussed in Linda Walbridge, ed., *The Most Learned of the Shi'a: The Institution of the Marja' al-Taqlid* (New York: Oxford University Press, 2001). Abbas Amanat, "In between the Madrasa and the Marketplace: The Designation of Clerical Leadership in Modern Shi'ism," in *Authority and Political Culture in Shi'ism*, ed. Said Amir Arjomand (Albany: State University of New York Press, 1988), is an excellent analysis of the factors shaping the relations between clerics and fol-lowers in Shi'i Islam. There are very few comparative studies on Shi'is in the Arab world. Abbas Kelidar, "The Shi'i Imami Community and Politics in the Arab East," *Middle Eastern Studies* 19 (1983): 3–16, and Graham Fuller and Rend Rahim Francke, *The Arab Shi'a: The Forgotten Muslims* (New York: St. Martin's Press, 1999), are the first such attempts. Two writers have offered tentative assess-ments of the impact that the U.S. invasion of Iraq could have on Shi'is, and on Shi'i-Sunni relations, in the Middle East and in Pakistan: Vali Nasr, "Regional Implications of Shi'a Revival in Iraq," *Washington Quarterly* 27 (Summer 2004): 7–24; and Reuel Marc Gerecht, *The Islamic Paradox: Shiite Clerics, Sunni Funda-mentalists, and the Coming of Arab Democracy* (Washington: AEI Press, 2004).

Iran and the Legacy of the Revolution

Nikki Keddie has dedicated a good part of her life to the study of Iran. Her re-cently updated *Modern Iran: Roots and Results of Revolution*, 2d ed. (New Haven: Yale University Press, 2003), is among the best of this category of books. Roy Mottahedeh, *The Mantle of the Prophet: Religion and Politics in Iran*, 2d ed. (Boston: One World Publications, 2000), is an absorbing book that illuminates the uneasy relations between church and state in Iran, and the uncertainties of clerics about the change spurred by the revolution. Two perceptive journalists have captured the realism that has replaced the revolutionary fervor of the late 1970s and 1980s, along with the strength of the Iranian reform movement despite the recent campaign against it by the hard-line clerical establishment: Robin Wright, *The Last Great Revolution: Turmoil and Transformation in Iran* (New York: Vintage Books, 2001); and Elaine Sciolino, *Persian Mirrors: The Elusive Face of Iran* (New York: Free Press, 2000). Bahman Baktiari, *Parliamentary Poli-tics in Revolutionary Iran: The Institutionalization of Factional Politics* (Gaines-ville: University of Florida Press, 1996), traces the evolution of the national assem-bly as an institution contributing to sociopolitical stability in the Islamic Republic between the 1980s and the mid-1990s. Detail and analysis on Khomeini's views of Islamic government as developed between the early 1940s and the late 1970s may be found in Vanessa Martin, *Creating an Islamic State: Khomeini and the Making of the New Iran* (London: I. B. Tauris, 2000), and Hamid Algar, *Islam and Revolution: Writing and Declarations of Imam Khomeini* (Berkeley: Mizan Press, 1981).

Iraq

A discussion of the Shi'i learning circles in Najaf and Karbala in late Ottoman Iraq may be found in Meir Litvak, *Shi'i Scholars of Nineteenth-Century Iraq* (Cambridge: Cambridge University Press, 1998). Yitzhak Nakash, *The Shi'is of Iraq*, 2d ed. (Princeton: Princeton University Press, 2003), highlights the strong Arab tribal identity of Iraqi Shi'is as well as the distinct religious and organiza-tional forms of Shi'ism in twentieth-century Iraq and Iran. The unique characteristics of Iraqi Shi'ism are discussed further in Faleh Jabar, *The Shiite Movement in Iraq* (London: Saqi Books, 2003). Chibli Mallat, *The Renewal of Islamic Law: Muhammad Baqer as-Sadr, Najaf, and the Shi'i International* (Cambridge: Cambridge University Press, 1993), focuses on this important Iraqi cleric and thinker, who was executed by the Ba'th in 1980, and discusses Sadr's views on Islamic constitutionalism and the role of religious leaders. The essays of Talib Aziz in *The Most Learned of the Shi'a*, and in Faleh Abdul-Jabar, *Ayatollahs, Sufis, and Ideologies: State, Religion, and Social Movements in Iraq* (London: Saqi Books, 2002), shed new light on Sadr's political theory. Sadr's ideas on Islamic government, and those of Khomeini, may be contrasted with 'Ali Sistani's rulings and statements following the U.S. invasion of Iraq, posted on his Web site (http://sistani.org), to underscore their different views regarding clerical participation in politics.

Lebanon

Fouad Ajami, *The Vanished Imam: Musa al-Sadr and the Shia of Lebanon* (Ithaca: Cornell University Press, 1986), is a masterful account of the changing fortunes of the Shi'i community sparked by Sadr. The role of Sadr as a community leader is discussed further in Majed Halawi, *A Lebanon Defied: Musa al-Sadr and the Shi'a Community* (Boulder, Colo.: Westview Press, 1992). Augustus Richard Norton, *Amal and the Shi'a: Struggle for the Soul of Lebanon* (Austin: University of Texas Press, 1987), focuses on the Amal movement established by Sadr. Amal's rival, Hizballah, has attracted a great deal of attention. Martin Kramer, "The Oracle of Hizbullah: Sayyid Muhammad Husayn Fadlallah," in *Spokesmen for the Despised: Fundamentalist Leaders of the Middle East*, ed. R. Scott Appleby (Chicago: University of Chicago Press, 1997), explores the political ideas as developed through the early-1990s of the cleric who acted as Hizballah's mentor in its early days. The transformation of Hizballah from a revolutionary movement into a political party is sketched in Amal Saad-Ghorayeb, *Hizbu'llah: Politics and Religion* (London: Pluto Press, 2002); Sami Hajjar, "Hizballah: Terrorism, National Liberation, or Menace?" (Washington, D.C.: Strategic Studies Institute, U.S. Army War College, August, 2002), http://au.af.mil/au/awc/awcgate/ssi/hizbala.pdf; Judith Palmer Harik, *Hezbollah: The Changing Face of Terrorism* (London: I. B. Tauris, 2004); and Ahmad Nizar Hamzeh, *In the Path of Hizbullah* (Syracuse: Syracuse University Press, 2004). Christoph Reuter, *My Life Is a Weapon*, trans. Helena Ragg-Kirkby (Princeton: Princeton University Press, 2004), documents the decrease in suicide bombings by Hizballah against Westerners and Israeli targets since the 1990s.

The Persian Gulf

Two helpful articles on the Saudi Shi'is are Madawi al-Rasheed, "The Shi'a of Saudi Arabia: A Minority in Search of Cultural Authenticity," *British Journal of Middle Eastern Studies* 25 (1998): 121–38, and Madawi al-Rasheed and Lou-

louwa al-Rasheed, "The Politics of Encapsulation: Saudi Policy towards Tribal and Religious Opposition," *Middle Eastern Studies* 32 (1996): 96–119. There is a good anthropological study on Bahrain with useful information on the Shi'is: Fuad Khuri, *Tribe and State in Bahrain: The Transformation of Social and Political Authority in an Arab State* (Chicago: University of Chicago Press, 1980). The role of Shi'is in the early stages of the 1994–99 uprising in Bahrain is discussed in Munira Fakhro, "The Uprising in Bahrain: An Assessment," in *The Persian Gulf at the Millennium: Essays in Politics, Economy, Security, and Religion*, ed. Gary Sick and Lawrence Potter (New York: St. Martin's Press, 1997), 167–88. Shi'i opposition groups have used the Internet effectively to promote their cause. The Web site of the Bahrain Freedom Movement, http://vob.org, has updated information in English and in Arabic. The Shi'is of Kuwait are discussed in Fuller and Rahim Francke, *The Arab Shi'a*.

Acknowledgments

In the decade that it took to complete this book, I have accumulated many pleasant debts. My colleagues in the Near Eastern and Judaic Studies Department at Brandeis University showed remarkable patience in accommodating my research leaves. Marc Brettler, Bernadette Brooten, Avigdor Levy, Antony Polonsky, and Ben Ravid were particularly supportive, and I thank them for their collegiality. I would also like to note the support that I received through the Mazar Award for faculty research in the humanities, arts, and social sciences at Brandeis.

A membership in the School of Historical Studies at the Institute for Advanced Study in Princeton during 1998–99 enabled me to get the project off the ground. Patricia Crone took a keen interest in my topic and made my stay at the institute both productive and enjoyable. A workshop that we organized on nationalism among minorities in central Asia and the Middle East helped me to develop some of the themes discussed in this book. While at the institute, I benefited from the sound advice of Michael Walzer, and I thank him for inviting me twice to contribute articles to *Dissent*. A generous research grant from the U.S. Institute of Peace for 2004–5 helped me concentrate on the final stages of writing. I completed the book as a fellow in the Woodrow Wilson International Center for Scholars in Washington, D.C., during January–May 2005. The collegial working environment at the center was beyond expectations. Lee H. Hamilton, President and Director of the center, was always accessible and welcoming. Michael Van Dusen, Robert Litwak, and Rosemary Lyon were unfailingly supportive. Haleh Esfandiari, Director of the Middle East Program, was exceedingly kind, ensuring that I could pursue my writing uninterrupted. My research assistant, Ariel Ahram, was most helpful in some last-minute checks of the Arabic press.

I thank the many librarians and archivists who facilitated my research in the Firestone Library at Princeton, the Widener Library at Harvard, the Library of

Congress, the British Library, and the Arabic newspaper archive at Tel-Aviv University. Thanks are also due to the Controller, H. M. Stationary Office in England, for permission to quote copyright material in the Public Record Office and the India Office in London.

A number of people have been generous in providing counsel, in commenting on my work, and in sharing with me their knowledge of Islam and the Middle East. I am grateful to Şahin Alpay, Shaul Bakhash, Gene Garthwaite, Ellis Goldberg, Etan Kohlberg, Joseph Kostiner, Meir Litvak, Kanan Makiya, Richard Norton, Hazim Saghiya, Frank Stewart, Ezra Suleiman, Judith Yaphe, and Sami Zubaida. Michael Cook has closely followed my writing in the course of two decades. He read the manuscript twice with utmost care, making pointed and stimulating comments. I have benefited tremendously over the years from his intellectual wisdom and insightful ideas.

It has been a pleasure to work again with the staff at Princeton University Press. They all did their best to bring the book to completion in a speedy manner. My editor, Brigitta van Rheinberg, was an enthusiastic champion of the project from its infant stages. I value her input and sound judgment, as well as her consistent support through the years.

Writing a book is not always an easy exercise. How wonderful it was, then, that in those tough moments I had Beth, and Neta and Talya, by my side. This book is dedicated to them.

Index